THE

POWER

OF

PODCASTING

THE

POWER

OF

PODCASTING

TELLING STORIES THROUGH SOUND

Siobhán McHugh

Columbia University Press
New York

Columbia University Press
Publishers Since 1893
New York   Chichester, West Sussex
cup.columbia.edu

First published in Australia by UNSW Press Ltd, in its UNSW Press imprint

Library of Congress Cataloging-in-Publication Data
Names: McHugh, Siobhán, author.
Title: The power of podcasting : telling stories through sound /
Siobhàn McHugh.
Description: New York : Columbia University Press, 2022. | Includes index.
Identifiers: LCCN 2022013910 (print) | LCCN 2022013911 (ebook) |
ISBN 9780231208765 (hardback) | ISBN 9780231208772 (trade paperback) |
ISBN 9780231557603 (ebook)
Subjects: LCSH: Podcasts. | Podcasting. | Webcasting.
Classification: LCC PN4567.7 M34 2022 (print) | LCC PN4567.7 (ebook) |
DDC 791.46/6—dc23/eng/20220329
LC record available at https://lccn.loc.gov/2022013910
LC ebook record available at https://lccn.loc.gov/2022013911

Columbia University Press books are printed on permanent
and durable acid-free paper.
Printed and bound by CPI Group (UK) Ltd, Croydon, CR0 4YY

Internal design Josephine Pajor-Markus
Cover design George Saad

Aboriginal and Torres Strait Islander readers are advised that this book contains the names of people who have died.

Chapter 6 discusses the theme of suicide.

Contents

Contents

The seductive power of sound

I once interviewed an extraordinary Australian woman, Ingrid Hart, who had entertained US troops in Vietnam during the war. In the audio trade, Ingrid was what is called good 'talent'. She had amazing stories to relate, full of detail and feeling, and she told them eloquently, in the mellifluous voice of the singer she still was.

One story was about a night when Ingrid and her band were to be escorted from a base at Qui Nhơn on the coast to An Khê in the high country. It was a treacherous route, vulnerable to attack by communist Viet Cong forces, and therefore usually negotiated by helicopter. But on this night, only a truck and a jeep showed up. Ingrid was unimpressed. 'You mean to tell me we're going through the hilly terrain in *that*?' she snorted at the US escort. Worse, the rear gunner, supposed to keep watch, failed to show. 'They did have an M16, which I was used to firing, and a bulletproof vest. So I volunteered to be the rear gunner', Ingrid, the cabaret artist, tells me now, deadpan.

Listening intently, as I always do when recording an interview, I absorbed this huge statement. An interview goes two ways: there's a time for interrupting and a time for giving the talent free rein. If someone is a bit incoherent or shy, I will let them get to the end and then go back and try to fill in the gaps they've left. But Ingrid was not going to be put off by a question, I could see. So I asked the obvious one: 'How were you so used to using an M16?'

She replied with enthusiasm. 'Well, being on bases all the time, you get to know the guys, and they have target practice. And being adventurous, I wanted to find out what it was like to fire a machine gun. Those M16s, they're magnificent guns! They're so accurate, so light, there's no recoil, nothing. We used to go to the riverbank, line up some cans.' Here Ingrid made a rat-tat-tat noise. 'Fabulous!' she added pensively, before resuming the story. 'So I'm sitting there like Rambo, with this M16, and we're slowly winding up the hills. And I tell you if anything had moved, in those bushes – anything – I'd have killed it.' She paused. 'I can realise now, the feeling of survival – what you don't even *realise* in civilian life. If anybody was there behind the bushes, I would have *known* it would be enemy, and I would have shot.'

In crafting Ingrid's interview for an audio story, I had many choices. I could have run the voice straight, lightly edited as above to cut repetition and remove 'crutch' phrases, such as 'you know'. In that form, it would provide useful insight into a little-known aspect of the Vietnam War: the mettle of a female entertainer, the psychology of being in a conflict zone.

But if I really wanted the listener to place themselves in Ingrid's shoes, I needed them to *feel* the tension as the jeep wound up each hill and past each bush that could be concealing an enemy shooter (from Ingrid's point of view). I found some throbbing, synth-driven music and lined it up to start after 'I volunteered to be the rear gunner'. Instantly, a sense of expectation arose: something was about to happen. I let the music run by itself for a phrase or two, building anticipation, then faded and held it low under the next bit, the question and answer about how Ingrid knew how to use a M16. The music phrasing worked perfectly. A drum roll followed Ingrid's exclamation 'Fabulous!' and we were off again, sitting in the jeep, scanning the terrain for snipers. On it would go, phrase by phrase.

After 'if anything had moved, in those bushes – anything – I'd have killed it', there had been a natural pause. (Ingrid was a performer and knew how to create an effect.) I could mirror this with the music, because it fortuitously changed at that point to a sighing chorus of women. As they exhaled, over the percussive synth, Ingrid's words had time to sink in. *This woman, a cabaret singer from Sydney, had been prepared to mow down anything that moved in the night.* That realisation demanded acknowledgment. Now, ideally, I might bring the music up to its reverberating end – a definitive end is better than a fade, as it inherently sets up anticipation of what is to come next.

And here it comes: Ingrid's voice, unadorned, ruminative, reflects on how the war zone changed her on that night, as she ponders a universal truth. 'I can realise now, the feeling of survival – what you don't even *realise* in civilian life. If anybody was there behind the bushes, I would have *known* it would be enemy, and I would have shot. Something happens to you in a war zone which is completely different to the way you are at home, having fish and chips!'

I have only one final adjustment to make. I will take that natural pause that she left after 'I'd have killed it' and instead insert it after 'I would have shot'. This will, in my view as the author/auteur of the piece, allow the narrative to reach a higher truth, communicate the *emotional* truth of what Ingrid is saying.

But what if I had a different view as auteur? What if I wanted to make a political point from this story, to inflect it away from the gung-ho attitude of Ingrid–Rambo, and make the listener see it from the viewpoint of the local Vietnamese, whose region has been invaded by a gun-toting, bomb-dropping US military? I also happen to have soundtracks I recorded while on my own field trip in Vietnam: out in the countryside, chickens mooching about making varied chicken noises. If I remove the music track and replace it with the clucking of chickens, Ingrid's story starts to sound very different. She is now an intruder, a menacing presence in this bucolic landscape, where the locals just want to raise chickens.

Taking things a step further, just as an illustration: what if I keep the chickens, and then creep in the music under them? If I start it at 'Fabulous!', the listener will sit up – looks like the chickens are going to get it in the neck! By playing around with where I drop in the music, and at which acoustic point – synth, drum or vocals – it is introduced,

I can make the chickens seem either sinister or vulnerable. And then there are the infinite possibilities raised by using a different musical choice. Adding in the sound of a machine-gun burst would further alter the impact and interpretation of Ingrid's story.

At one end of this spectrum lies artistry aligned with authenticity; at the other lies distortion and misrepresentation. And you, dear listener, will probably never know how manipulated, benignly or otherwise, you have been. That is the prerogative of the audio producer, who builds this invisible framework – the same one that also scaffolds great narrative podcasts.

Academics, fans and critics have spent many decades analysing how their favourite writers and film directors produce alluring story, but the craft behind storytelling in the audio medium is arcane. You usually only learn by doing it. And those who acquire 'The Knowledge' tend to talk about it only to other insiders, who speak the language of jump cut, music bed, atmos pause. Plus, outsiders assume it's easy – it's only *audio,* after all, not some hifalutin art like film, or canonical text like a book. Audio comes naturally, doesn't it? We can almost all talk.

But audio (and it's a lot more than 'just talk') has its own grammar and logic. Radio has been around for a century now and the people in that medium had to learn how it worked pretty quickly – otherwise listeners switched off. You wrote for it like you talked, in a conversational, informal way. You knew when to keep a listener hanging with a well-judged pause. You adjusted your tone and tempo to your time slot: morning radio was quick and lively, everyone rushing to work. Drive time was more relaxed, chatty. Late night was whisper-intimate, just you and listeners communing in the ether. Shock jocks, when they arrived, were shouty. Sports commentators built the drama, created sound pictures, as the famous Sydney rugby league caller Frank Hyde learned to do after a blind listener complained he couldn't figure out what was happening: 'It's long enough, it's high enough and it's *straight between the posts*' was his famous call. Sometimes the pictures in people's heads were so real, they could convulse a nation – as on Halloween in 1938, when

Orson Welles so convincingly delivered an adaptation of HG Wells's novel *The War of The Worlds* that listeners phoned the police to see if Martians really had invaded the US.

Radio's flirty first cousin, podcasting, arrived quietly as a tech innovation in 2001 and as a term in 2004, then exploded as a pop-culture phenomenon in 2014. That year, two events serendipitously collided: Apple embedded a purple 'podcasts' app in its smartphone, making listening easy and ubiquitous; and the American show *Serial* converted investigative journalism into gripping, episodic narrative, sparking millions of downloads. Right now there are over two million 'podcasts' on iTunes and more than 43 million distinct episodes online. Every man, woman and their dog seems to have a podcast, every brand wants one, and politicians, educators, entertainers, journalists, corporates and ideologues of all kinds are playing in the podcast pond.

This book is my attempt to distil the magic of narrative podcasts, and the podcasts I survey have one common denominator: storytelling. You can tell a story in many formats: through an empathetic interview, a poetic sound-led work inflected with voice, a beautifully written first-person essay or memoir, even the ubiquitous 'chatcast' or 'chumcast', when two or more hosts who have chemistry, presence and focus reflect on a theme. The epitome of the form, for me at any rate, is the highly crafted narrative podcast, be it fiction or nonfiction.

There is an ineffable quality to a compelling podcast that guides my discussion. It's something to do with mastering the medium of sound, connecting with the audience and being real. Although a lot of my own experience comes from Australia, these core principles of making lean-in podcasts are pretty universal, as I discovered when I recently ran a free online course called *The Power of Podcasting for Storytelling*. It had more than 35 000 participants from 150 countries, and while cultural differences obviously came up in terms of the content they wished to make, it was a joy to see not just how participants engaged enthusiastically with the learning materials I presented, but also how they interacted generously, dispensing advice and support to each other.

The feedback on the course convinced me of the appetite that's out there – from Nigeria to Japan, from Pakistan to Mexico, from the US to the UK – for a deeper understanding of the seemingly simple medium of audio. To get there, I'll introduce you to diverse podcasters from around the world who, to me, make listenable, likeable or remarkable podcasts. I'll share my own insights on where a podcast idea starts, sometimes simply by being inquisitive or being a good listener. Interviewing is a vital part of delving into a story: I love sitting down with a stranger, feeling when to stay quiet but also figuring out the right questions to ask. It never ceases to amaze me how deep a relationship can form in that setting, in the space of only an hour or two – but I've learned from my mistakes there too and have drawn on my experience of doing hundreds of interviews to guide you. But if interviews are often the spine of a true story, other kinds of research supply the heft: digging through records, finding evidence in letters, official documents and personal memorabilia.

Then comes the artistry: how to combine all these elements in such a way as to keep the listener agog rather than overloaded, confused or, worst of all, bored. I'll give you my tips and I'll also bring you the views and expertise of podcasting friends and colleagues. Today's feted podcasters didn't just emerge in some audio big bang: they stand on the shoulders of pioneering broadcasters from the 1930s on, who influenced each other and moved with the technology to evolve new ways of telling audio stories. I'll trace some of that history, from the first tearful radio news broadcast describing the implosion of the *Hindenburg* airship in New Jersey in 1937, to the global village of audio storytellers today.

To illustrate this under-appreciated art of audio storytelling, we'll go inside how one venerable newspaper, *The Age* in Melbourne, shifted its investigative journalism from a print format to make three hit narrative podcasts: *Phoebe's Fall*, *Wrong Skin* and *The Last Voyage of the Pong Su*. I was on board as a story editor and consulting producer for a wild and rewarding ride. I'll show you our breakthroughs and our misjudgments, including actual before-and-after scripts, until finally we got all our moving parts working in glorious harmony. All three podcasts had more than a million downloads and won a slew of awards, so they clearly chimed with the audience. I'll help you understand why.

In addition, I analyse two absolute classics of the genre: *Serial* is one, of course. The other is *S-Town*, another gamechanger, hailed as 'a nonfiction novel for your ears'. Finally, I'll look at trends in the podcasting industry, from the push for diversity, equality and social inclusion to the explosion in news digests and the corporatisation of what was once a homespun medium. I'll end by giving you some recommended listening, in different genres.

It's no surprise to me that when people get the podcasting bug, they fall heavily for it. It's often because they underestimated just what sound can do, in some deep, subconscious place we all carry within. Walter Murch makes a living from film: he coined the term 'sound designer' for his work on *Apocalypse Now* and won two Oscars, for Best Sound and Best Film Editing, for *The English Patient*. But without the right sound, he reckons, the visuals can't fire. That's because, he says, we are 'suckled by sound'. Sound is absolutely elemental – hearing is the first sense we develop, still in the womb, and the last sense to leave us as we die.

So whatever stage you're at, whether it's listening in your earbuds, beavering in the studio or roving around with a microphone gathering your sounds, let's podcast – with passion!

1
Podcasting: Why, who, what

Podcasts come in all sounds and sizes and deliver a mind-boggling range of content, from personal storytelling to pop-culture punditry, from sharing deep knowledge to the 'vanity casting' of corporate brands. But what the good ones share, in my view, is that they engender a feeling of intimacy and authenticity, connecting with us through the lure of story and the power of voice.

Most people listen to podcasts to gain knowledge and/or to be entertained. Most of us also enjoy the sense of being connected to the host, our new best friend. I'm not really a visual person – perhaps because my audio antennae are overdeveloped – but I had a go at representing this in a Venn diagram. As you can see, the common denominator throughout is audio – which is why understanding audio is at the heart of this book.

Some folk go for a 'vodcast', a sort of podcast-with-visuals, watched on platforms from YouTube to TikTok. The American comedian Joe Rogan, for instance, attracted 47 million views on YouTube (and counting) for a 2018 episode of his interview show featuring Elon Musk, but regularly gets an estimated 190 million downloads a month of the same show, *The Joe Rogan Experience*, in its audio-only podcast form (now available in full only on Spotify). Rogan's episodes often run to two or three hours. One disadvantage of watching them as video is the huge amount of data that will chew up. Another is screen fatigue, which is more pertinent to me: I spend far too much time already stuck to my computer. One of the great benefits of podcasts is that they accompany you as you do

The pillars of podcasting

other things – walk the dog, chop veggies, commute to work. But I also prefer podcasts to vodcasts any day because audio frees my imagination and gives me a purer connection with whomever is being interviewed. I am untainted by how they look and not ambushed by preconceptions, whether conscious or not, about appearance. Instead, I can focus on what they say and how they sound, and take in more meaning that way. Far from being 'less than' video, the audio medium gives you more, in many ways. And that's what this book will help you discover.

Why people podcast

The world of audio has three parts, as the BBC Sounds app reminds us: music, radio, podcasts. Within the podcast universe, or podsphere, there are multiple genres. Listening platforms sometimes categorise these by content: news, society and culture, true crime, comedy, educational, tech, lifestyle and health. Others try to sort podcasts by format: interviews, repurposed content, panel discussions, solo commentary, nonfiction narrative storytelling, hybrid and talk shows. The Bello

Collective, an association of audio aficionados, had only four categories for its Top 100 annual podcast list in 2020: narrative nonfiction, fiction, conversation and experiential (which could be read as 'experimental', including the more poetic 'turn towards sound' art).

In one sense these tags are meaningless: one person's 'talk show' is another person's interview or conversation format, and 'narrative nonfiction' spans everything from cutting-edge investigative journalism to luminous memoir to the trashiest true crime. One of the most popular formats, in which two or more pals riff off a theme and make you feel like you could be their friend too, has been cleverly named a 'chumcast'. Julie Shapiro, a Boston-based podcasting executive and key figure in audio storytelling, thinks she coined the term. 'I used to have a taxonomy of shows', she tells me. 'It was chum/chatcast. They're interchangeable.'

If there are numerous ways to classify the podverse, there are almost as many reasons why people want to make a podcast. Renae 'Rocket' Bretherton's motive is one of the best: 'Being heard. I had never had an opportunity to be heard before'. Aged 40, Rocket has spent most of her adult life in prison, and was in Darwin Correctional Centre in northern Australia when producer Johanna Bell and her StoryProjects team began developing the *Birds Eye View* podcast. Over two years, they would collaborate with some 70 women from the prison. Rocket's dark humour and raw honesty were particularly affecting. *Birds Eye View* won Australian Podcast of the Year in 2020, and has had some 250 000 downloads. 'I love that my story has reached all around the world', says Rocket, in reply to a survey I conducted online. A former ice addict, she's on the outside now, drug-free for almost three years. 'The podcast helped me change my life for the better. I feel like my story has been validated and I feel understood now. It's an amazing, freeing feeling and as many people as possible should be given that opportunity.'

In Los Angeles in 2020, writer Elizabeth Versace spent her days looking after her elderly father-in-law, 'Papa', whom she adored. It was the year of pandemic, and with time on her hands, she took my online podcasting course. It inspired her to record a script about the gentle rhythms of life with Papa, her partner and their cats: Papa's walker scraping across the floor, his last words every night, 'I love you'. She wrote to me, 'I wanted to take my storytelling to the next level, but didn't know what form that would take ... there was not a genre that satisfied me – until podcasting'. Elizabeth launched her podcast, *Bone Tired,* in late 2020. Papa died soon afterwards, first giving her his blessing to proceed, and she has continued to podcast 'first-person essays on being a full-time caregiver in an age of pandemic'. Though it has a modest audience, Elizabeth tells me that making the podcast has changed her life.

My husband points me to the person who got him into podcasts. Jeff Wright was a high school teacher in Ottawa, Canada, obsessed with the legends of Ancient Greece, which was where he learnt to 'craft a story and perform for an audience', he says. After doing hundreds of live shows for students, he graduated to paid gigs – and then to podcasting. *Trojan War: The Podcast* is a 20-episode, 25-hour epic, which sought to retain 'the vibe and the feel of my live shows, which meant *not* reading a script, but knowing a story, and telling it'. The monologues have two parts: in the first, Jeff gives a straight telling of the story – 'The Apple of Discord', 'The Birth of Achilles'. In the second, addressing an imaginary audience, he debates the story's accuracy – with himself, offering 'value-added insights and a lot of geeky fun'. When brand new to podcasting, Jeff set himself low expectations. 'I hoped that immediate family would feel obliged to listen, and possibly a few friends.' But his audience grew quickly, and even included serious classical scholars. 'That *Trojan War* has done considerably better than that remains a constant source of bewilderment and delight', says Jeff. He is being humble: *Trojan War* and its equally epic follow-up, *Odyssey,* have jointly clocked up about 927 000 downloads.

Meanwhile in Italy, my audio colleague Cristina Marras cheerfully admits she is addicted to podcasts. A freelance audio producer, she loves podcasts with 'unorthodox subjects/storytellers/ways to tell the story – anything that surprises me'. In making her own *3'grezzi (3 raw minutes)* podcast (mostly spoken-word reflections, sometimes accompanied by location sound), Cristina loves 'the freedom of expressing myself. It is an unbelievably satisfying activity. Of course I love it when my podcast is downloaded or when I receive feedback, but that's not my main objective … podcasts is not the way I earn money'.

All these podcasters are hobbyists, using podcasting to express something they're passionate about. Even with listener donations and impressive downloads, Jeff Wright makes almost no net income from the 50 hours of podcasts he has created. He'd 'make more money in two weeks of slinging burgers at McDonalds', he tells me ruefully. But money is not what motivates him:

> What I do receive, in non-monetary remuneration, is priceless.
> A week does not go by when some podcast listener, from
> somewhere in the world, writes me a long email about my pods,
> and the impact/effect/sometimes 'joy' it has brought to their lives!
> And then I write back; and then they write back to me. In short,
> every week of my life I receive a 'slow drip of validation', for a
> product I released onto the world over five years ago! That –
> not the cash flow – is the genuine reward.

This is the true power of podcasting. Whether your podcast gets two dozen downloads an episode or four million, as the *New York Times'* narrative news show *The Daily* does (see chapter 5), the *currency* of podcasting is pretty much the same: the intimate sense of connection that audio can build via voice, especially when that voice is speaking right into your ear, in your headphones or earbuds.

This is also what excites Chenjerai Kumanyika, an African American hip-hop artist, activist, academic and journalist based at Rutgers University in New Jersey. In 2014, Chenjerai attended a workshop on audio storytelling hosted by Transom, a US-based public media think-tank and training organisation. During a week-long workshop, as he prepared to write his first ever public radio piece, he felt suddenly stymied. 'I realized that as I was speaking aloud I was also imagining someone else's voice saying my piece.' Someone white. Because white voices were the ones he had mostly heard on American public radio. 'When the vocal patterns of a narrow range of ethnicities quietly becomes the standard sound of a genre, we're missing out on essential cultural information', Chenjerai writes. 'We're missing out on the joyful, tragic, moments and unique dispositions that are encoded in different traditions of oratory.' Chenjerai's words are from a manifesto he wrote for Transom in 2015 on the lack of diversity in public radio.[1]

Around the same time, the killing of Michael Brown in Ferguson, Mississippi, in 2014 had fomented passionate debates about race and racism and triggered the #BlackLivesMatter movement. Over at the Center for Documentary Studies at Duke University, North Carolina, veteran former public-radio producer John Biewen was preparing a new series of his *Scene on Radio* podcast. Called *Seeing White*, it would be a penetrating analysis of how race was socially and politically constructed in the US. John, who is white, invited Chenjerai to be a collaborator, to critique the podcast content from his own cultural perspective in their robust Q&As. The podcast's power was recognised when *Seeing White* was nominated for a prestigious Peabody Award in the US, and the audio and an associated study guide have since been adopted by many educational institutions as a comprehensive but accessible way to understand the fraught history and politics of race in the US. Chenjerai went on to co-host his own podcast, *Uncivil*, which 'ransacked' the history of the American Civil War and reclaimed stories left out of official accounts. This one won Chenjerai and his co-host, Jack Hitt, a Peabody.

The reach and impact of these podcasts made a deep impression on Chenjerai. As he told the podcast *BackStory*, 'As someone who is a critical scholar and an organiser, I'm thinking a lot about how we form the analysis that we need to have of issues of power and inequality. And it turns out there's not really a lot of spaces for us to come together and do that in a sustained way. Social media is not great for that, things turn negative very quickly'. But podcasting offered a very different space –

one that might break down the insidious silos in which people were increasingly barricading themselves.

Podcasting is a place where people have kind of agreed to listen and reflect and think and may even be willing to change their minds and reconsider things. I think that's powerful.

– Chenjerai Kumanyika, on *BackStory*, 2020

Shiny eyes and great ideas: Podcasting formats that work

One of the exciting things about podcasting is that it allows newcomers to audio, like Chenjerai, to compete with and sometimes outdo the established old hands. To harness podcasting's power, the first requirement is not tech know-how – it's wanting to transmit a passion for something. Is it a story you're bursting to tell, an undying obsession, maybe a biopsy of your own life? A Chinese broadcaster who doesn't want to be named took a workshop with me and instantly got the radio/podcast difference. Her daily radio show, she said, was 'like a task. OK, I have to go work now – ding ding ding'. But making a podcast was something she would keep for when she had 'shiny eyes [and] great ideas'. I reckon that's a winning formula!

Narrative and storytelling podcasts

Narrative podcasts rely on plot (what happens), characters (to whom it happens), voice (who is telling the story) and sound (how it comes together as audio). They also need a strong structure to support an episodic format. Just as aspiring writers are advised to read the works of great authors in order to develop their own way with words, an easy way to get a feel for narrative podcasts is to listen critically to some exemplars.

Examples range from audio drama series, such as Gimlet's early production *Homecoming*, or the BBC's eco-sci-fi offering *Forest 404*, to expansive nonfiction storytelling on a fascinating range of topics, from the soft power possibly exerted on post-Soviet Russia by the CIA via a pop song (*Wind of Change*) to a complex saga of how two women reclaimed their power following a sexual assault (*Canary*). Australian journalist Marc Fennell has nailed nonfiction storytelling, delivering a breezy mix of deep reportage, sassy commentary and assured production in the hit podcasts *It Burns*, which tells the story of 'the scandal-plagued race to breed the world's hottest chilli'; *Stuff the British Stole*, a pithily titled exploration of colonialist predations around the world; and *Nut Jobs*, an investigation into a $10 million almond heist. Out in almond country in California for *Nut Jobs*, Fennell meets PI Rocky Pipkin: 'Tell me that is not the best name you have ever heard', Fennell begins. He has a knack for summoning a character with colour and concision. 'Rocky Pipkin has a face that's equal parts fiercely curious and "I do not approve of you dating my daughter".' In Rocky's 'peak bland' office, Fennell notices the PI is carrying a gun. 'If someone's watching me and they decide they want to do something stupid, I'm prepared to defend myself', Rocky explains. After a beat to let that sink in, host Fennell chimes in, wryly: 'Noted!' This sort of chatty but astutely observed writing makes for compelling listening.

There are also hybrid narrative forms, such as *Appearances*, a 'one-woman audio show that straddles the line between fiction and truth', produced by Mermaid Palace, from Radiotopia. In it, fictional host Melanie Barzadeh (Sharon Mashihi) describes her quest to become a mother while coping with the vagaries of her Iranian-American family, all of whose members she role-plays, along with candid chats with her on/off boyfriend. It messes with conventional storytelling and has an assured feel. We unpack the factors that go into a good storytelling podcast in detail in chapters 5 to 8, but here are a few starter tips for working in the narrative podcast genre.

Tips for starting a narrative podcast

1   Pick a story with interesting, three-dimensional characters who will give you frank, in-depth interviews. (See chapter 4 for advice.)

2   Make sure the story is complex, with twists and turns, satisfying rabbit holes and occasional bum steers. Hint: this all derives from deep *research*.

3   Who is hosting and why? This matters! The host should have a strong connection to the story and be emotionally invested in it – and reveal that interest.

4   As you turn your idea and research into the audio recordings that will form the podcast, learn to Think Through Your Ears. Don't just knock on the door; record yourself knocking on the door, and someone answering. Record (with their permission of course) *scenes* with the people you interview: capture them bantering with family, answering the phone, working out at the gym, making a cup of coffee. These scenes are invaluable as episode openers to establish a character, or as bridging moments, to take the narrative to a new place.

5   Write like you talk. That does not mean a script is one big splat – far from it. It means you don't use words you wouldn't say to someone over coffee: so forget 'utilise' (go for 'use') and change 'I believe we are acquainted' to 'Don't I know you?' Your speech rhythms are likely to include shorter phrases, maybe with 'crutch' words such as 'hey', or 'you know what I mean' tacked on. You should be able to read the script and sound natural, as if you're talking to a friend or favourite relative.

'Chatcast' or 'chumcast'

If, on the other hand, your podcast is a 'chatcast' genre, the crucial thing is that the hosts bounce off each other well and that there's a defined theme. Examples include *Call Your Girlfriend*, in which tech expert Aminatou Sow and journalist Ann Friedman catch up on what's going on in their lives and the world, just as any friends who live apart might – hence the tagline, 'a podcast for long-distance besties everywhere'. It helps that they are funny, articulate and informed. Others in this genre include the long-running *My Brother, My Brother and Me*, in which the three real-life McElroy brothers host 'an advice podcast for the modern era', and *The Read*, in which bloggers Kid Fury and Crissle cover hip-hop and pop culture's most trying stars while conducting a mutual therapy session about life in the big city.

Chumcasts can be niche – or amazingly popular. Twenty-somethings Zara McDonald and Michelle Andrews quit their jobs at media company MamaMia to go professional in 2018 with *Shameless*, a pop culture/celebrity podcast 'for smart women who love dumb stuff'. With no real marketing budget, they visited a few universities in Melbourne and tacked posters for the show to the doors of women's toilets, guessing that female students would enjoy their shtick. By September 2020, the podcast had been downloaded more than 15 million times and was voted most popular podcast in Australia: it clearly spoke to young women in a way they perhaps hadn't even realised they craved.

An even more successful chumcast had a highly unlikely premise: in *My Dad Wrote a Porno*, unassuming Londoner Jamie Morton reads a chapter each episode of *Belinda Blinked,* a painfully amateur 'erotic' novel written by his dad, a retired builder with a lamentable understanding of the female anatomy. Jamie discusses it, over wine and amid much hilarity, with two savvy friends, James Cooper and Alice Levine. Episode One sets the tone. Belinda attends a job interview and is asked to strip. As she takes off her thong, 'her vaginal lids pop open', reads Jamie. A bemused James asks Alice if a vagina has lids. 'I have never thought of it as a Tupperware box', she reflects. Since its launch in 2015, *My Dad*

Wrote a Porno has become a cottage industry, with live shows around the world. By 2021, it had had 280 million downloads and had been made into an HBO special.

Crashing the podcast party

Besides chumcasters, people in other media are discovering that the seemingly humble podcast can do things that showier or more traditional media formats cannot. They can liberate you from the stranglehold of raising a film budget, for starters. An hour of Australian television drama, for instance, costs around $1–1.5 million to make. An hour of podcast, even at the highly produced narrative nonfiction end of the spectrum, costs a tiny fraction of that. Take *My Only Story*, a narrative podcast from South Africa in which host Deon Wiggett conducts a 'live investigation' into the schoolteacher who raped him. It's not as grisly as it sounds, due to Deon's light touch describing South African culture and his frank insight into his younger self. It also has good journalistic and audio production standards, as its Bronze award at the New York Festivals confirms – their radio awards date back to 1957 and they added a podcast category in 2017. Seeking to recoup funds, the team posted their production schedule and costs online. Applying a very basic hourly rate of US$50 – a bit less than what AIR, an association of independent audio producers, recommends for a reporter/producer with two to five years' experience – their costs run to about $46 635 per hour of podcast.[2] That includes music licensing costs, equipment and travel, but the vast bulk of it is people's time. Still, it's tiny compared to a film budget.

Lower costs are partly why you see documentary filmmakers increasingly turning to podcasting to tell a story: shows like the true-crime *Someone Knows Something* from CBC in Canada, or the voyeuristic but pacey *Missing Richard Simmons* by Dan Taberski. At the other end of the privacy spectrum, *Not By Accident* by independent Australian filmmaker Sophie Harper documents her deeply personal, three-year journey into single motherhood via IVF. In a winning move, the podcast is introduced by three-year-old Astrid, born as a result of the IVF.

But the appeal of making a podcast is not just a matter of economics. Ruby Jones, an Australian journalist, had the rare experience of publishing the same story as a serialised television documentary and as a podcast at the same time. *Unravel True Crime: Barrenjoey Road* (2018) investigates the disappearance in 1978 of a teenage girl on Sydney's Northern Beaches, and a spate of linked rapes and abductions. The seven-part podcast ran to about four hours; its treatment as a TV series, *Barrenjoey Road*, ran as three one-hour episodes over three weeks, in a prime evening slot and online. Yet as Ruby Jones told the hosts of *Behind the Podcast*, the reaction from the podcast listeners far outweighed the reaction from the TV audience: 'The response from the podcast was so huge. Everyone who emailed me, they never really talked about the TV show. They spoke about the podcast – listening to it and the things it had made them think and feel … that's when I realised the power of it'.

Media personalities outside film and television also began bringing their content to the podcast space. Canadian author Malcolm Gladwell had published five bestselling books when he launched his *Revisionist History* podcast in 2016. Billed as 'a journey through the overlooked and the misunderstood', it has been so successful that Gladwell talked for a while about giving up writing. Instead, in 2018 he and partner Jacob Weisberg founded Pushkin Industries, a podcasting network with simple aims: 'We would put artists and creators first. We would produce work that we care about and believe in. And we would have fun'. Behind the high-profile partners, the network relies on skilled audio producers, editors and engineers to adapt their work for an audio medium: collaboration is at the heart of great narrative podcasts. With Pushkin up and running, Gladwell returned to books; in 2019, he published yet another bestseller, *Talking to Strangers*.

Audrey Gillan and *Tara and George*

Scottish journalist Audrey Gillan was a reporter with the *Guardian* in the UK when she first became interested in storytelling through sound. Noted digital creative Francesca Panetta was at the *Guardian* too, developing cutting-edge storytelling via audio, virtual reality and immersive media, and it got Audrey thinking. But then she turned to screenwriting and travel journalism, and was living a busy life as a freelance journalist based in London when she became aware of two homeless people camped on the doorstep of a house in her historic Spitalfields neighbourhood. Sheer curiosity drove her to buy an audio recording kit, she told me. 'Just thinking, "I'd really love to know their story", and mulling it over and then just basically getting the balls up to go and sit down and doing some interviews ... not really doing it very well at the beginning and then keeping on going with it, but not knowing what I was doing.'

Their names, Audrey found out, were Tara and George, and the house belonged to iconic art duo Gilbert & George, who sometimes made coffee for the two middle-aged rough sleepers. Over the next two years, in sunshine and bitter cold, Audrey slowly pieced together Tara and George's chaotic personal history and touching, if volatile, relationship. But what to do with the 'shoebox full of tapes' she had acquired? As luck would have it, she was introduced to Alan Hall, founder of Falling Tree Productions and an acclaimed audio feature-maker.

The pair spent six weeks going through the audio Audrey had marked up. At first Alan 'was disappointed by the sound quality', Audrey tells me. But in among the recordings were nuggets of gold. As producer, Alan created a structure for a six-part series, and got it commissioned by BBC Radio 4 in 2018. As it evolved, Audrey began to grasp how audio storytelling worked. One epiphany was that she did not have to spell everything out through narration:

> Alan was bringing out the sound of the street. I was sitting on
> the pavement. And so you can hear the pavement, where I was

sometimes scared of the noise ruining the interview – somebody skateboarding by, or the bin men. Alan made that a part of it. And sometimes that would be synchronicity ... like Tara would be telling you about her child, and then suddenly a mother is walking past Tara with a child and the child cries, and I'm like, 'How did that happen?'

Alan's experience with the materiality of sound also led him to suggest including scenes that Audrey was at first dubious about. Understandably, given her tough circumstances, Tara's mental and physical health were fragile. At one point she lunged at Audrey while the recorder was running. 'Tara was going to batter me', Audrey explains. 'And you can hear me getting sort of scared and aggressive and very Glaswegian! And to me, it was embarrassing that it was more like *me*, rather than me-as-broadcaster, and I thought, "We can't use that."' But Alan saw the scene as authentic and important. 'He said, "It's a big turning point. It's a real illustration of her character, but also [that] you're really vulnerable as well."'

Moments like this added rare emotional depth and honesty to the series, which they named, simply, *Tara and George*. Critics recognised its raw power. It won Radio Programme of the Year at the 2019 British Broadcasting Press Guild Awards and is now a BBC podcast – not a bad start to Audrey Gillan's podcasting career. She has become a big fan of audio. 'It's an immersive visual medium. And it's a visual medium in the sense that it incites the imagination, because you're not seeing it – your imagination is creating the visual from what you're hearing.'

Podcasts have it over newspaper articles, she reckons, when it comes to hearing voice. 'You can hear people punctuate their sentence; you can hear the emotion of their punctuation in their sentence. I don't think flat words on a page are able to convey that.' But mere voice is not always enough to be engaging, if the content is dull. 'So much of [podcasting] isn't actually a visual medium because it's just two blokes sitting in their mum's garage in their Y-fronts talking a lot of shit.'

Adapting to the form: Mark Dapin

Understanding the medium of audio is something that comes through in the work of multi-award-winning author, historian, screenwriter and journalist Dr Mark Dapin, who has adapted various art forms and content to a podcast/radio format. Mark has worked in a remarkable range of genres, from gonzo journalist, humorous columnist, feature writer and men's magazine editor to noted military historian and social historian, novelist and poet. As audio content, he has written short fiction for ABC Radio National and curated an RN crime fiction podcast, *Untrue Crime*. He was also responsible for the eight-part RN broadcast/podcast, *Myths of War*, in 2020.

I met Mark in memorable circumstances a few years back in our mutual Sydney suburb. I was getting my hair coloured and had left the salon, mid-dye, to grab a coffee next door, when he walked by. Mark favoured a distinctive baseball cap and I recognised him from an author photo I had seen. In his recent PhD thesis he had cited a book I had written about Australian women in the Vietnam War, and had given it short shrift, mainly because it was not a scholarly work. The book was written as a mainstream social history, not an academic publication, but I guess being dismissed did sting a bit.

So I bailed him up and introduced myself. If he was fazed by a strange woman whose head was covered in tinfoil appendages, querying his PhD, Mark didn't show it. He explained that his supervisor had expressed criticism of my book, which Mark found valid. At this point, Georgia, my hairdresser, banged on the window. It was time to rinse off the dye. I went to end what had been a friendlier than expected exchange. But Mark had recognised our common ground as freelance social historians and wanted to keep talking. He followed me into the salon and sat alongside me, chatting away, as Georgia rinsed and snipped. 'Hmmm', he observed. 'If I were writing a profile of you, I'd begin with: "The first time I met Siobhán McHugh, her hair changed colour literally in front of my eyes".'

It was the first of numerous serendipitous encounters that led to a few beers and friendship. And so Mark generously agreed to reflect on his podcast experiences here.

 Q&A with Mark Dapin

> *What does podcasting give you that other media formats don't?*
>
> As a journalist and author of literary nonfiction, I make more use of direct quotation than most similar writers. I edit my interviewees only lightly. I try to make my stories flow around their words, rather than force them to play a predetermined role in my narrative. It's important to me that working-class (and other marginalised) speech patterns, vocabulary, imagery, argot and humour should colour and inform the more formal structure that I impose upon them.
>
> Ideally, with podcasting, I can take these ideas several steps further. While I can, obviously, choose the quotations I use, I can't easily line-edit or abbreviate them. Therefore, the voices of my subjects are more authentic and unmediated. The listener hears their accents, inflections and timing – and can better make their own judgment on their credibility and, I guess, value.
>
> I am uncomfortable with some aspects of the role of narrator. Ideally, I would 'explain' nothing. I would only contextualise. My interviewees would explain things to me.
>
> *With* Myths of War, *what were the pros and cons of adapting your material for a podcast?*
>
> *Myths of War* was not an adaption of written material – although some of the episodes concerned subjects I had written about previously (for example, Vietnam). I used

specialists in various areas of military history to discuss controversies within their own fields. If I had written a book about Australian military mythology, I would have had to undertake far more original research and I would have gone back to many more primary sources. Podcasting allowed me to pluck informed analysis straight from the experts' mouths, rather than clumsily plunder their work and then shamelessly appropriate their ideas as my own, augmented with a few oral-history interviews masquerading as adequate original research.

How easy/hard was it to literally find your own voice?

I was hired for my 'distinctive voice', which Radio National then set about trying to change – but I did not think this was necessarily a bad thing. During our studio sessions, my producer recalibrated my rhythms of speech by waving his arms around like an orchestra conductor. I enjoyed this as it made me feel like a musical instrument. People who know me have said I did not sound like myself, but I guess most radio announcers do not speak in real life in the way they might come across on the airwaves – just as horseracing commentators don't blabber on at 100 kilometres an hour over breakfast at home. I suppose, however, that altering my intonation was a compromise that acquaintences did not expect me, specifically, to make.

I was more concerned that some of my jokes disappeared during the mixing process. I was not used to being edited at that level and without close consultation. I probably did not react well to outside editorial input – but then, it's not something I've ever sought. At a more senior level, the editorial process barely seemed to function.

What did you learn from making Myths of War*?*

Before I began to work on *Myths of War*, I should have given a presentation to everyone who might be involved at any level, setting out my vision for the show. I should have explained it would involve fairly complex ideas about the interplay between popular culture and popular memory, leavened with a humour that might sometimes seem inappropriate but nevertheless was integral to the package.

As a freelancer, how workable is podcasting for you, in terms of time and money issues?

I thought it paid alright. An episode paid about the same as a long magazine feature.

With 'Big Steel', your fictional story for Untrue Crime, *I thought the actor [Mark Coles Smith] got the character – they gelled. How did you like the audio treatment of the story?*

It was great. Sophie Townsend put all that together and she was wonderful. I was also very pleased with an earlier short fiction that Townsend produced for me, 'The Canner'.

The collaborative approach Mark describes is common in professional audio storytelling. The discerning ear of an experienced producer (such as the ABC's award-winning Sophie Townsend: see chapter 10) will always be of benefit. But how do you get to *be* a producer in the first place? Where do you learn your trade? In the next chapter, we will explore how audio storytelling evolved, and how art, craft and technology are intertwined.

2

Appreciating audio storytelling:
The backstory

In a delightful twist, the man who created the first replayable sound recording was partially deaf. Unable to keep up easily at school, Thomas Alva Edison became a voracious reader and autodidact. Though he had no formal education past the age of 12, he would patent (singly or jointly) over a thousand inventions – more than any other individual. They included the incandescent light bulb, a revolutionary product, but Edison was always fondest of the phonograph, a contraption he made in 1877 out of rolling tinfoil, a horn and a stylus. To his own surprise, the device captured him reciting the nursery rhyme 'Mary Had a Little Lamb'. 'I was never so taken aback in my life', he observed. 'I was always afraid of things that worked the first time.'

Edison was still in his heyday when another transformative moment in the history of sound occurred: Guglielmo Marconi transmitted the first transatlantic radio signal in 1901, from the UK to Canada. Early radio offerings included terse ship-to-shore messages, an Austrian music show in 1904, a Christmas Eve broadcast from Massachusetts in 1906, and a poorly transmitted opera recital from the Metropolitan Opera in New York in 1910. In 1920, radio manufacturer Westinghouse broadcast the first licensed radio show from its own station, KDKA, in Pittsburgh. By the end of 1922, there were 576 commercial radio stations in the United States. Public radio broadcasting would not come to the US on a large scale until almost 50 years later, when National Public Radio (NPR) was established in 1970.

In other parts of the West, things were different. In the UK, the British Broadcasting Corporation (BBC) was created in 1922, to famously 'inform, educate and entertain' the nation. Other public broadcasters would be established in subsequent decades from Europe to Australia (1932), Canada (1936) and beyond.

So why does this matter? Well, because it offers insights into the foundational principles of audio storytelling culture.

Public radio and the greater good

Much of what I consider the engaging storytelling side of radio – and of early podcasting – evolved in the public broadcasting sector. While public radio took on very different roles in individual countries, it is commonly associated with what media historian Paddy Scannell calls 'an inclusive public good'.[1] Unlike commercial media, which are there primarily to make money, public broadcasters have an ethical underpinning, a responsibility to serve the community and uphold basic journalistic ideals. Public broadcasting 'gives without any expectation of a return', Scannell tells us, and is infused with 'paradigms of love and communication'.[2] And at the risk of sounding Pollyanna-ish, I have found those same qualities in abundance in the kind of audio professionals with whom I have communed over 40 years.

It's entirely unscientific and I have no way of proving it, but I just think we audio-storytelling folk are generally a good bunch, softer than the average media apparatchik, more inclined to care about fairness and social justice. It sounds absurd, I know – but maybe not. After all, the twin pillars of podcasting are intimacy and empathy, and they are rooted in radio too. Of course not every public radio person is a bleeding heart, and clearly there are generous souls in television, film, photography and newspapers. But as a sweeping generalisation, I've found audio types tend to be decent folk. Maybe it's because people with bigger egos have traditionally gone into TV or print, where their image or by-line figures more prominently. Maybe it's because audio storytellers genuinely love the medium, despite the fact that for decades it was seen as far less 'sexy' than TV or film. Maybe it's because audio craft takes infinite patience, and yet until the advent of the internet, months of work would be gone in half an hour, disappearing into the ether in what BBC producer Lance Sieveking complained of way back in 1934 as the 'ghastly impermanence' of radio.

As backup for my highly irrational theory of the public service–oriented virtues of audio folk, take a look at the very first mission statement of NPR. It was written in 1970 by the network's new program director, Bill Siemering, and it begins:

> National Public Radio will serve the individual: it will promote personal growth; it will regard the individual differences among men with respect and joy rather than derision and hate; it will celebrate the human experience as infinitely varied rather than vacuous and banal; it will encourage a sense of active constructive participation, rather than apathetic helplessness.

It concluded:

> The total service should be trustworthy, enhance intellectual development, expand knowledge, deepen aural esthetic enjoyment, increase the pleasure of living in a pluralistic society and result in a service to listeners which makes them more responsive, informed human beings and intelligent responsible citizens of their communities and the world.[3]

Now that's a place I'd like to work! NPR did shine a light on many critical issues and continues to offer solid journalism. But lack of diversity, gender imbalance, pay inequality and other issues would undermine its idealistic origins, culminating in veteran NPR broadcaster Celeste Headlee's blistering manifesto, 'An Anti-Racist Future: A Vision and Plan for the Transformation of Public Media' in 2021 (see chapter 9). Bill Siemering foresaw the challenges. He warned back in 1970 that his shining vision would be reduced to 'platitudes and good intentions unless there is the strong commitment, creative energy and specific strategy to implement them'.

Highlights of early radio programming

NPR turned out to be far from perfect. The BBC, ABC, CBC and European networks also had their ups and downs. But collectively, these public broadcasters have produced outstanding audio storytelling, in both fiction and nonfiction formats, for about a century. Here are some highlights.

Some of the first 'radio features' emerged at the BBC in the 1930s. These were imaginative audio works that blended actuality with narrated information usually delivered by actors. A proto-feature series, *Crisis in Spain*, was made by Archie Harding in 1931, while in 1936, *The March of the 45* by producer DG Bridson recreated the tragic 1746 Battle of Culloden, in which the English defeated the Scots, in a three-and-a-half-hour 'panorama feature'. The left-wing Harding, considered 'a very dangerous man' by the BBC Director-General John Reith, was banished to Manchester after a 1933 program, *New Year over Europe*, offended the Polish ambassador with a reference to Poland's military spending. Undaunted, Harding worked there with Bridson and a remarkable woman called Olive Shapley to include marginalised voices. They once put Durham coalminers live on air, but only after Shapley showed them a placard that cautioned: 'Do not say bugger or bloody'. Thereafter, the BBC ruled that all discussions should be scripted.[4]

The Bard: Norman Corwin

Prominent among early US broadcasters was Norman Corwin, known as 'The Bard of Radio', whose long career began in 1936 at CBS. He wrote and produced radio plays before making two hugely influential wartime shows: *We Hold These Truths*, a government-sponsored drama, was a patriotic tribute to the Bill of Rights, broadcast in 1941; and the commissioned radio play *On a Note of Triumph* that aired on VE Day, 8 March 1945, another show celebrating the victory of the forces of good over evil. In 1947, Corwin made an inventive documentary, *One World Flight*, based on 100 hours of interviews in 16 countries, laboriously recorded on magnetic tape over a four-month trip. Unusually, he wove in actuality: Italian demonstrators demanding work, Australian sheep shearers and Aboriginal singers, traffic on a Prague street. Corwin died in 2011, aged 101.

My kind of radio is that which takes into account the
intelligence of my audience. I do not believe in talking down.
I also brought to the microphone my concerns;
my feeling about society; my feeling about war and peace;
my feeling about man as a species that is developing and
for which we cherish hopes, frequently dashed,
as they are at the moment.

– Norman Corwin, 'Norman Corwin on war, poetry, and
radio: A conversation with Tony Kahn', Transom, 2001

In the postwar era, the radio feature – a more impressionistic, poetic version of a radio documentary – flourished in Europe and as far afield as Australia, where writer Colin Simpson included natural sounds like a buffalo hunt and a mass flight of geese in his 1947 series *Australian Walkabout*, which took ABC listeners to the top end of Australia. In the UK, the 1950s were a golden age, with writers such as Samuel Beckett, Dylan Thomas and Louis MacNeice writing plays and poetry for the BBC. On the nonfiction front, the producer Denis Mitchell, originally from South Africa, moved to the UK and produced innovative audio montage explorations of ordinary people's lives.

The curious: Studs Terkel

Not surprisingly, these audio experimenters influenced and enriched each other. The work of Norman Corwin and Denis Mitchell, for instance, mightily impressed another broadcasting giant, Louis 'Studs' Terkel. Over his own long life (he died in 2008, aged 96), Studs' 5000-plus interviews were broadcast on the WFMT Chicago radio show he hosted for 45 years and adapted for noted books on American history and culture, and are now preserved as an active public archive.

What I love about Studs is how diverse his interviewees were. He spoke to 20th-century legends and luminaries such as Dr Martin Luther King Jr, Simone de Beauvoir, Buster Keaton, Dorothy Parker, Bob Dylan, Betty Friedan and Muhammad Ali. But he showed equal enthusiasm for a woodcutter, a gravedigger or a truck driver. He conferred on all he interviewed the respect of deep listening. An anecdote he often recounted described beautifully how validating that is. He was out and about in Chicago one day when he saw a woman with several children staring into an empty shop window. Ever-curious, Studs politely asked what she was looking at.

'Oh, dreams, I'm just looking at dreams.'

So I've got my tape recorder and I switch it on and I say 'Good dreams, bad dreams?'

And she starts to talk ... and when she stops talking after eight, maybe ten minutes or so, one of them [her children] says, 'Hey mom, can we listen to what you said?' ... so I play it back and she listens to it too.

And when it's over, she gives a little shake of her head and she looks at me and she says, 'Well until I heard that, I never knew I felt that way.'[5]

In 2011 I was thrilled to sit in Studs' Chicago living-room, at the table where he worked, and interview his son Dan about Studs' life and work. This privileged access happened due to the warmth of the audio storytelling community, whose kindred spirits look after each other. I was put in touch with Dan Terkell by Sydney Lewis, a writer who had edited Studs' work for many years, and whom I had met through her work at Transom when I visited its Massachusetts headquarters. (Transom, the organisation founded by 'the godfather of public radio' Jay Allison, was where Chenjerai Kumanyika would issue his manifesto on lack of diversity in public broadcasting – see chapter 1. Transom's nine-week audio storytelling workshop, which ran each year from 2011 to 2020, was legendary, allowing a small group of 'hard working, curious, story-driven, wanna-be radio producers' to have a deep immersion in learning how to craft audio.)

Thanks to Sydney's introduction, Dan Terkell would then drive me and my husband Chris around Chicago for hours, pointing out Studs' favourite haunts and providing a running social history. We stopped at Bughouse Square to pay a proper tribute. Studs' ashes are buried there, near Speakers' Corner, a symbol of his lifelong championing of the underdog and challenging of authoritarianism. He showcased his philosophy in a beautifully composed documentary, *Born to Live*, which won the 1962 Prix Italia, the highest radio accolade.

Cross-fertilisations in audio

So, Norman Corwin influences Studs Terkel, and both of them influence Jay Allison, who plays *Born to Live* every New Year's Day on the Atlantic Public Media WCAI radio station he founded at Transom's home, Woods Hole in Massachusetts. And Allison, in turn, has shaped generations of new producers. I love these synergies, this whispering of audio creativity across oceans and borders, even in a pre-internet age. Here's another one: in 1944, Norman Corwin made a docudrama called *The Lonesome Train*, about the transportation of Abraham Lincoln's corpse to his hometown in Springfield, Illinois. It was released as a recording on Decca Records, and made a big impression on a BBC producer called Charles Parker. Parker had grown up in a conservative religious, military tradition, but he became radicalised after the war. He soon ran up against folk singer and agit-prop theatre performer Ewan MacColl, who would write the immortal love song 'The First Time Ever I Saw Your Face' for singer Peggy Seeger, who first performed it in 1957. Together with Charles Parker, MacColl and Seeger then devised a groundbreaking BBC series called *The Radio Ballads*, broadcast from 1958 to 1964.

The Radio Ballads are a portal to a rich, vibrant world that hitherto had gone virtually unremarked. The series of one-hour, non-narrated montages vividly portrays the lives of ordinary people: coalminers, train drivers, fishermen, people with polio trapped in 'iron lungs', travellers (outcast gypsy tribes) and teenagers. Each program broke – spectacularly – the unwritten rule that working-class voices should not be heard on the air. Amid the cacophony of accents and emotions, we hear the actual world these people inhabit: the creaking of the boat's ropes, the tap-tap of the mining, the terrible in-out whoosh of the mechanical lung that allows the polio victim to talk.

That series, in turn, influenced a whole new round of people, including me. I based my 2009 podcast/documentary series *Marrying Out*, about Australians who suffered bigotry for marrying across the sectarian Catholic–Protestant divide, on *The Radio Ballads'* blend of deep oral history, evocative sound and specially composed soundtrack. I was delighted to tell Peggy Seeger that in person, when she gave a rip-roaring concert in Sydney in 2012, aged a sprightly 77. I was even more delighted when she emailed to say she and her partner had enjoyed listening to *Marrying Out* as they drove around Australia, her partner's Belfast origins chiming loudly with its theme. *The Radio Ballads* continue to inspire younger generations. The annual Charles Parker Prize is today awarded to students who produce the best imaginative audio features, and the winners are mentored by a BBC producer to polish the piece for broadcast – a wonderful opportunity.

On and on the cross-fertilisation and conversations go. In Europe, from the 1960s, producers grasped the revolutionary opportunities offered by the arrival of portable tape recorders and seized the chance to leave the formality of the studio and record soundscapes and actuality. These composed, sound-rich 'features' were often imaginative treatments of an idea rather than the more linear, narrator-driven approach associated with documentary forms. *Glocken in Europa* (*Bells in Europe*), made by the German producer Peter Leonhard Braun in 1973, is a classic of the genre and has been translated into 15 languages. This 51-minute 'acoustic film' meditates on the role bells have played in the history and culture of Europe. Braun started experimenting with 'documentary sound sculptures' in the 1960s, influenced by pioneering radio work from the UK, France and elsewhere. In 1974, he founded the still-running International Feature Conference (IFC), a forum at which radio feature-makers of an artistic bent could share and critique their work.

Every year, producers who consider themselves 'auteurs' (authors) of a feature in the same way that a director shapes a film, gather at the IFC to be inspired by, assess and discuss exemplary audio works. Crucially, the public broadcasters have supported this work, notably in Scandinavia, Eastern Europe, France, Germany, the UK and Australia, and not so much in the US – though early NPR producers such as Joe Frank and

Larry Massett (his 1985 *A Trip to the Dentist* is still a riot) were highly innovative. By the 1990s, US producers such as David Isay (founder of the StoryCorps conversational/oral history project) and Stacy Abramson were pushing boundaries with works like *The Sunshine Hotel*, an immersive piece about the residents of a New York dosshouse. *Ghetto Life 101*, in which Isay gave two young black teenagers in a Chicago housing project a tape recorder, was a revelatory 1994 documentary drawn from the audio-vérité they recorded. Its intimacy reminds me of another extraordinarily raw piece, *Jason and the Thunderbirds*, a cinematically up-close portrait of tenants of a Glasgow public housing estate, made by Mairi Russell for the BBC in 1992. Extracts from dozens of these remarkable artistic audio features were assembled on one boxed CD set in 2004 to mark the 30th anniversary of the founding of the IFC: a collector's item I am lucky to have.[6]

The digital revolution: Third Coast, critical listening and *RadioDoc Review*

The new millennium birthed what would become a seminal organisation for lovers and makers of audio stories. The East and West Coasts of the US had long been cultural hubs. But in 2000, Johanna Zorn and Julie Shapiro launched an audacious initiative in Chicago, a city they saw as part of the 'Third Coast'. The Third Coast International Audio Festival (TCIAF) was founded as an independent, nonprofit arts organisation, 'serving a global community of storytellers and makers'. Since then, Third Coast has 'steadfastly advocated for the medium of audio, the art and craft of sonic storytelling, and the people who build our world in sound'.

The timing of Third Coast's launch was propitious. The internet had finally percolated through to ordinary people around the world, and the talks, programs and discussions on the Third Coast website could be widely accessed. Among its activities were an annual competition and biennial festival, at which noted audio producers would deconstruct their art and craft before an audience of aficionados and peers; a radio show, posted online, called *Re:sound*, which gathered 'found sound' from around the world and remixed it into a weekly best-of; and a Filmless Festival, where selected audio works were 'screened' as communal listening events.

Julie Shapiro was not from a solid NPR background at all. 'Through college, my primary interest in listening was to music and I DJ'd at college stations', she told me in 2011, when I visited Third Coast on Chicago's famous Navy Pier. Driving around the US after college, really listening to public radio for the first time, she realised 'how sound conveyed message and narrative and story'. *This American Life* had just started, 'telling the kind of stories we could all relate to and imagine telling ourselves'. A brush with North Carolina public radio, a break in New Zealand (a country Julie still loves – look out for her 2015 audio feature *The Search for Tiny Libraries in New Zealand*) and a stint at the vibrant Center for Documentary Studies at Duke University followed; Julie also organised an experimental music festival and self-published a magazine in which she played with unusual ways to tell stories.

Julie's CV turned out to contain the perfect mix when she moved to Chicago in 2000, serendipitously just when Johanna Zorn had got the green light from WBEZ radio to start the Third Coast Festival and was seeking an assistant. The job involved a lot of careful listening. 'We curate', Julie told me. 'We are taking the work that other people make and trying to share it with as many people as possible and encourage the makers to push themselves to embrace creativity.' Aesthetics of audio was a fundamental concept. Julie summarised it this way: 'Important radio can sound beautiful'. I took this to mean that even if you're dealing with a serious real-life issue, you can still lavish attention on the composition of the piece. 'There's a real sense that radio's for news information. It has to be delivered in a certain way', Julie elaborated. 'We're always trying to challenge people's expectations in that realm.'

The importance of audio critique

A year after Third Coast launched, in 2001, producer John Biewen arrived at Julie's old stamping ground, the Center for Documentary Studies, and would later become Director of Audio there. A long-time maker of documentaries at NPR, John had been having similar thoughts to Julie about the boring associations factual audio stories had acquired. 'The word "documentary" might have evoked thoughts of sonic Brussels sprouts', he memorably wrote.

John's allusion was not a compliment. I laughed when I read it, in the preface to *Reality Radio: Telling True Stories in Sound*, the book John co-edited. In it, a bunch of acclaimed audio producers in North America, Europe and Australia reflect on their art and craft, offering a rare and precious insight into how some of the best in the business plied their trade. The common denominator John notes of this seminal book's contributors: they all 'use sound to tell *true* stories *artfully*'. So rare was it then (2010) to find this kind of serious engagement with audio storytelling that I wrote to John from Australia seeking a pre-publication copy. He kindly obliged.

Around that time, John produced a documentary for *This American Life*, about a massacre of 38 Dakota warriors in 1862, the largest mass execution of First Nations Americans ever. Called *Little War on the Prairie*, it revealed another shocking truth to John: it happened in the town he came from – Mankato, Minnesota – yet he had never heard it mentioned while he was growing up. From this intriguing premise, John wove a fascinating and appalling tale. I listened to it closely and charted my reactions: historical allusions I didn't quite get, moments where I was particularly shocked or moved, points I wanted more information on. It was more narration-dense than the sort of montage-led European and Australian features I was used to. There were also places where in my mind's ear I could 'hear' opportunities for sound or actuality, but these didn't eventuate. A reason for one of these omissions was clear: a final climactic First Nations American ceremony could not be included because of cultural protection. While beautifully produced, John's approach to storytelling sounded different to my ears in other ways, such as its use of music. Grateful for his kindness in sending me the advance copy of *Reality Radio*, I decided to write out in detail how his show landed to an Australian listener and email him my thoughts.

I worried when I saw his reply in my inbox that maybe I had crossed a line, been too critical. But he was delighted! Like most creative folk, he craved feedback. Comments from family and friends are always welcome, but we know in our heart they might just be being nice. An honest, in-depth critique from a peer that comes from a place of demonstrated knowledge is invaluable – even if it does hurt at times. It's the only way to test your process, to think about whether you have to kill this darling, or switch a slab around, or even rejig the whole thing. If you're lucky, that's the sort of advice you get from an executive producer, in time for you to make changes. But even when a show has been broadcast, there is great merit in having a dispassionate analysis from someone who understands the form and can point out the strengths and weaknesses of your work.

I discovered this when John returned the favour and sent me his critique of a complex documentary I had recently made in collaboration with an anthropologist, Jacqui Baker, about the gratuitous killing by police of petty thieves in Indonesia. Called *Eat, Pray, Mourn: Crime and Punishment in Jakarta*, it revisits Jacqui's PhD research into these horrifying extrajudicial killings through the eyes of three women who have lost loved ones. I converted their wrenching personal stories into a flowing audio narrative, animated by the rich soundscapes Jacqui recorded of the Indonesian slums and villages where the women live, and brought further to life by her reflective script. The interviews were in Bahasa (Indonesian) language, so I had to work hard to float the character of the women through the tone and emotion in their voice, before the translation took over. John's critique described how he was moved by the fieriness of the main protagonist, Yeni, a noodle-seller who was fighting for justice for her murdered brother, Yusli. But there were other parts where he wanted more guidance, such as on Indonesian history and politics. He noted other production aspects, some of which appealed to him and others about which he had reservations.

Though I also had had wonderful collegial input during production, we both realised how important an expert outsider critique was too, to help us see how we could extend ourselves in new storytelling projects. An idea formed.

RadioDoc Review

In July 2013, I was at a radio studies conference just outside London with a secret mission: to launch a new open-access journal. It would bring academics and industry folk together to develop a forum for high-quality critical analysis of crafted audio stories. I wanted it to elevate readers' understanding of our art in the same way that an informed, perceptive book or film review deepens our appreciation of literature or cinema. I had a name: *RadioDoc Review*. But I needed top-class reviewers and a board with the credibility and authority to select works worthy of a review. All this would be pro bono, done for love of the audio medium and of audio narrative formats, just to celebrate and develop the art of audio storytelling. But how to persuade people of such eminence to sign up?

The conference keynote speaker was lauded media historian David Hendy. I'd read his insightful chapter on the radio documentary form in an academic anthology.[7] I liked how he described documentary as 'the built programme par excellence' and how he had noted its inherent struggle to deliver a 'creative interpretation' of the issue or idea it explored. 'It offers authenticity, but it also denotes artifice', he wrote. David had also made the first ever narrative history of sound and listening, a marathon 30-part BBC radio documentary series called *Noise: A Human History*. If David Hendy came on board, surely the rest would follow.

David's keynote was warmly received and afterwards, he moved through the appreciative crowd. I waited until he was on his second glass of wine, bathed in approbation. Then I sidled up and introduced myself. After a few flattering remarks, I stammered out my idea for the journal. Would he do me the honour of being on the editorial board? It would not be onerous, I hastened to say (all academics are fearfully overloaded). Just nominate a work once or twice a year, suggest a reviewer, peer-review a critique. Glowing with bonhomie, he said yes, congratulating me on the idea.

After that, they fell like nine-pins. I approached other experts at the conference, explaining that David Hendy was on board this new venture. Would they like to join us? They would. Later, I invited specialists from industry as well as academia. Recent audio chums like Julie Shapiro and John Biewen threw their caps in the ring. I wrote an open email to the Radio List, a specialist radio studies group, asking for expressions of interest from potential reviewers. Soon we were all set, with an international board and a flash website administered from my university.

I formed a subcommittee to develop *RadioDoc Review*'s own guidelines for writing reviews of an audio documentary or narrative. Michelle Boyd, an African American sociologist in Chicago who had an interest in how audio stories could illuminate social justice issues such as police brutality, was one volunteer. Gail Phillips, a longstanding Australian radio academic and former broadcaster, was another. We adapted some characteristics from film theory and also applied our own concepts, building in consideration of storytelling strength, originality, production of empathy and emotiveness, research and reporting depth, complexity of story and form, craft and artistry, ethics, public benefit, audience engagement and impact. Our criteria have since been adopted by other analysts.

In January 2014, *RadioDoc Review* published its first critique: of a wry 30-minute feature called *Poetry, Texas*, made by Pejk Malinovski, a Danish-born producer based in the US. The title came from a small town in Texas called, yes, Poetry, which had caught Pejk's eye on Google Maps. Coming from three generations of poets, he set off to investigate the place. I was elated when the review came in; it was written by Seán Street, the first professor of radio broadcasting in the UK and a noted feature-maker and writer. Seán set the broader philosophical context:

> Documentaries and features are about stories, but although they share much common ground, they often occupy very different worlds ... in many radio cultures a documentary is a journalistic framework for seeking answers to questions, whereas a feature may often be an impressionistic hybrid that can contain drama, music and poetry, moving often towards not necessarily answers, but more questions.[8]

RadioDoc Review (*RDR*) has since published dozens of articles offering groundbreaking critical analysis of the audio feature/podcast narrative form. The works selected are, as anticipated, evolving into a de facto audio canon, and the journal's articles are increasingly being set as texts in the new podcasting subjects being developed at universities. But it is the *community* of audio-loving readers that *RDR* has spawned that most thrills me. Whether it is via social media hook-ups, or the seductive real-time global download map on the front page, people are bonding via *RDR* due to a passion for audio storytelling.

Besides English, *RDR* has reviewed audio works in Spanish, Portuguese, Polish, German, Norwegian, Farsi, French and Danish. Audio-makers have come from all over Europe, the US, Canada, Latin America and Australia. Reviewers have come from the same regions, along with South Africa and China. In February 2020, I stood aside as editor to be replaced for three years by the indefatigable Neil Verma. Neil has a remarkable record as a researcher, critic and teacher of sound studies and audio stories, and also practises as a sound artist. Based in Chicago, and of Indian American heritage, he is bringing new perspectives and diverse voices into play, including broadening the remit of *RDR* to showcase work by emerging scholars and people of colour. It's wonderful to see *RDR* re-energised and recognised: in 2021, it was described by eminent scholar Michele Hilmes as 'offering consistently high-level review and criticism of international audio work, often bringing historical and contemporary documentaries into juxtaposition'. Hilmes nominated *RDR* alongside significant digital technology projects such as PodcastRE, the US Library of Congress's Radio Preservation Task Force, the WNYC digital archives and the American Archive of Public Broadcasting as helping to liberate 'not only the contemporary poetics of sound but also its historical roots'.[9] The next chapter delves further into that continuum, exploring the close links between radio and podcasting.

Audio and podcasting festivals and events

There are new events happening every week, but these are some of the most prominent podcast industry and audiophile events.

Podcast Day 24 (Sydney/London/North America)
This international 24-hour event brings together organisers of various radio and podcast events, with an excellent range of speakers from three continents, creators, industry executives and media organisations, keeping the talk going in various time zones. <www.podcastday24.com/about/>

Podcast Movement (USA)
Billed as the world's largest podcasting community and a 'hub for podcasting news, resources and the best podcast events', this entity and associated conference has been running since 2014. Industry-oriented. <https://podcastmovement.com/about/>

Podcast Academy (Los Angeles, USA)
A newcomer, the PA launched a flash awards ceremony in May 2021, the Ambies. Their overall mission is to 'support podcast

makers and advance the cultural merit of the medium'. A good online attempt to connect podcasters around the world. A membership fee applies. <www.thepodcastacademy.com>

International Podcast Day (Online)

Begun in 2014, this group organises social events, festivals and meet-ups across the world around 30 September. Easy to track on social media using #InternationalPodcastDay! <https://internationalpodcastday.com>

She Podcasts (USA)

This group of self-empowering female podcasters began as a Facebook group and podcast in 2014 and launched a three-day gathering in 2019. Over 15,000 members. <www.shepodcasts.com>

Third Coast International Audio Festival (Chicago, USA)

Dubbed 'the Sundance of audio', this is for people who make and/or love to listen to creative audio stories. It has conference elements, where experts divulge their secrets or debate issues in the audio world, and listening sessions, often with the maker present. And it has awards! <www.thirdcoastfestival.org>

HearSay Audio Arts Festival (Kilfinane, Ireland)

This heralded event is an unlikely premise for an audio festival: world-class audio in an Irish mountain village. It brings together audio makers of all disciplines from all over the world, with the people of Kilfinane, who have been welcoming HearSay since 2014. Has awards too! <www.hearsayfestival.ie>

International Feature Conference (Mostly Europe, Australia)

This critical-listening gathering of top and up-and-coming audio feature-makers has been running annually since 1974. Features are competitively selected for 'screening', listened to communally and robustly critiqued in groups. Great for understanding the art and craft of audio and for networking. <https://ifc2.wordpress.com>

Radiodays Asia (Various locations)

A savvy radio-based organisation that increasingly has podcast elements, rare in the region until recently. <www.radiodaysasia.com>

PodFest China

An annual conference hosted by JustPod, a Chinese podcasting company. The 2021 Shanghai event was attended by c. 500 and supported by leading podcast platforms Xiaoyuzhou and Ximalaya. <chinapodfestchina@gmail.com>

Asia Podcast Festival

A slick new organisation that runs workshops on tech, content and monetising aspects, and holds awards and an annual conference. <https://www.asiapodcastfestival.com/>

Asian American Podcast Festival (Online)

A new initiative in 2021, 'for Asian Americans from all over'. <https://aapodcasters.org>

Awards and prizes

Prix Europa: Founded in 1987, open to all European residents, no entry fee. Audio categories include Documentary, Documentary Series, Fiction, Fiction Series, Investigation and Music. <www.prixeuropa.eu >

Prix Marulić: An international festival of radio drama and radio documentary drama with an emphasis on sophisticated sound art and radiophonic treatment, run by Croatia's public broadcaster Hrvatska radiotelevizija (HRT). <https://prix-marulic.hrt.hr>

Prix Italia: The oldest and most prestigious audio prize in the world, established in 1948. Audio categories: Drama, Documentary/Reportage, Music. <www.rai.it/prixitalia/>

New York Festivals, Podcasting categories: Established in 1957, this huge festival covers radio content in formats from around the world. Podcast awards were added in 2017 and come in 18 categories. <https://radio.newyorkfestivals.com/Competition/Categories>

Peabody Awards: Established in 1941, the Peabody Awards honour 'excellence in storytelling that reflects the social issues and the emerging voices of our day'. Radio/podcast categories cover Documentary, Entertainment, News, Children's/Youth Programming, Public Service and Arts. <https://peabodyawards.com>

Pulitzer Prize: Established in 1917, the Pulitzers added an audio journalism category in 2020. <www.pulitzer.org>

British Podcasting Awards: Established in 2017, the BPAs have awards in many categories. <www.britishpodcastawards.com>

Australian Podcasting Awards: Established in 2017 as the Castaways, these awards now link to the BPAs and aim 'to discover great podcasts wherever they come from'. <https://australianpodcastawards.com>

Webby Awards: Established in 1996, the Webbys honour 'the best of the internet'. Their huge Podcast section has more than 30 categories/formats. There is a popular vote as well as a jury award. <www.webbyawards.com>

AIBs: The Association for International Broadcasting (AIB) Awards recognise 'the world's best journalism and factual productions across television, radio and digital'. There are five audio categories, including Podcasts. <https://theaibs.tv>

Asia-Pacific Broadcasting Union (ABU) Awards: The ABU's members in 69 countries broadcast to more than three billion people – around half the world's population. Audio awards are made in seven categories. <www.abu.org.my/abu-prizes/>

3

Radio, podcasting and intimacy

If you want to experience live radio at its most sublime, check out the Radio Garden. You can find the website, or download the free app to your phone. It manifests as a globe, covered in green dots. As you zoom in, each dot reveals a town or city, and you start to hear a local radio station. I swivel the globe. In Kampala, Uganda, it's 8 am and two deep-voiced men are talking politics in English in between playing pop on HOT100 FM. In a little town called Le Faou in north-western France, it's 7 am and Radio Évasion is playing funky jazz piano. In Miami, Florida, Radio Hit Latino greets the small hours with a Latina crooner. And in Kabul, Afghanistan, three days after the city fell to the Taliban in August 2021, it's a relief to hear three stations playing pop music at 9:30 am.

I was at the radio studies conference in Utrecht, the Netherlands, where Radio Garden was first displayed in 2016. It was part of a research project, Transnational Radio Encounters, commissioned by the Netherlands Institute for Sound and Vision, that set out to explore how radio communicates across borders. There are more than 35 000 stations just a click away on Radio Garden's interactive map, and even in an internet age, it feels uplifting and somewhat magical to be able to commune with real people all over the world in real time.

Liveness has always been a huge part of radio's appeal. From 1993, 'internet radio' allowed broadcasters to reach listeners much further afield than the old sound waves of terrestrial radio could travel. Besides streaming live content, listeners would soon be able to avail themselves of radio-on-demand, as broadcasters uploaded shows to the internet to be downloaded whenever the listener preferred. Some radio formats transitioned seamlessly to an online existence, becoming early de facto podcasts. Long-form interviews conducted engagingly with interesting subjects, for instance, remain evergreen: thus, for many years, Australia's most popular podcast was *Conversations*, hosted by Richard Fidler on the ABC. Like other great interviewers, such as Terry Gross on NPR's *Fresh Air*, Fidler brings an intense curiosity, empathy and attentiveness to the encounter, along with warmth and wit.

But over time, other players began to populate the podcast space, developing 'native' podcast-first content tailored to the emerging medium. In the US, former radio journalists and artists developed independent podcast networks such as Gimlet (now owned by Spotify) and Radiotopia in 2014. That same year, the runaway success of the made-for-podcast hit *Serial* made traditional radio sit up. Though radio and podcasts have a lot in common, they are different creatures. This chapter explores how radio adapted to a more 'podcasty' mode, and what distinguishes that form.

Kissing cousins: How radio fits with the podcast industry

Major radio organisations, such as NPR and iHeartRadio in the US, consistently feature in the top ten of most downloaded podcasts. iHeartRadio owns massive hit shows such as the *Stuff You Should Know* franchise, which began podcasting in 2008, while NPR has had huge success with the news digest *Up First*, created as a bespoke ten-minute podcast in 2017. In 2020, NPR's podcast sponsorship revenue was expected to surpass revenue from broadcast sponsorships for the first time – a breakthrough moment.

Other radio organisations learned to adapt to the new listening mode that podcasting afforded and the additional audiences it could attract. The Canadian national broadcaster, CBC, moved quickly, launching CBC Podcasts in 2015. It would develop award-winning and innovative shows such as *Alone: A Love Story*, a raw first-person account of a woman's life post-divorce; *Tai Asks Why*, in which the 12-year-old host asks searching scientific questions; *The Shadows*, a playful fictional anatomy of a relationship; and *Finding Cleo*, an investigation into the disappearance of an Indigenous Cree child. *Alone* and *The Shadows* contained content that would not meet most public broadcasting standards for content transmitted to, say, a general daytime audience – another advantage of switching to podcast. *Finding Cleo* was a long and involved investigation that required complex cultural context about First Nations peoples; podcasting is perfect for these sort of stories, because it allows producers to go off on tangents and fill in backstories, confident that their audience has a declared interest in this topic because they have *chosen* to listen.

Australia and the ABC

Australia's ABC launched its podcast production house, Audio Studios, in mid-2017. Successful output included two innovative kids' shows, *Short & Curly*, 'a fun-filled ethics podcast for kids and their parents', and *Fierce Girls*, which includes episodes where girls under 12 write and narrate short stories about female heroes in sport, arts and science; a feminist panel show, *Ladies, We Need to Talk*; and two investigative series, *Trace* and *Unravel*. *Trace*'s first series saw host Rachael Brown examine a cold case in which a woman was murdered in a Melbourne bookshop. The podcast exposed a poor police investigation and the sexual abuse of the young son of the murdered woman, and it won Best Documentary at the Australian Podcasting Awards in 2018. In the second series, *The Informer*, Rachael and her colleague Josie Taylor followed the extraordinary story of a Melbourne lawyer who had double-crossed her gangster clients to be a police informer.

Podcasting also offered new opportunities for Indigenous content, previously largely focused in a one-hour weekly slot, *Awaye!*. Indigenous journalist and Muruwari man Allan Clarke made two major podcasts on the untimely death of two Aboriginal boys: *Blood on the Tracks*, the first in the *Unravel* series, was a multimedia project about the death of a 14-year-old boy, which allowed his family to air their grief and frustration at length and at last. *Thin Black Line* examined the death of a young dancer who had been apprehended by police. Produced at a time when there was growing support in Australia for the #BlackLivesMatter movement, and against a backdrop of shocking rates of deaths of Indigenous people while in custody, the podcast was a moving and sensitive account of a tragic death that might have been averted if police had not racially profiled a group of kids drinking in a park.

While drawing on the ABC's array of excellent journalists, Audio Studios' founding commissioning editor and manager Kellie Riordan saw a clear distinction between the on-demand podcast approach and ABC Radio's linear mode. 'On-demand is all about the mobile phone and what a person decides to download when they go for a run, or are on the train, or when the kids go to bed. It has to be specific and tailored', she noted. The ABC, like most established public broadcasters, had a rusted-on, loyal audience. But Riordan sought fresh ears, via slick marketing. 'We spend a lot of time making great audio but we also need to spend more time telling great stories in episode titles, program descriptions, and the social space', she said at the launch. ABC Audio Studios podcasts would be marketed on standard platforms but also on a newly created ABC Listen app, which offered live and time-shifted radio content alongside well-presented podcasts. The strategy has paid off, with ABC podcasts winning gongs in recent years, after a sluggish start. Its *Unravel* unit has had several hits, including *Snowball*, a comedic scammer story that introduced us to a New Zealand family among the most likeable in podcasting.

The UK and the BBC

The BBC uploaded its first podcast in 2004, a Radio 4 show called *In Our Time*, and by 2017 the BBC's podcasts had been downloaded 240 million times. That year, the UK communications regulator Ofcom approved the broadcaster to make dedicated podcast-first content, distinct from radio programs. BBC Audio in Bristol was one of the first podcast teams out of the traps, producing *Blue Planet II* and *Evil Genius*. But as an executive noted in 2018, there were still nearly two million podcast listeners in the UK who did not consume any BBC Radio output. Partly to address this, Jason Phipps, former Head of Audio at the *Guardian*, was appointed the BBC's first Commissioning Editor for Podcasts in 2018, and the BBC Sounds app followed. BBC Sounds offered transformative opportunities for in-depth BBC storytelling. Prior to that, Radio 4 and World Service carried the burden of representation across the UK with limited slots available on traditional linear radio. Now, instead of one 40-minute speech documentary, you could pitch a ten-part podcast from wherever you were based.

By 2020, the BBC reported that more than half a million young people aged 16–34, a coveted sector, were using Sounds each week, and there had been a 21 per cent increase in podcast listening – although it conceded that might have been related to the COVID-19 pandemic. Its top ten podcasts were a mixture of genres: *That Peter Crouch Podcast*, in which former star footballer Peter Crouch chats with two mates about all things football, was the top performer. A news digest was second, followed by a historical panel show, *You're Dead to Me*. More chat shows, interview formats, entertainment shows, literary fiction and true-crime genres rounded out the list. Of the latter, one, *The Missing Cryptoqueen*, felt the most rooted in a 'podcasty' narrative journalism style, rather than something you might have heard on BBC Radio.

The Missing Cryptoqueen investigates a cryptocurrency scam and the woman responsible for a multi-billion-dollar international fraud, Dr Ruja Ignatova. Painstaking research underpins the podcast, but it is delivered by host Jamie Bartlett and producer Georgia Catt in an irreverent way that invites listeners to join them on a quest that is at times fun, at times sinister. Reviewing it in *RadioDoc Review*, Claudia Calhoun writes, 'Part of the excitement was the sense that the story was evolving in real time ... As in *Serial*, the integration of asides is a key strategy of this present-tense storytelling'. Her perceptive review continues:

> This sense of immediacy is amplified by the confessional nature
> of the narration. Bartlett often speaks into the microphone in a
> fast, breathless whisper, as if he is talking to himself and that the
> listener just happens to be there ... Bartlett often voices his thoughts,
> describes his concerns, and expresses his fears. On the hunt for
> Dr. Ruja, we hear Bartlett turn away from an unhelpful interviewee,
> then sigh to no one in particular, 'This is going to be tough; this
> is going to be hard work'. Choices like these give the listener the
> feeling that they are inside the story with Bartlett, as close to him as
> producer Catt.[1]

A 'bonus' episode, which dropped online months after the series officially finished, added to the live feel, featuring a bugged recording of the Cryptoqueen, now in hiding, holding forth with sweary abandon. It was the sort of language one could not imagine hearing live on the august airwaves of the BBC, but it suited podcasting perfectly. In this way, podcasts are to radio what series on Netflix and other streaming services are to live TV.

BBC Sounds has made use of this freedom, hosting a frank and fruity panel show in which three women of colour talk about sex, *Brown Girls Do It Too*, and a wildly inventive show, *Have You Heard George's Podcast?*, which won awards in fields as diverse as arts and culture, comedy and 'smartest podcast' for its Ugandan British host, George Mpanga (aka George the Poet). *Brown Girls Do It Too* won Podcast of the Year at the British Podcasting Awards in 2020, while *Have You Heard George's Podcast?* was the first program made outside the US to win a coveted Peabody Award. It also made the unusual journey of morphing into a radio show, when BBC Radio 4 picked it up following its early success as a podcast.

 ### The 11 Commandments of Podcasting

The BBC's podcasts unit published an appendix of 11 cheeky commandments that distinguish podcasts from radio. It's a smart and succinct guide:

1   A podcast is not a radio programme even if radio programmes can be made available to the public as podcasts.

2   For a younger generation who will never own a radio, podcasts are their radio [but] reread rule 1.

3   The story and topic will always be the guide for the length of a podcast.

4   Podcasts are built for the headphone generation, be respectful, warm and gentle inside their heads.

5   Use your f-bombs wisely; be informal, be intimate [but] the freedom to use raw language does not mean it's an obligation.

6   Podcasts are a visually powerful form of audio, they can be cinema for the ears.

7   The angels are in the detail, podcasts tell big, thorny and emotionally complex stories, real and made up.

8   Podcasts offer clarity in chaos; in a manic news cycle, podcasts offer focus and context.

9   Podcasts are tribal; they bond and deepen communities.

10 Regardless of where they spring from podcasts are natively global digital forms of audio.

11 Podcasts are agile; they can take all the rules above and change them, except rule 1.[2]

The BBC World Service outstrips its sister stations in podcasting. Its *Global News* podcast is the BBC's most downloaded podcast, with more than 220 million downloads in 2020 and a worldwide following. The World Service's weekly base of more than 350 million listeners has also allowed it to tap new audiences for podcasts such as *Kalki Presents: My Indian Life*, with Bollywood actor Kalki Koechlin, which reached young listeners in India, while *The Comb* and *Africa Daily* cater for African audiences.

Meanwhile back at BBC Sounds, another storytelling podcast hit in 2020 was *On the Ground*, hosted by Audrey Gillan, on her second major audio adventure (see chapter 1 for the story of *Tara and George*). This time Audrey's audio collaborator was journalist Dan Maudsley. *On the Ground* vividly revisits Audrey's experiences as a war correspondent for the *Guardian*, embedded with British troops in the Iraq War of 2003. The podcast opens with gripping archive of the bombing of a British patrol by an American plane. One young British soldier died in the tragic 'friendly fire' incident and others were badly injured. Over the series, Audrey unpacks how the incident occurred, but the podcast largely focuses on the relationships between the soldiers, the experiences of the journalists who accompanied them and the long-term impact of the war on all of them. This kind of deeply personal and emotive content is what podcasting does best.

Episode Seven, 'Survivor's Guilt', has Audrey interviewing Danny, a soldier who comforted her when they both came under attack and could have died. Danny is speaking openly for the first time, and trying to deal with what is probably post-traumatic stress disorder. Audrey also has difficult memories to confront. For such a highly sensitive interview, you need peace and quiet. But it was not easy to find, Audrey remembers. Initially they met at a restaurant, but it turned out to be too noisy, so they went to Danny's home:

He lived in one of these more posh blocks of flats with a concierge, and we went to the clubroom. And there was a guy doing a Skype call in the clubroom. Then we went to his flat. His girlfriend was there, the washing machine was on. So we got the washing machine off. And she said she would go to the gym. And then we sat down and did the interview.

The interview is deeply affecting, as both Danny and Audrey re-inhabit their terror and trauma on the day. In one incident, in which two men died, they watched in vain as soldiers attempted CPR. 'It's hard to explain seeing your friend that, you know, that you play football with, that you've been out drinking with, just – there's nothing there', Danny says haltingly, recalling how a helicopter came in to retrieve the two men. One was already dead; the other would die shortly afterwards in hospital. Audrey attended both their funerals. 'And then the helicopter's gone, and that's when it kind of kicked in, what had happened, all the realism kicked in', Danny continues.

'Did you not come sit next to me?' Audrey asks. 'Yeah, that's when I started, I started cryin'', says Danny.

'Do you remember if I was?' she asks. 'I think you was', he says. 'I think I was too', Audrey agrees.

'I think we had a moment and cried, on the bank', Danny affirms. 'And I think I remember you rubbing my back.' He makes some throat noises that hang in the silence. 'But then, that was literally moments, and then we were off again.'

Audrey told me she felt torn about revealing such naked emotion:

I said to Dan [Maudsley], 'We need to be careful with it. We can't use all that and see me breaking down in it'. You hear [Danny] remembering things that he didn't remember until I sat down with him. And you hear me getting quite raw and upset as well. And I would cover all that up in a written piece, probably ... Whereas with the tape – it's unvarnished.

Audience, timing, host and voice:
Radio vs podcasting

One of the signature tropes in podcasting is the centrality of the host, as a character in their own right. Radio presenters have historically been popular figures with dedicated followings, but podcast hosts do not have to abide by the proprieties of broadcasting – they can reveal themselves as real people, with foibles, fears, strengths and weaknesses. Even the term podcast 'host' versus radio 'presenter' is a giveaway. A host is someone who invites you to their home, or some personal part of their life; a 'presenter' is a professional communicator.

Pre-podcasting, a radio documentary presenter would normally stick closely to the topic in question, with tightly honed narration flowing into interview excerpts or layered over relevant sounds. But in a narrative podcast, where show duration is not a constraint, there is room for meta-scenes that allow listeners to peek into the host's life and 'witness' the production procedure. Thus *On the Ground* has Dan Maudsley quizzing Audrey on her journalistic process in Iraq, and Audrey cooking Dan a meal. 'I felt quite uncomfortable with it a lot of the time, to be honest with you. It's not my style', says Audrey, who did not know Maudsley was recording at the time. 'Like he's coming up the stairs: "Hiya!" Lots of people really like it. Some people hate it.'

Deciding what's in and what's out is one of the most significant creative and editorial decisions a podcast producer makes. In some cases, such as in Audrey's emotion-choked interview with Danny, there are ethical aspects to consider. What effect will it have on your interviewee for this knowledge to be made public? Conversely, having dredged up these difficult memories, what is the point of someone doing the emotional labour of describing these terrible incidents if they are not used to advance the public understanding of what goes on in war? (See chapters 4 and 6 for more on ethical implications.)

Besides permitting graphic or explicit material, there are other subtle differences in how audio content is created for radio or podcast.

Eleanor McDowall, an award-winning producer and co-director of Falling Tree Productions, is very aware of this. She has produced diverse shows for BBC Radio that have gone on to secondary lives as podcasts: *Short Cuts*, 'short documentaries and adventures in sound' presented by comedian Josie Long; *Lights Out*, 'documentary adventures that encourage you to take a closer listen'; and *The Enemy Within*, a 30-minute documentary for the *Between the Ears* program, that explores 'the inner lives of women who care for soldier partners who have returned from warzones suffering from post-traumatic stress disorder'.

By contrast, Eleanor has three series that are podcast natives: *Field Recordings*, a pandemic-inspired, sound-rich podcast 'where audio-makers stand silently in fields (or things that could be broadly interpreted as fields)'; *Radio Atlas*, 'a curated feed of innovative audio from around the world' in which audio works in many languages are subtitled via a website that ensures that sound and translation are sensitively synced; and *Goodbye to All This*, a 12-part 'story about life, love and loss'. (See chapter 10.)

I asked Eleanor to consider how the podcast/radio outcome affected her storytelling. She confirmed that the one crucially important factor was time:

> In radio, everything is held within the confines of the broadcasting clock. Ideas are explored in blocks of 15, 30, 45 minutes precisely. But in podcasting time is fluid, unconstrained. On *Field Recordings*, for example, episodes range from 30 seconds to 54 minutes long – the space expanding or contracting as the idea demands. When I'm editing for radio I can almost sense the timings in my body without looking as I pace something out, knowing what that duration feels like, thinking about how to hold the feeling whilst expanding or contracting work to fit the parameters of the time frame.

The listener dynamic also varies between the worlds of radio and podcasting, something an independent producer like Eleanor has to consider carefully. 'Radio is often used as a near-constant companion throughout a day, and I often think that one of the things that impacts work getting commissioned – through to editorial guidance before it's broadcast – is the impulse to stop listeners from *turning it off* rather than encouraging anyone to tune in.'

The episodes on *Goodbye to All This* vary from 19 to 38 minutes, the length determined by what the episode theme demands or can sustain. 'Doing the podcast edit felt liberating in some ways as the only question I had to ask myself was about what pacing felt right, when might a listener need longer to hold a moment or process something that had happened, when might something run quicker to keep its humour', Eleanor observed.

In radio, you're encouraged not to alienate anyone, to translate everything for a presumed 'neutral' imagined listener ... often quietly conceived of as white, cis, middle class, male and straight, whose invisible presence determines what is seen as needing explanation and what is not. In podcasting, no one hears your work without the excitement of seeking it out, of tuning into what you're doing. This can mean that you set the terms of who your imagined listener might be, giving freedom for a greater plurality of styles and ideas.

– Eleanor McDowall, Falling Tree Productions

But what if you have heaps of material, which nonetheless has to be condensed to a one-off feature rather than a series, because of a commission? What are the pros and cons? I had firsthand experience of this constraint when Eleanor made a 28-minute documentary, *A Sense of Quietness*, for the BBC's *Lights Out*. It explored four women's experiences navigating the laws around abortion in Ireland over a

35-year period – including mine. Bear with me while I take a podcast-style wander down a rabbit hole for a moment, as we consider whether a story is best rendered as multi-episode long-form or a one-off, pared-back program.

A Sense of Quietness: Distilling the story

Ireland in the 1980s was a strongly conservative Catholic country, and it had always made abortion illegal. But in 1983, a movement arose to make an amendment to the Constitution of Ireland to put the life of the unborn child on a par with that of the mother. It meant that a woman, rather than her baby, could be allowed to die in childbirth.

The Eighth Amendment campaign divided the country like nothing since the Irish Civil War some 60 years earlier. I was then producing a popular morning show on Irish national radio, RTÉ. We were warned that we could not discuss 'The Amendment'; it could only be addressed by news formats. The last hour of our show featured an interview with some person of note, who would recount their life story and play three favourite pieces of music (a format shamelessly ripped off from the BBC's *Desert Island Discs*). At a production meeting, I proposed having a woman who had founded a family planning and women's health clinic, Anne Connolly, one week; and, for balance, a woman from the Society for the Protection of Unborn Children the following week. In neither case would we discuss The Amendment, but their background would be of interest given the coming referendum.

My manager approved the plan and the interview with Anne Connolly went off without incident – if anything, it was rather bland. But influential Catholic figures immediately complained to the Director-General of RTÉ and, carpeted, my manager lied about having approved the guest. By lunchtime that day I had been suspended. The referendum passed, making abortions so illegal in Ireland that not even a pregnant child rape victim threatening suicide would be granted one. I, meanwhile, was put out to grass on a country music show and generally branded a 'troublemaker' with limited career prospects – an outcome that led me directly to emigrate to Australia.

Fast forward three decades. I am teaching journalism in Australia and assign students an exercise to write a profile feature. Most portray standard community figures, but one stands out: a piece about a gangster's 'moll' who runs a racket in fake luxury handbags. The author, Brianna Parkins, has a keen ear for dialogue and an observant eye. It opens like this:

> 'Fake', declares Linh confidently, her voice a delicious, tobacco-softened drawl with a light accent. She sounds somewhere between a Bond girl and a husky Mae West. She flicks heavily lined eyes on a group of young girls in the suburban food court.
>
> 'So fucking fake, but the little one might be real.'
>
> She's talking about the monogrammed Louis Vuitton handbags that burden the girls' slight shoulders.

The feature is so original I want to enter it for a student award. But there are numerous grammar and punctuation errors. I correct a few and send it back to Brianna to complete. She replies that, unlike better-off students who lived at home, she had to work late in a hospitality job to pay rent, was tired and hadn't the time. I must have been in a particularly unsympathetic mood for I replied, curtly, that I had left home at 16 and worked 40 hours a week as a waitress to put myself through college. 'It's about professional self-respect', I told her. 'You either have it or you don't – up to you.'

I duly received the fully subbed feature. It did not win an award (an error of judgment, in my view), but it put Brianna on my radar. She was feisty, funny and smart, and though she once threatened to lead a demonstration if I changed an assignment, we grew close. A few years later, in 2016, I was astonished to see a picture of Bri, wearing an evening gown and a sash, in an Irish-Australian newspaper. She had been selected as the Sydney Rose of Tralee. The Rose of Tralee was an eccentric pageant founded in the 1950s to promote tourism by bringing the 'Daughters of the Diaspora', young women all over the world whose families were Irish emigrants, back to Ireland. They were selected on the basis of personality, not looks, or so the official spiel ran. The nominated 'Roses' would gather in Tralee, with their families, to be interviewed on live TV about their backgrounds, heritage and aspirations.

The Rose of Tralee Festival was a hugely popular television event, akin to the Eurovision song contest. I would never in a million years have expected to see a fearless feminist like Bri in a setting she herself described as a 'Kate Middleton Impersonation competition'. But she had her own logic: the Sydney community paid her airfare and her selection convinced her grandmother to accompany Bri back to Dublin for the first time since she'd left, in poverty, 50 years before. Brianna wanted to do her family proud in their native home.

Since 1983, a new movement had formed in Ireland to repeal the Eighth Amendment that had entrenched the illegality of abortion. Brianna had observed it with interest from afar. Now, live on stage at the Rose of Tralee Festival, before a massive national audience, her moment came. Amid otherwise anodyne interviews, she told a surprised compere: 'I think it is time to give women a say on their own reproductive rights. I would love to see a referendum on the Eighth coming up soon. That would be my dream'. Bri later remembered a hush, but in fact the audience was whooping and applauding.

In Australia, I saw the kerfuffle unfold on Twitter – people revelling in Brianna or reviling her. I posted about my firebrand graduate on Facebook. Eleanor McDowall noticed it. I posted again when a referendum to 'Repeal the Eighth' was announced. Bri took unpaid leave from her job at the ABC to return to Ireland to support the Repeal campaign.

On 26 May 2018, Ireland voted by a 2:1 majority to make abortion legal. Two months later, I met Eleanor McDowall in person for the first time, at a radio studies conference in Prato, near Florence. There I bonded with her and other female audio creatives, and told them the long looping story of Ireland's abortion laws and the links between me and Brianna that spanned 35 years since that first referendum. The next day, Eleanor approached me about making a documentary about the whole saga. I emailed Bri, who was in straightaway.

The 28-minute documentary Eleanor made for BBC Radio 4, *A Sense of Quietness*, features the voices of four women: Brianna Parkins; Anne Connolly, the women's rights campaigner we'd interviewed in 1983; me; and an anonymous woman who describes heading to the UK from Ireland to have an abortion in 2016. Waiting at the airport on her return, she scrolled through her phone and saw Brianna's rallying call at the Rose of Tralee. It made her feel whole again, she told Eleanor. *A Sense of Quietness* is spare and beautiful, and has won huge acclaim: a Prix Europa, an Amnesty International UK Media Award, and a Third Coast Competition bronze award.

But I sometimes wonder how it might have been as a podcast. A natural performer, Bri would have made a terrific host, and the story was awash with complexities and compelling characters. It also had copious opportunities for actuality – indeed, Eleanor recorded reams of tape that went unheard, including my meeting with Brianna at uni years later when she coincidentally gave a guest lecture to my students of her old subject. There was Bri living her take-no-prisoners life, calling out media fakery in her day job, partying on with her partner and share-house mates, and staying close always to her Irish Australian family. It even had a perfect cyclical ending: Brianna was offered a job as a TV host in Dublin, the city I left for Sydney all those years ago. She continues to be a colourful presence there.

There were also remarkable backstories of the first wave of feminism in the 1970s and '80s, including a famous train ride across the border to Belfast, Northern Ireland, to buy hundreds of condoms (illegal in the Republic of Ireland), which the returning women provocatively declared to bemused Customs officials were all for their 'personal use'. And there were heartbreaking accounts of savage misogyny and repression: Joanne Hayes was coerced into saying she had killed a baby who was in fact stillborn; Miss X was a schoolgirl who became pregnant after being raped and, though she was suicidal, was stopped by authorities from going to England for an abortion.

In the 28-minute radio feature, this level of intricacy does not come out. My three hours of interview alone comes down to six minutes, as it must – all long-form storytelling involves reducing tons of material to a tiny fraction that is assembled creatively and coherently for maximum impact. *A Sense of Quietness* is a feat of crystalline, linear storytelling, which exposes the shocking era when anyone performing an abortion in Ireland would be imprisoned for life. But as a multi-episode podcast, it could have taken us into the labyrinthine depths that underpinned the brief shining moments that achieved change.

Podcast or one-off show?

Which format is preferable: podcast or one-off show? This is the kind of decision an audio producer has to make, based on money, time, creative expression, editorial goals, preferred audience, exposure, preference of commissioning bodies and, crucially, the story fit.

I asked Eleanor why she made that particular choice for *A Sense of Quietness*. 'The boring pragmatic answer is that we had a half-hour slot available within our first ever *Lights Out* series and so I was considering building something for that space in particular rather than conceiving of a pitch for something that could expand into a series', she replied. 'But I agree – there's such a rich and deep history there that it could easily expand!'

On further reflection, though, Eleanor is pleased with her decision:

> I think there was something particular about holding all four voices
> within that same half-hour moment. I'm very interested in social
> justice stories told collectively – rather than pinning a story of

social change to the actions of a single heroic individual, or a single moment in time. To have a feeling of how the actions of individuals slowly build a cumulative power. If each woman's story was told in its own half-hour I wonder if part of that feeling of community, of that shared focus on what happens to women when they just *speak* about their right to choose, the shared cause with each individual sparking something in another, might have been diluted.

Podcasts are intimate

Audio has always been the most intimate of mediums. It's a lot to do with the connecting power of voice, which allows us to hear so much more than words. We can detect how someone *feels* as well as what they say: their tone, their timbre, their delivery all provide clues that help us develop a sense of who is speaking. Accent can build character, as can idiom and rhythm: all provide sensory information that is missing on the page.

Sound adds its own magic: it's porous and enveloping. You don't have 'earlids' that can switch it off, as the Canadian composer R Murray Schafer points out. He memorably wrote that 'hearing is a way of touching at a distance'.[3] This was based on an actual calculation that shows that at low frequencies (around 20 hertz), audible sound gives way to felt vibrations. But it makes sense to me too as a poetic concept.

All these factors enable audio to create uncanny intimacy, as anyone who has worked in radio knows. Though audiences might number in the millions, a radio personality speaks only to one listener. US president Franklin D Roosevelt harnessed this intimacy back in the 1930s and '40s to deliver personalised 'fireside chats' to the nation over the wireless. The way sound was conveyed ethereally over airwaves was part of its mystique, its ability to make listeners feel viscerally connected to what they were hearing. Julie Snyder, who worked at *This American*

Life for 16 years before co-creating the hit podcasts *Serial* and *S-Town*, calls radio an 'empathy machine'.

But podcasting turns those qualities up to 11, for two reasons: first, people usually listen privately, often through headphones, so the podcast voice is speaking right into our ears, maybe even our ear canals if we're wearing earbuds. Second, podcasters *know* someone has actively chosen to listen to them, which gives them the confidence to be themselves and makes them more relatable.

Manoush Zomorodi is an Iranian American journalist who hosts TED's *ZigZag* podcast, 'a business show about being human'. She summed up the difference between being a radio presenter and a podcast host in one revealing word: hugs. When her earlier show, *Note to Self*, about human stories in the digital world, was broadcast on WNYC, a public radio station in New York, Zomorodi's interaction with listeners was cordial but distant. But when the show took on a second life as a podcast, even though the content was exactly the same, the response was very different. Fans at public events would throw their arms around her, wanting hugs! She told a conference in Sydney in 2016 that she put it down to podcasting's easy, accessible delivery mode: 'I walk home from the subway with them. I'm *with* them'. The lack of gatekeepers introducing the show further bonds listeners. 'We are buds', she says. 'We are friends.'

'The host relationship is more crucial than we even knew. It's just gone off the charts. And after the [pandemic] year of solitude and isolation, that pull of a relationship you feel with a host is so so meaningful'.

Julie Shapiro,
Vice President of Editorial, Radiotopia and PRX

Tech tips: Recording interviews with a portable recorder

The technical side of audio is relatively simple, so spend some time getting up to speed. It will pay off in spades in terms of how listenable your podcast is. You can delve deeper into practical aspects via NPR's excellent, free *Ear Training Guide for Audio Producers*.[4] For more on the interviewing relationship, see chapter 4.

1 **Get to know your equipment**. Don't get caught out by leaving the recording device blinking on pause and finding out too late that you've had the most amazing conversation but have not recorded it. Learn what the buttons and knobs are for and how they work by playing around with test recordings at home, checking YouTube demos and, er, reading the manual!

2 **Wear headphones when recording**. *This is vital!* Make sure they are turned up high, so you are hearing your surrounds through the headphones, not the naked ear. They are the only way you can know what your actual recording is sounding like – whether the voice is being drowned out, for example by wind or traffic, in which case you have to intervene (by moving somewhere else or asking your interviewee to repeat a phrase). Don't worry what you look like. People will get used to it.

3 **Get your mic up close when interviewing**. About a hand's span from the face is good. If the voice is off mic, it will sound emotionally distant as well, and you will squander half the powerful intimacy of voice just by being too far away. No smartphones left on a table!

4   **Be creative about how you record an interview.** If it's a deeply personal story, some audio producers might get the interviewee to lie down, in order to be more relaxed; they may even turn off the lights and use a candle.

5   **Know the difference between 'good noise' and 'bad noise'.** Remember that you can't get rid of any background noise: it is baked into the interview. Good noise might be birdsong or an old-style ticking clock – it does not drown out or distort, and can add a nice sense of place. Bad noise is generally wind, traffic or the neighbour with the leaf blower: it just pollutes the tape. Move away, or ask leaf blower man politely to take a break.

6   **Record ambient sound separately from the interview.** So, if someone does karate, but this is only an incidental part of their interview, don't record their whole life story in a karate studio. It will sound incongruous behind them talking about their childhood, for example. Record them at home in a neutral setting; later, accompany them to a karate session, be a fly on the wall and get a 'clean' recording. You can weave this sound in and out of the interview at appropriate moments.

7   **In general, pick a sound-neutral setting for a long personal interview.** Choose a home, not a pub, restaurant or shopping mall. When you arrive, take stock: how can you minimise noise? Turn off the TV mindlessly running in the background; silence phones. If possible, turn off air conditioning and fans. Turn off generators or fridges, or move away from them. Then restore order before you leave! (I once got an elderly man to turn off his fridge, as it juddered like a jet engine at intervals. He did a great interview about having launched the first tourist cruises of the Great Barrier Reef in the 1940s, and then sent me

out on the boat with his son. We were miles out to sea when I remembered I hadn't turned the fridge back on, and the week's supply of his Meals on Wheels in the freezer would be melting in the tropical heat. This was before mobile phones, but his son sent a ship-to-shore message and disaster was averted, much to my relief!)

8   **Take charge.** If the interviewee positions herself miles away in an armchair and you have only one mic, ask her instead to sit diagonally across a table from you, so you can easily get the mic up close without invading body space. Alternatively, you can use lapel mics, but I prefer physical closeness and strong eye contact in most settings. If she drums fingers nervously, or rustles papers, ask her nicely to stop – you will hear it on your headphones, but your interviewee will probably not be conscious of it.

9   **Don't be afraid of silence.** This is not live radio and you don't have to jump in to fill a pause. That may derail someone's thought process, or stymie a reflection. Sit there quietly and companionably before going to the next question. Silence can promote deeper conversation.

10   **Give non-verbal acknowledgment and reactions.** Do not say 'uh-huh' or 'I see' every two minutes as you might unconsciously do in a conversation. Instead show your understanding via eye contact, facial expression and nodding your head. Laughing along with a joke is fine, but your verbal tics may be very irritating to the listener later.

4

The aerobic art of interviewing

I once interviewed a man who worked down a coalmine outside Sydney, shovelling shit – the human alternative to a Portaloo. A burly bloke in regulation singlet and shorts, he spoke matter-of-factly about hanging around deep underground, waiting for his mates to have a crap. I asked him what he did to pass the time. He pulled a delicate piece of white crochet out of a pocket, pointing out the intricate patterns with the enthusiasm of a mother expounding the charms of her children. I was astonished, having subconsciously written him off as Macho Man. Instead he showed me that you can transcend your circumstances. Surrounded by shit, he created beauty.

I love how interviews deliver such surprises and expose our preconceptions. In another setting, I interviewed a German plant operator called Otto Blank, one of many European immigrants who helped build the Snowy Mountains Scheme hydroelectric project in Australia after World War II. I knew very little about Otto – just that he had served in the German army, was a champion boxer and rode a motorbike. I was piecing together the history of the project because it had been the cradle of multiculturalism in Australia, and Otto had answered an ad I placed looking for former workers. Early on, I asked a fairly obvious question: 'Why did you join the army?' His answer floored me. 'Because I thought the food might be better than in the orphanage.' Otto was 17 when he signed up, hungry and alone. To my shame, I realised I had been thinking of him as a rampaging militarist, from the cues of boxing, motorbike and, yes, a German in that era. In fact he was thoughtful and funny, telling me how the local Australian police were put on full alert one day because the Germans had all bought guns – to hunt rabbits, to supplement the ghastly canteen food.

Aerobic listening

The best interviews create an accelerated form of intimacy, in which you as interviewer get to ask very personal questions without seeming rude. It's a contract: you want to know their story and they have agreed to tell you. People agree to be interviewed for different reasons: some, like Otto, just want to place their word on the record for posterity. Others want to convey their expertise, assist in exposing a crime, right an injustice or simply expand social history. Some may have played a crucial role in an event, or had a unique experience, which they feel is in the public interest to share. Others may want to describe their professional role, as artists, scientists, athletes, politicians or whatever, out of pride in their occupation or their contribution. Still others will seek out any media exposure, to promote themselves and their cause.

But while their motives and backgrounds will vary hugely, they will all have one thing in common: they will enjoy the privilege of being listened to by *you*, the interviewer. And I mean *really* listened to – with such close undivided attention that someone once termed it 'aerobic listening', because if you do it right, it will be exhausting in the way that listening in a conversation never is. Few of us are ever really listened to in daily life. People are distracted, daydreaming or bored, and words are only half heard. When someone *really* listens to you, it's like a force field. And that lean-in, high-processing listening is the gift that will give you your first and best chance of getting a 'good' interview – one where your subject opens up, reaches for memories, dispenses anecdotes, crackles with opinions, pauses to reflect, and generally puts flesh on the bones of all the facts you already knew and adds a good few you did not.

The crucial importance of active listening came home starkly to me when I had the unusual experience of watching someone re-interview people I had interviewed. I had made a radio documentary series for the ABC, *The Irish in Australia, Past and Present*, which traced the history and influence of what had been Australia's first ethnic minority. A TV production company developing a similar concept hired me as an associate producer, incorporating much of my research and my network of interviewees. I was to write out a brief for the TV presenter, a chisel-jawed chap we shall call Robbie, and include a suggested list of questions. Early on, we were filming in the former residence of a famous archbishop, Daniel Mannix. I introduced Robbie to Mannix's biographer, Niall Brennan, a warm and garrulous man. As he shook Niall's hand, I noticed Robbie was looking over Niall's shoulder to check his image in the mirror.

The men settled into big leather armchairs and the interview began. 'Niall, can you tell me about Daniel Mannix's upbringing in Ireland?' Robbie asked, the first question I had penned. Niall began to enthusiastically recount how the outspoken nationalist had grown up in a politically fraught era. Robbie was nodding in acknowledgment but his eyes were vacant. Niall began to lose steam. He looked over to me, sitting in the corner to ensure no major points were missed. I leaned in, evincing avid interest, and Niall recovered his mojo – then 'Cut!' The cameraman stopped filming, as Niall had swivelled out of eyeline. This happened a few times, until finally the director had me squat down, off camera, behind Robbie, to be a human focus for Niall throughout the interview. Robbie had performed the questions with crisp elan but then switched off, leaving Niall unable to communicate – until I was wheeled in.

That experience also clarified for me why I prefer interviewing for audio, not TV. Audio does not care if you're bald or beautiful, old or young, fat or thin: appearance does not come into it. This allows both parties to relax and be less self-conscious, which in turn fosters connection and facilitates revelatory responses. In short, audio is hugely liberating.

Ten keys to a strong interview

1 **Research**. Prepare informed, interesting, well-worded questions.

2 **Flexibility**. Follow the flow, not your list (but have a list as a guide).

3 **Avoiding repetition**. Stick to small talk until recorder is running. They will sound stale and half-hearted if repeating.

4 **Curiosity**. You must *want* to know.

5 **Attention**. Aerobic listening!

6 **Empathy**. Suspend judgment.

7 **Balance**. Ask the hard questions – eventually.

8 **Control**. Don't cede it. A small digression is easily edited out, but if people keep going off-topic, I bring them politely back on track. You're here for a purpose, not a gossip.

9 **Clarity**. Ask again if you don't understand. Don't be afraid of seeming stupid. Much better to ask them to clarify than to realise too late that your listeners aren't going to get it either, because the topic was not explained well enough.

10 **Intimacy**. Don't ask the sensitive stuff until you've developed a rapport.

And finally, before you finish: ask if there's anything else they'd like to add. If they get passionate once the tape is off, ask them if you can turn it on again. That's usually the best bit!

Audio also allows you to avoid the intrusiveness of a hi-tech film operation: lights, cables, directors, camera operators. Usually, it's just me and my trusty recorder, sitting in someone's kitchen, or in a quiet outdoor setting – or, in pandemic times, recording over the internet. Some podcasters like to have a producer handle the recording side, so they can focus entirely on the conversation, and that works too. Personally, I like the closeness of one-on-one, and have trained myself to monitor the technical side via wearing headphones (which lets you hear in real time how the recording actually sounds) and glancing periodically at recording levels, controls and so on. I also carry lots of spare batteries! If I'm feeling paranoid about a super-important interview, I will run a backup recording on a second device, and even stash a whole other recording kit in the car, in case of dire emergency. I once won a car in a Kellogg's Corn Flakes competition at odds of 66 000 to 1, so if there is one person who will get the statistically improbable machine malfunction it will likely be me! Seriously though, there is nothing worse than that awful pit-of-the-stomach realisation that the searing one-hour interview you just conducted has not been preserved, because you forgot to un-pause the button when a phone call interrupted things. So do yourself a favour and play around with the equipment *before* you head out.

Over the next sections, I'll give you my insights on how to handle a wide range of interview situations.

Curiosity and the 'line of difference'

The next most important thing to bring to your podcast interview, besides aerobic listening, is its first cousin: curiosity. The legendary Studs Terkel (see chapter 2) thought it so important he wanted this epitaph: 'Curiosity never killed this cat!' As an interviewer, you are a licensed stickybeak. You need to *exude* interest in who the person in front of you is, what happened to them, and how it affected them and others. If you take the whole-of-life-story approach to an interview, you are ultimately trying to find out what makes someone tick, and distil that essence. It's a tall order. People can feel your sincerity – or its opposite – in this regard and will respond accordingly. A genuine urge to know and understand the person speaking into the mic, combined with focused and non-judgmental listening, builds trust, which in turn develops into an unspoken but palpable pact of intimacy as the interview continues.

The 'exchange of gazes'

The eloquent Italian oral historian Alessandro Portelli, my friend and inspiration, describes an interview as 'an exchange of gazes'. You, as interviewer, may be the one asking the questions, but you are also being observed and sized up – and that will affect how things unfold. The dynamic in every interview depends on that specific pairing.

The exchange happened for me very significantly on a tropical island in Northern Australia. Palm Island looks and sounds idyllic, but it has a violent, troubled past. The Queensland Government established an Aboriginal Reserve there after a cyclone destroyed a mainland Aboriginal settlement in 1918. People from numerous Aboriginal and Torres Strait Island nations – some of them culturally at odds – were sent there and the Reserve took on a penal air. Right into the 1970s it operated under apartheid-like conditions, with black residents not allowed to walk down Mango Avenue, where the white superintendent lived. In 1957, seven men led a strike against appalling conditions that saw them forced to work for no wages. They were deported in chains to the mainland. By 1991 when I got there, only one of those seven men, Bill Congoo, was still living on the island. I was hoping to hear his story.

The ABC Radio budget only allowed for about four days on the island. On day one, I found out where Bill hung out, and put in a request via a community worker for an interview. The response came back; he would do it, but not today. Day two was the same. In the meantime I recorded interviews with other residents, who described the ghastly, punitive regime they had laboured under, having committed no crime. One of them gave me the name for what would be a two-part series: *Palm Island, A Punishment Place.*

On day three, Bill wandered past again, but he was still seemingly not disposed to be interviewed. Due to my then scant knowledge of cultural differences, I had not realised that Bill's 'yes but not now' was actually a resounding 'no'. On the last day, in desperation, I went up to him as he walked by. 'Bill, could I please talk to you? I just want to hear about what happened. I don't know the story and I think most Australians don't know it and would really like to hear it.' Something in my voice got through and he looked at me as if seeing me for the first time. 'They took away our land, they wouldn't let us speak our language – you wouldn't understand', he finished, hopelessly. 'But Bill, I'm Irish – they did the same to us!' I exclaimed. 'What – you're Irish?' he said. 'Siddown! Have a beer.' And a few minutes later, we were sitting cross-legged, side by side on the beach, as Bill stared out to sea and related the brutal history of the strike and its aftermath, a vital record of a terrible crime against him and his people, now archived at the National Library of Australia. Why tell me? It turned out there had been an Irish priest on Palm Island who had exhorted Bill and his mob, 'Don't let the bastards beat you, Bill', and kept their spirits up. It was true too, though, that we had been co-colonised by the British, who had also dispossessed the Irish and tried to eradicate their culture. My simple but heartfelt affirmation had been enough to make a connection, through a shared oppression.

Finding empathy

This affinity between Aboriginal and Irish people was one I would later explore with Senator Patrick Dodson, a Yawuru man from Broome in Western Australia who has won the Sydney International Peace Prize. In the radio documentary *Reconciliation: From Broome to Belfast*, Patrick articulated links he observed between the Irish struggle to heal the damage caused by centuries of English colonialism and the struggle by Aboriginal and Torres Strait Islander peoples to gain recognition and equality in Australia. For the documentary, I recorded a moving speech he gave outside Dublin in 2000 to a gathering of young people of diverse religious and cultural backgrounds, brought together to help undo bigotry. He told them: 'We're quite adept at picking out what it is we don't like about other human beings. The harder challenge is always to find, well, what is the common ground? How do we train our minds, and our emotions, and our desires to look for the common ground with someone that we normally wouldn't bother to spend the time of day with?'

Being different from someone you are interviewing is not necessarily a bad thing. What's important is acknowledging and examining the difference. 'Let's enable people to have their say, but also to be challenged and let us also be prepared to be challenged by someone else's point of view, and if we can meet in a humane way in relation to those differences that will arise in that exchange then we've done something', Patrick Dodson concluded. On another continent, listening to the stories of Kentucky communities, oral historian Alessandro Portelli applied the principle of the 'line of difference' in order to permit a more meaningful exchange when he found himself, a white man, interviewing a black woman whose grandmother had been a slave. The point is, your background will play into how an interviewee responds to you, so be aware of it and engage with it, rather than act like it doesn't exist.

Power and hierarchy are real presences in personal relationships, and while they cannot be wished away, they cannot prevent us from doing our work either. Democracy is not to pretend these unequal differences are not there; democracy is to face them squarely and to take responsibility for them in the process of working to deconstruct them.

– Alessandro Portelli, *The Battle of Valle Giulia: Oral history and the art of dialogue*, 1997, p. 78

During a lifetime of interviewing around a thousand people, I have felt the intimacy of strangers with those far removed from me in terms of age, life experience, and social and cultural background. I think it occurs through simple empathy – placing myself in someone else's shoes and attempting to understand what they are feeling. The pain of a Cambodian woman recounting how her son starved to death before her eyes under the Khmer Rouge was no different from the pain of an Aboriginal woman describing being kidnapped from her family, or a white Australian woman recalling how her Protestant father had to put her and her baby brother in an orphanage when her Catholic-raised mother had died in childbirth, due to the religious prejudice of the era. Likewise joy, anger, regret, pride – the *feelings* are universal, however different their context.

Empathy both simplifies and complicates things. It allows you to thrill to the messy contradictions that are real people. The genial farmer who is also an implacable racist, the bloodless lawyer who unexpectedly reveals a passion for light opera, the ruthless media mogul who retains the sadness of a wounded child – these are all people I have met. When you interview people, you have to be open to their frailties as well as their more obvious strengths.

Empathy obviates the need to like or dislike someone. You can clinically record a distasteful action by your subject without abhorring them – judgment is withheld. Instead you seek to understand their point of view. This does not mean you let them off the hook. You still ask the hard questions, but because the interviewee feels you can truly see and hear them, you're more likely to get a real answer.

About 20 years ago, I stumbled across what became a documentary on the Stolen Generations in the Kimberley region of Western Australia (*Beagle Bay: Irish Nuns and Stolen Children*). I was introduced to several Aboriginal women who had been taken from their families and reared by Catholic nuns as part of the assimilation policy of the day. Their stories of separation and loss were heartbreaking, but to my surprise and even irritation, they had nothing but praise for the nuns. Didn't they realise, I thought, that they were victims of cultural dispossession at the hands of church and state? Confused, but still clutching my righteous anger at the religious women who had inculcated these girls with their white Christian beliefs, I interviewed one of the nuns. Having read of grim contemporary children's homes run by sadistic overseers, I was unprepared for her description of how the nuns and the girls shared limited food and resources and jointly battled isolation, poverty, and the sexism and rigidity of the church hierarchy. Instead of religious doctrine, Sister Pat spoke of how she loved the girls and tried to give them a rounded education, even teaching them Shakespeare in secret.

But the elephant was still on the lawn and this is how the question came out, spoken slowly and evenly, for I was trying to avoid an accusatory tone: 'Did it ever occur to you to wonder why these children were being taken from their parents?' Sister Pat paused, then gave a deep sigh. These sounds alone spoke volumes and set up the contrite reflection that followed. 'No. I don't think it did. Religious life didn't allow for that. We didn't have access to newspapers or the wireless. We were told they were there for education. How they got there, we didn't question.' Later, she expressed profound regret for having been part of what she described as 'a terribly wrong' policy.

The truth of that is evident in Phyllis Bin Bakar's story, as she recounts how, when she was three, her mother took her to the hospital because she had a fever. When her mother returned, Phyllis was gone, passed on to the welfare authorities. Phyllis would not see her mother again until one day, as a grown woman, she was working as a cleaner and was told she had a visitor. Somehow, her mother had tracked her down. 'My mother came once to see me. But she was hurt, I could understand, she was upset', Phyllis told me, her voice heavy with melancholy. 'With all the hardship and the loss of her child – she just looked at me and said, "You're not my daughter". It was a long time, you know?' Phyllis never saw her mother again. She carried the grief of that absence all her life. 'That was the first and the last I've seen her. She was broken up inside. I mean, taking a child away at a small age ... she had a broken heart. And that's how she went to her grave, with a broken heart.'

The program illuminated the complexity of the situation – the Aboriginal women lamented the loss of their families and their culture but insisted the nuns had loved them and given them a great start in life; Sister Pat knew in hindsight the grave implications of what had been done, but also felt the sisters had provided a stable and nurturing environment. Had I been blinded by moral outrage and dismissed Sister Pat as an Enemy of the People, how much less would I have learnt about the paradoxical reality? Had I not been able to sit quietly with Phyllis in her pain, she would not have referred me on to other women, to build a bigger picture of the trauma they suffered.

Interviewing and the 'driveway moment'

The precious trust that develops over a well-executed, long-form interview was very apparent to me when I recorded another female Australian veteran of the Vietnam War, Jan Graham, for my book and radio series *Minefields and Miniskirts*. Jan spent ten years in Vietnam covering the war as a journalist with wire agencies such as Associated Press. Like the entertainer Ingrid Hart, she had answered an ad I put in the *Sydney Morning Herald*, seeking Australian women's stories of the war. When I rang her, she grilled me for over an hour on my background and my intentions, clearly trying to decide whether to confide in me. She was both tough and vulnerable, and she swore, laughed and cried as she gave me preliminary details of some of the remarkable things she had witnessed in that decade. In that first phone call I recounted a few of my own journalistic stories, to show my mettle. In the end, my Irish background clinched it – she had Irish heritage, she said, and was proud of it. Thanking the Lord that the Irish were largely seen as harmless/likeable ratbags, I made an appointment.

Jan cancelled that first appointment I had made for an interview with her. And the second. She had plausible reasons (a bad cold, a fall in the shower), but had she cancelled the third, I would not have asked for a fourth. I could sense that she was in some way dreading talking about her experiences, even though she had initiated the contact. On the day, I arrived at her home in the western suburbs of Sydney to find her husband pottering about. I always prefer to interview married couples individually – otherwise they inevitably fall into well-rehearsed routines – and so we banished him to the cellar, where it turned out he had a ham radio. As Jan poured out her guts to me in the living room upstairs, he would unwittingly (and unbeknown to me) inflict a persistent buzz on the tape, at a frequency I could not pick up on my headphones at the time.

We started, as I usually do, with general non-threatening 'orientation' questions that established her family background, her early career and how she came to be in Vietnam in 1965 as the war took off. She laughed as she recalled the drive into Saigon (now Ho Chi Minh City) from the airport, and how she recoiled at all the bloodstains on the streets. 'Turns out it was betel nut juice', she explained wryly. On we went to stories of the other journalists there, the daily US army briefings known as the Five O'Clock Follies because of their glossing of the truth, the booming nightlife in Saigon, the 'firefights' across the river that they watched from the rooftop bar in the Caravelle Hotel, strangely dissociated from reality.

About an hour in, she started talking about the times outside Saigon, when she was embedded (as we would now say) with American troops. The stories got darker and darker. She met a well-heeled Chinese Vietnamese man who boasted that he could break every bone in someone's body without leaving a bruise. She accompanied an elderly lady to the site of a massacre at Huế and watched as she searched through dozens of corpses shot through the neck, until she identified her son by his bent little finger. She stumbled on the interrogation of a man 'with a scraggy grey beard and a patrician face', a suspected Viet Cong informer. And she identified the body of her own GI lover, a member of the elite 'Green Berets' whose body had been mutilated.

At times Jan cried, reaching for a box of tissues. I often had tears in my eyes, too. I offered to pause the tape, indeed stop the interview, but she waved the idea away. It was as if, now that she had committed to talking about this stuff, she would not, or could not, stop. In between relating shocking incidents, she reproached herself for not having been more interventionist, for having bought the US line, for serving up copy that described 'plenty of bang-bang' along with cosy platitudes about how Joe Bloggs from Minneapolis had had a great Christmas. 'Depicting the Vietnamese as human beings is what they did not want to know.'

Towards the end of the afternoon, when we were both emotionally drained, Jan told me one last tale. She had been travelling with an American GI on his last day of deployment 'in-country'. On his way to the airport, the soldier ducked into a paddy field to check out a suspicious movement. When a concerned Jan followed him, she found he had been blown up by a mine. She cradled his mutilated body, and during the 15 minutes it took him to die, in his shocked state, he mistook her for the wife he had been on his way home to see, and proclaimed his eternal love for her. Jan described the scene and re-enacted the conversation. The tape is virtually unedited, though (unusually) I shortened some pauses as the tension was unbearable.

I have published two print versions of the interview: one with a standard layout, and the other with lots of white space around it in an attempt to render the poetic cadences and rhythms of her voice, and the spaces, gulps and snuffles in between. I know, from numerous experiments, at conferences, with students and with thousands of participants in my recent online course, that neither print version has anything like the impact of the audio.[1] More than 90 per cent of my course respondents thought the print had less impact. One man said it all. 'When I read Jan's story, I feel sad', he wrote. 'When I hear it, I cry.'

After Jan's interview went to air on the ABC, people who had listened in their cars wrote in saying they had to pull off the road, as they could not focus on driving because they were so immersed in her harrowing story. Others recounted how they could not leave their car until she finished, though they had reached their destination. This is what in America they call 'a driveway moment', when what you are hearing is so compelling, you cannot switch it off. It is the strongest example I have personally recorded. I think it is so forceful for two reasons: the story itself, with its sudden, ghastly, tragic turn and the awful role Jan was assigned as surrogate wife; and the raw emotion that surfaces as she tells it, which may partly be because Jan was recounting it for the first time. She told me later that not even her husband had ever heard much of what she told me, so she was dredging up the details in the moment. That carries huge visceral charge.

I spent hours with an audio engineer trying to filter out the buzz from the ham radio signal on the original cassette tape and eventually gave up. Recently, I've been told it would probably be possible to remaster it digitally and clean it up – but it would feel inauthentic to tamper with it now, more than 25 years on. It is now part of how I remember Jan and hear her voice.

The post-interview relationship is a delicate one. Mostly, I find it is a professional encounter and boundaries are observed. I will, of course, communicate with interviewees afterwards, about when the podcast or other material is being published, and related matters. Some will send me Christmas cards for a while – Ingrid Hart sent them for decades. A few I will see socially from time to time, one or two crossing over to become friends. I think Jan found her interview unburdening, and was happy with how she came across, on air and in print. She continued to phone, and we had long conversations for years.

Questions matter

I always make a list of questions before I do an interview. But that doesn't mean I stick to it. Just devising questions is a great way to get into the headspace of the person you'll be meeting. You start to think your way into what you know of their experience, and you identify the key themes you want to explore, or information you need to extract. A list of questions also serves as a checklist, to ensure you don't leave out some important aspect. And it can help you keep the ball rolling if your interviewee suddenly dries up and throws back to you earlier than expected.

But what you actually ask the person, and when, will be guided by them, not you! It is intensely annoying to hear someone say something extraordinary in an interview, and then to hear that it's not pursued because the interviewer is on autopilot and just moved on to the next question on the list. Imagine this:

> **Interviewee**: It was the fourth of January 2018 when I bought the house. I remember it because I got bitten by a shark that same day.

> **Gormless interviewer**: [blandly] And when did you move in?

What every listener is thinking is: 'What – you got bitten by a *shark*? How did that happen?'

I'm exaggerating, of course, but not too much.

Some years ago, I audited the oral history collection of the Historic Houses Trust of New South Wales, who maintain and document a range of public properties. A lot of the tape was (understandably) banal, as curators tried to gather information on when various decorative touches were applied to the historic buildings. So when I heard the following exchange as the elderly owner of a big country house on the outskirts of Sydney showed a curator around, I sat up.

> **Owner**: This room belonged to Aunt Katherine. That's her boa on the back of the door.

> **Curator**: Oh. Which one was she?

> **Owner**: Ran off with her lover, a White Russian. Murdered in Manchuria, 1932.

Lovers? A White Russian? *Murder*? And in Manchuria? Where even *was* Manchuria? Who was this mysterious Aunt Katherine, with her elegant boa? I was agog.

A pause followed. The curator said 'Oh', in a tone of disdain. Then, with a rush of enthusiasm, she exclaimed: 'What a *lovely* lino! When was this put down?'

And that was the end of poor Aunt Katherine.

Another historic house, a beautiful weatherboard building called Meroogal, in Nowra, south of Sydney, had been occupied by women of the Thorburn family for four generations. It was built in 1886 for a widow and her four daughters. The youngest passed it on to her three nieces in 1956, and one of these passed it to her daughter, June, in 1977. June sold it to the Trust in 1985 and had been interviewed 12 times about the remarkably well-preserved domestic practices of the female occupiers over the previous century. There was the finely embroidered lace, meticulous recipes for a sponge cake in which the eggs had to be beaten on a plate with a knife, descriptions of singsongs around the piano at night. Over hours of tape, June divulged the rich detail of her relatives' lives – but nobody asked her the question that preoccupied me: why did none of these women (except June's mother) get married? Statistically, it was unusual for so many women in the one family to remain unmarried. Photos showed them to be attractive and in good health, and diaries recorded their busy social lives.

Finally, the Trust commissioned a 13th interview, in which I got to pose that question. In the case of her great-aunts, June, told me, it was partly the dearth of young men after World War I. One had, in fact, proposed to Great-Aunt Tot, but he wanted her to move to England with him and she could not bear to leave her family. In her aunts' generation, one trained to be a nurse and did not want to forsake her occupation, as married women were expected to do. Then June clinched the argument: the Thorburn women were known to be choosy! They weren't going to marry any old chaps, particularly when they had each other and a lovely home in perpetuity. We made a short film of June's interview, which can be viewed at Meroogal today. I'm pleased to have resolved that longstanding puzzle.

The fresh question

It's important to ask questions that fill in the gaps, but it's also vital not to bore your interviewee stupid by having them repeat stuff they've said many times before. 'Ordinary people' usually don't mind going over things – in fact they may relish the opportunity to revisit some fond memory. But celebrities are a different matter. They're hard to interview, not just because of ego and aura, but because they've heard it all before. A friend of mine, Caroline Baum (her cleverly titled podcast, *Life Sentences*, features interviews with biographers), tells a wonderful story about this. An arts journalist, Caroline was hosting a TV show where one evening the star attraction was to be the writer Frank McCourt. McCourt had had a huge global hit with his memoir, *Angela's Ashes*, which describes his tough childhood in a tenement in Limerick, Ireland, in the 1930s. The book was at the top of the bestseller lists for two years, and by the time McCourt showed up at the Sydney TV studio, arriving straight from the airport, he'd been interviewed countless times. Caroline remembers he looked exhausted and irritated, clearly not in the mood for yet another interview. As the 'Recording' light gleamed red, she had a brainwave. Ditching her list of questions, she leaned forward. 'Frank McCourt, what's it like to have gotten filthy rich from writing about your dirt-poor youth?' McCourt shot upright, electrified. 'It's shocking!' he exclaimed. 'I worry about it all the time – what to do with the money, and have I really earned it?' They were off and running – thanks to that one original question, which tapped into a moral quandary he really wanted to talk about.

The hard question

Then there's The Hard Question, the one you know they don't want to hear. Asking it is never easy (unless you're a bully at heart, as some media interviewers seem to be), but it's particularly hard when your interviewee is scary, or famous. Architect Harry Seidler was both. Scary not just because of his international reputation, but because of his renowned intolerance of fools and philistines – and when it came to architecture, I had zero cred. But three weeks of intense research acquainted me with the basics of the Bauhaus and, having absorbed the colourful details of Harry's journey from Austrian refugee to Australian aesthete, I began a marathon filmed interview, commissioned by the aforementioned Historic Houses Trust. On that spring Saturday in the surrounds of the famous modernist house Seidler had built for his mother, curators watched as I engaged with the testy artist, his intellect still formidable at 83. I had prepared 30 pages of questions and quotes, committed to memory for the day.

The technical crew was late setting up, and between that and the bum crack on display as the audio engineer laid his cables, the great man was distinctly tetchy as we began. Instinct told me to jettison the chronological order I'd planned. Instead I plucked a quote from Walter Gropius, Seidler's mentor – that good architecture incorporated 'firmness, commodity and delight' – and asked him to nominate examples. He frowned. Gropius, he said, was merely rehashing the words of Vitruvius, from ancient Rome. My first question and I was 2000 years out! But I had homed in, however clumsily, on one of his obsessions and he was off, expounding on the solidity, minimalism and aesthetics of his favourite buildings. Although we could not have been more ill matched, my research enabled me to bat the ball back and forth. More importantly, my curiosity and interest were real, and they fed his passion. By the time we broke to change reels at the end of an hour, we were bonded, oblivious to the audience, locked in the exchange of gazes.

Desperate not to break the spell and return to banal chitchat while the crew moved about, I offered to tell him a real Irish joke. He winced, but I took the risk. This was no ordinary joke. A Dublin university student goes to London to work on the building sites during the holidays. The foreman looks at his weedy frame and suspiciously pale skin. 'You done this before?' he asks. 'Sure', lies the student. 'OK then – what's the difference between a girder and a joist?' The student smiles. 'That's easy. Goethe wrote *Faust* and Joyce wrote *Ulysses*.' Seidler exploded in what a watching curator said was the biggest laugh he'd ever seen him give. We resumed the interview on the warmest terms.

The trouble was I then had to ask him about his bête noire, the infamous Blues Point Tower skyscraper adjacent to the Sydney Harbour Bridge, whose brutal plainness had attracted much criticism and even been satirised as a totalitarian condominium. Basking in our new-found connection, Seidler warbled happily to me about its proportions, its economy, and how much the residents loved their views and their living environment. That was my in. 'But don't you think that's a little Marie-Antoinette-ish?' I heard myself say. 'What about the rest of us, who are looking at it from the outside?' (Somehow I refrained from saying what had first come into my head – 'who *have to* look at it from the outside' – for I was no fan of the tower.) He bristled. 'They are entitled to their opinion', he said icily. 'I still say it's one of my finest buildings.'

Before his hauteur could escalate, I slipped in a question about Neue Donau (New Danube), the massive social housing project he was building in Vienna at the time. As I hoped, he became animated again, enthusiastically unfolding his vision for his native city. By the fourth hour, so solid was the ground beneath us that I felt able to ask him about the delicate topic of a reputed family feud. In an emotional tribute to his late brother, he explained that the 'feud' had never happened. When we finished, I felt as if I had seen into his soul – a humbling experience that I have had more than once during an interview.

Finding the passion

The late American writer Janet Malcolm marvelled at 'the careless talk' that interviewees let slip to journalists, their 'childish trust and impetuosity'. She obviously never met a laconic Australian bushie. The most taciturn man I ever met was a retired depth sounder, whose 40 years in the Public Works department had been spent swinging a lead line, the method by which river depths were gauged in the pre-digital age. His former employer was documenting the work and flew me to Jim's home up the coast to interview him.

Jim and his wife Wendy met me at the airport. All the way to their house, Wendy talked nonstop at breakneck speed, while Jim drove, steadfast and silent. I knew I had to get rid of her – but how? 'As soon as your little interview is over', she prattled, 'we'll have a barbecue'. A strategy formed. 'Barbecue?' I interrupted. 'That's very kind, but I'm a vegetarian.' A pause. She was shocked, but not defeated. 'What do *they* eat?' she asked, suspiciously. I cast about wildly for something she would not have. 'Tofu', I said solemnly. 'I only eat silken tofu.'

As soon as the door shut, I sprang into action. I had maybe 40 minutes, I reckoned, while she trawled the hippie co-ops in their rural valley.

> **Me**: So Jim – can you tell me about your lead-lining days. Firstly, what is lead-lining?
> **Jim**: It's uh, you know, the line goes in the water and you count how long.
> **Me**: How long what?
> **Jim**: How long the line is.
> **Me**: The whole line or part of it?
> **Jim**: Part.
> **Me**: Which part?
> **Jim**: The part in the water.
> **Me**: Why do you that?

Jim: What?
Me: Count how long the part in the water is?
Jim: That's lead-lining.
Me: But what does it tell you?
Jim: How deep the water is.
Me: How?
Jim: How what?
Me: How does the length of a line in the water tell you something about the depth – I need you to explain this for people who don't know.
Jim: There's a lot that don't know alright.

On and on and on, fragment by tortuous fragment, it went. I focused on easier themes – daily routine ('the usual'), eating and sleeping arrangements ('camp, you know') accidents ('had a few') and mates ('Paddy was a character').

Me: Tell me about Paddy.
Jim: Oh a right character.
Me: What did you talk about round the campfire at night?
Jim: Jeez he could talk!
Me: Can you remember any yarns?
Jim: The things he'd say!

I moved on, without much hope, to the rivers. Wendy would be back any minute.

Me: What's your favourite river of all the ones you've navigated?
Jim: Done a lot, yeh.
Me: You mentioned the Clarence – what's that like?
Jim: King tide is good.
Me: What would you do waiting for the king tide?
Jim: Full moon too sometimes.

We were like motorists on different sections of the freeway, passing over and under each other but never intersecting. Forty years of living with the garrulous Wendy on weekends and the enigmatic Paddy during the week seemed to have numbed Jim's instincts for communication. I would have given up but my plane didn't leave for hours, and having so duplicitously got Wendy out of the house, I felt honour-bound to continue until her return.

As always in an interview, I had been listening super-intently to every word Jim said. With enormous effort, I searched my mind for every crumb Jim had dropped and rolled them all into one long desperate question:

> When you were out on the Clarence River, on a king tide, under a
> full moon, with Paddy there beside you, swinging the lead line ... did
> you ever think about what it was all for, the people who'd been to
> these places before you, and the ones who would come after ... ?

I was struggling to make a word picture that would somehow kickstart long-dormant emotions. Before I got any further, Jim jolted in his chair, suddenly agitated.

> Yerr, there was this little girl, she was only eight and she died of a
> snakebite. I read it in her father's diary, he was a surveyor and he
> come out this way in the 1860s and he camped right where we done.
> Paddy always knew the best spots. He'd been in the army see, had to
> get out 'cos his nerves went after the Japs got him, but he could tell
> how much she'd rise in a flood just by looking at the banks further
> down ...

On and on it went, a stream-of-consciousness soliloquy about Jim and Paddy's adventures on land and water, in bushfire, drought and floods, crossing the bar at a harbour mouth or rowing up a river tributary, diligently gathering figures for the faceless men at head office.

These days, they get it to within two decimal points and they think they're bloody great – but we gave it 40 years and we done a bloody good job.

He sat back, exhausted. I felt drained too, by his passion. We heard a key in the door – and into the scene waltzed Wendy, bearing a dripping packet of tofu. She stopped and almost sniffed. The current between Jim and me was still crackling. Eating near-mouldy tofu while they tucked into delicious steaks seemed a small price to pay. As I left, Jim gave me a sweet, childlike smile that made my heart sing.

When I told that story to my students, one, a psychologist, ventured an explanation. 'When you fed him back that word-picture, it was confirmation that you had heard him – obviously a rare thing – and it enabled him to access those buried memories. He felt validated enough to allow them out.'

I don't know if that's what happened. It sounds as plausible as anything else. But ever since then I have believed that there is passion in every one of us. It might seem unlikely on the surface, and it might take a lot of time and effort to tap into – but it's there.

Damned lies and faulty narrative

If you're assigned an interviewee, you just have to make the best of what you've got. But often you'll have the luxury of being able to pick who to talk to. I always vet prospective interviewees via a 'dummy' phone call. I'll say, 'I'm thinking of doing a project on X and I heard you were there at that time. Can you run me through a typical day?' If they come alive with the memories and have detailed recall of dates and names and places, that's a great sign. I'll cross-check the facts, and if they're right, they're in! If they are glum or hesitant or downright hostile, they're unlikely to warm up with a mic in front of them. In that case, I will can it right there: 'Thanks a lot – I might get back to you.' No need to let them know they've been rejected.

Deliberate misinformation

Sometimes the problem is not getting the person to talk but deciphering what you're hearing. Dissemblers will feed you misinformation in an attempt to distract or confuse you. When I was researching the Australian cotton industry, one of my final interviews was with a spokesperson for the cotton growers' body, what was then called the Australian Cotton Foundation – let's call him Mr B. For two years, I had been accumulating evidence about growers' use of toxic chemicals. I had heard from residents in cotton country how impenetrably scientific Mr B's answers were. I had in another life obtained a science degree, so I wasn't afraid of the lingo. But the volume of data was huge, and I knew I had to retain it mentally in order to pick up instantly on any telling admissions. Another return to the cramming days of uni exams, as I pored over dry government reports and scoured registries of agricultural chemicals!

On the appointed day, I asked Mr B first about a well-documented incident near Moree, in north-west New South Wales, in 1991. A team of chippers (people who weed cotton) was at work when a plane started spraying in an adjacent field. Soon a chipper smelled 'something like flyspray', and her eyes began to sting. The chemical from the plane was evidently being blown onto them by the wind. The supervisor radioed the news to the pilot and asked him to stop, but he would not. By the next morning, most of the chippers had experienced headaches, sore eyes and throats, and coughs – symptoms consistent with having been exposed to endosulfan, the active ingredient in the spray.

A government agricultural health unit fortuitously in the area examined 16 workers and filed a report. The case went to court – and despite the fact that the magistrate observed that there was no doubt that he 'deliberately sprayed pesticide' alongside fields where he was aware the chippers were working, the pilot walked away scot-free. This was because the woefully inept legislation required the workers to prove that he had not only deliberately sprayed them, but also 'wilfully' caused a risk of injury by a pesticide.

Nonetheless the case was embarrassing for the industry. Mr B played it down, telling me that 'none of those people, until the symptoms were described to them, exhibited any symptoms'. In fact, as I knew from reading the report, the agricultural health doctor took pains to point out that the chippers were interviewed in such a way as to eliminate any form of autosuggestion. When Mr B added that the pesticide used was 'a cholinesterase inhibitor', my antennae moved up a notch. (Cholinesterase is an enzyme, the blood level of which can indicate exposure to certain chemicals.) 'When they tested the people', Mr B went on, 'there was no depression of cholinesterase ... now that is a direct link of exposure. That is one of the points why the case was dismissed'.

From my reading, I knew that the chemical in question, endosulfan, was an organochlorine – a type that did not interact with cholinesterase. So to imply that because there was no depression of cholinesterase there must not have been any exposure to endosulfan was nonsense. Cholinesterase would be affected by totally different pesticides, like organophosphates.

When I pointed out this discrepancy, Mr B blanched. My mild manner and heavily pregnant state had perhaps led him to underestimate my understanding of the issues – on which I grilled him for the next 90 minutes, in what was one of the most satisfying interviews of my life. After my book came out, the laws on aerial spraying changed for the better.

Unintended misinformation

Misinformation is not always deliberate. Sometimes people will, in good faith, tell you something you know to be untrue. Critics of oral history often cite these factual aberrations as proof of the unreliability of personal testimony – but in fact, these 'errors', which Alessandro Portelli has termed 'wrong narrative' or 'faulty narrative', can be instructive. For example, when Portelli interviewed workers in the Italian town of Terni about the killing of a factory worker called Luigi Trastulli after World War II, the informants sometimes transposed the date and manner of the killing. But these 'mistakes' were significant. The date given related to another, key, battle in the ongoing fight between the workers and the Fascists, and the manner of Trastulli's death, often described as shot against a wall, arms extended, was permeated with strong cultural motifs, from the Crucifixion to the execution of partisans in the area a few years earlier. Analysing the changed 'facts', Portelli surmised much about the political environment of the day and how it had changed in the interim, which had caused his informants to subconsciously alter their view of what had happened.

I had a similar experience of 'wrong narrative' when gathering interviews from workers who built the tunnels of the Snowy Mountains Scheme. Person after person mentioned that men had died while lining the tunnels with concrete, and their bodies had been entombed in the rock. No one could offer me the full names of the supposed victims, and the locality and time of the supposed entombings varied. Yet the story persisted so strongly I felt it had to mean something.

Concreting was dangerous, and the migrants who played key roles were often desperate and vulnerable. Through the picture I built up, I surmised that what was real was the *fear* the mostly Italian miners had of being told to go behind the formwork (the arched mould for the concrete) and do the concrete lining, which could indeed be life-threatening. Migrants, being at the bottom of the pecking order, were most likely to do such work. One Australian I interviewed had quit the job rather than comply.

I examined 112 inquests into men who died in the Scheme's construction. None described someone dying while concrete lining a tunnel – but in one horrific accident concrete lining a dam shaft, three men, all migrants, were pinned under collapsed formwork. Their workmates had only two hours in which to get them out before the concrete set. The men could not be freed and died at the bottom of the shaft – effectively buried alive in concrete, as the 'myth' had held. So there had been a terrible truth at its core after all.

Technique and artistry

Those tunnellers remind me of another Italian, Michelangelo. In the Accademia Gallery in Florence, where his magnificent *David* stands, several of his unfinished sculptures are also exhibited. These striking, semi-sculpted figures are entitled *Prisoners* – they are still captive in the stone, powerful with potential. Of the act of setting free that was his sculpting, Michelangelo wrote:

> The great artist has no concept
> what a marble may have confined
> within its depths; that can be divined
> only by the hand subject to the intellect

Michelangelo believed that a block of marble already contained a work of art – his role was to liberate what was inherent. But the majesty, grace and beauty he saw in the stone that became *David* had remained invisible to sculptors who had previously tackled that same block.

As a sculptor wielding a tool, Michelangelo also relied on technique – and you should, too. The interview can be all or nothing to podcasters. A person sits across a table with stories to tell, ideas to impart, facts to confirm or deny, emotions to convey – but our ability to perceive who is before us, and to engage with what we are hearing, will critically affect what ensues. Perhaps it is not too fanciful to imagine the best interviewing as an art, whose purpose is to reveal the full humanity and depth of the person before us – depths that can be divined only by engaging the *heart* subject to the intellect.

One of the most common questions about podcasts is, 'How long should they be?' The answer is: as long as they need to be. It's the same with an interview. It should go for as long as it takes. I've recorded some great interviews in a mere 20 minutes, life-story interviews in two sessions of two and a half hours, and one that ran to 22 hours, over 11 sessions, for a biography. In general I seem to average one to two hours.

Should you ever ask a leading question? Only in certain circumstances. Generally speaking, you want people to paint word pictures, to tell you a story; you're not there to conduct an interrogation. So an open question such as, 'Can you describe what would happen on a typical shift?' or 'How much did you get to know the Vietnamese during your 12 months there?' or 'How were you treated by the soldiers when you were off-duty?' may be useful. But if you want a dramatic confirmation or rebuttal of some theory, a direct, closed question can be very effective: 'Did you ever get trained in safety procedures?' or 'Did you leak the email?' And if it's a confronting question, save it until you're deeper in, when you have built enough ground to get over a hump, as I did with Harry Seidler. Remember, if the interview is recorded, you can always resequence it when you edit, using a 'juicy' grab upfront to suck listeners in.

Do your research

One last thing: before you interview someone, show them some respect by doing decent research, so you can ask informed questions and get the most out of their responses. In 2019, I was pleased to be asked to go on the ABC's *Conversations* podcast, to talk about the publication of a new, updated version of my book on the Snowy Mountains Scheme, *The Snowy: A History*. This was partly because I knew going on Australia's most popular podcast would help sales, but mainly because I loved host Richard Fidler's interviewing style. In fact, I had set his interviews as exemplars for students.

Richard's producer, Nicola Harrison, dummy-interviewed me first, checking me out as talent. I regaled her with delicious details: the entrepreneur who converted an ambulance into a portable brothel that trawled the mountain camps, the sex workers servicing long lines of eager men, hawkers flogging beer and cigarettes. The woman whose house was to be drowned by the new dam, who was taken out in a boat for one last look before the land went under – and saw that a peach tree that had never borne fruit was now laden with peaches, as if having one last desperate attempt at life. The terrible accidents, the blizzards, the engineering wonders; the camaraderie, the stoushes, the drinking and derring-do. She booked me in.

On the day, the show was also going live, and Richard came out to the foyer about 20 minutes before we were due to start. We chitchatted and somehow I found myself telling him the story of prime minister Robert Menzies arriving in snowbound Guthega for the official opening of the Snowy's first power station in 1955. A fawning monarchist, Menzies had an un-Australian pompousness. Prior to his speech, the VIPs, in evening suits, were to be served cocktails. But as a worker had told me, the fridge had broken down, and shortly before the reception he saw a flustered drinks waiter running through the mess, shouting about needing ice. Later that night, he saw the waiter. 'Did you find any ice for the PM?' the worker asked. 'Yair', grinned the waiter. 'Got it out of the horse trough.'

Richard chortled a moment at the notion of the snobbish Menzies unknowingly sipping his horse-infused cocktail, before saying, accusingly: 'That's not in your book!' I was amazed. First, because I had not realised until then that we had somehow left it out of the new edition (it fell off a photo caption); and second, because it showed how microscopically he'd read the book. There and then I vowed, like a poker player, to see him and raise him. If he'd gone to that much trouble to engage with my book, I'd give him everything I had. For the next hour, on national radio, I fired on all cylinders, responding to his searching questions with story after story, secure in knowing he was really, really listening. It was very strange to be on the other end of the microphone, exposed to the very techniques I had practised and preached for decades. But I can now confirm: they really do work!

5

Milestones in the podsphere: From *Serial* to *The Daily*

Less than a decade ago, most people had never heard of podcasting. The technical prototype launched in 2001, when US software developer and self-styled media hacker David Winer put the finishing touches to the RSS (Really Simple Syndication) feed by which podcasts could be easily distributed online. Winer does not consider himself the 'inventor' of RSS, he told Brian McCullough, host of *Internet History Podcast,* in 2017. 'These things are iterative', he explained, in a fascinating interview in which he lamented people's inability to listen to and respect each other. Winer included himself in that assessment, describing how he had almost missed the idea, advocated by MTV star Adam Curry, that would lead to the dawn of podcasting as we know it: the ability to 'subscribe' to a feed and have an audio file automatically delivered to a device.

Winer met Curry at a party thrown by tech giant AOL in New York and, starstruck, admits to almost dismissing the celebrity presenter at first. 'It never occurred to me the guy had a brain', he told McCullough. But Curry had been playing around with Winer's pioneering software and had identified a crucial issue he called 'the last yard': getting a digital format from upload to download in a timely and efficient way. 'The problem was at that time the internet was very slow ... the click/wait problem was a real serious thing', Winer recalls. Curry suggested Winer attach audio files to his seminal RSS feeds, which could download in the background and turn up fully accessible on a device. In early

2001 Winer trialled the idea using Grateful Dead songs; it worked. 'I thought the world would explode', he recalled.

But to Winer's surprise, nobody took much notice. A couple of years later, Winer had a fellowship at Harvard to develop the 'blogging' concept he'd launched in 1999. In Boston, he met journalist Christopher Lydon, a colourful NPR personality who had quit his job at radio station WBUR after a dispute and started to post his interview show online. Fans could download the audio files as MP3 formats, but it was a clunky procedure. Winer linked his new RSS technology to Lydon's website, providing 'subscribers' with a continual feed: the world's first talk podcast (though the term had not yet been invented), launched 2003. *Open Source*, billed as 'arts, ideas and politics ... an American show with global attitude', is still running, as both a podcast and, ironically, back on Boston's WBUR as a live broadcast.

Winer speaks highly of Lydon: 'he's a brilliant interviewer, very patient, does his homework and his questions are very insightful'. But he told McCullough that in a sense, this professionalism was a deterrent to podcasting taking off as a new mass medium. 'Chris Lydon's podcasts did not inspire anybody to do podcasting ... because Chris's podcasts were so beautiful!' As with blogging, Winer believed that podcasting's raison d'être should be innately connected to RSS having been deliberately devised as an open, free, democratising force, available to any individual rather than controlled by corporate interests. 'The thing that pisses me off about podcasting, is that the people who do it don't understand why it's so great! Because it's open. Because nobody can tell you you can't do it!', he told McCullough.

In this experimental spirit, Winer reckons that proto-podcasts such as the unvarnished recordings of his road trip through the 2004 Democratic Party Convention, uploaded to his blog, were more likely to have encouraged punters to try this new 'audioblogging' affair. 'They were awful!' he laughed. 'Technical glitches ... just ranting. But people heard and over time ... it became like a serial ... That convinced people they could do it.'

Perhaps unsurprisingly, other pioneering podcasters had connections to technology. Among them were Stephen Downes (*Ed Radio*), Dave Slusher (*Evil Genius Chronicles*), Steve Gillmor (*Gillmor Gang*) and Doug Kaye (*IT Conversations*). Adam Curry, who would become known as 'the Podfather', launched his podcast *Daily Source Code* only in August 2004. Interestingly, Curry's podcast style was more casual than Lydon's NPR-influenced approach, and included the sort of personal reflections, meta-scenes and incidental references we are used to hearing today.[1]

You're using something that ONLY exists because somebody decided that it should be open. Otherwise you would be boxed in. And you'd have to sell it through them. And it would be all watered down and there'd be nothing interesting about it.

– Dave Winer, 'showrunner' of podcasting, on *Internet History Podcast*, 29 Oct 2017

Podcasting hit its stride in 2004–05. By then, Steve Jobs' Apple iPod had taken off as a portable media player that allowed users to download not only music but these new audio shows on the internet. Grasping for a word to describe this 'new boom in amateur radio' for a 2004 *Guardian* article, journalist Ben Hammersley suggested three: 'audio blogging', 'podcasting' and the perhaps overdramatic 'GuerillaMedia'. 'Podcasting' stuck – and most people date the word coinage as the starting point of the medium. 'Podcaster' was coined soon after, by Dannie J Gregoire, an audio tech enthusiast. In September 2004, the term 'podcasts' only had 24 results in a Google search. By the following year, it had 57 million hits. This surge saw 'podcast' selected as word of the year by *The New Oxford American Dictionary*, outgunning runners-up like 'bird flu', 'trans fat' and 'sudoku'.

Early adopters

Podcasters back then liked what indie podcasters like today: the lack of institutional gatekeepers regulating their content, the ease of getting their stuff to the public via the internet, and the opportunity to have listeners talk back to them online. They were defined by 'a free-flowing openness', summed up Nick Quah, one of the savviest podcasting commentators around, in May 2020 on his own podcast, *Servant of Pod*. 'You'd find some comedians, some minor media figures, some public radio people, and lots and lots of average-Joe tech-bloggers. Now, there's significantly more glitz. Today, you'll find celebrities, journalists, authors, social media personalities, athletes, big media companies – you name it.' Nick was talking to Adam Sachs, an early podcast executive. They lamented how podcasting was falling prey to the excesses of capitalism and profiteering – losing its glorious origins as meant for passion projects and hobbyists in their sheds. It was a somewhat unlikely conversation, given that Sachs now runs Team Coco, a major media company owned by comedian and talk-show celebrity Conan O'Brien.

But to set the scene, let's revisit a few early adopters who used the unregulated podcast space in an experimental way.

In the US, *Love + Radio* was created in 2005 by Nick van der Kolk and helmed by different producers over the years. It took full advantage of podcasting's lack of censorship to tell stories that were edgy, discomfiting or surprising – and always beautifully sound-designed. The first season had episodes about sex, anger, violence, urination and secrets. Over the years it has lived up to its motto: 'in-depth, otherworldly-produced interviews with an eclectic range of subjects, from the seedy to the sublime'. Both of van der Kolk's parents are psychiatrists, which he thinks may have planted the seed for an engagement with the weirder side of humanity.

Another durable format launched in 2005: *Slate Political Gabfest*. Its tagline today is 'where sharp political discussion meets informal and irreverent analysis'. I preferred its earlier incarnation, which *Slate* magazine's Andy Bowers envisaged as three friends who happen to be politically informed journalists chatting over after-work drinks. The hosts, David Plotz, Emily Bazelon and John Dickerson, originally worked together at *Slate*. Each show, in a freewheeling discussion, they would recap the big issues of the week, often interrupting and arguing points, just as friends would, before moving to a 'cocktail chatter' segment on miscellaneous, often trivial matters. Besides their informed point of view, the appeal comes from their ability to be 'natural' on mic and their blend of very different personalities. *Political Gabfest* would spawn a slew of similar formats, such as *Pod Save America*, created by former Barack Obama staffers after he lost office in 2016. (Hundreds of new podcasts about politics would then be created in the Trump years.)

The rise of the chatcast

The *Slate* formula, of having personable friends or colleagues riff off a theme, would spin off in numerous chumcast/chatcast directions, becoming perhaps the most prolific podcast template. It is the perfect formula for non-professionals to start up a podcast about some idea or cultural trope, some cause or situation they care deeply about. It takes months and even years of deep research to develop the best investigative/ storytelling podcasts, but a chatcast can succeed largely with the right pairing of hosts and well-positioned, strongly badged content. Take *Mothers of Invention*, in which two Irish women who probe and assess climate justice team up to portray 'feminist climate change solutions from (mostly) women around the world'. One is a comedian, Maeve Higgins; the other, decades her senior, is Mary Robinson, the former Irish president. It's an unlikely match but it works a treat, with Robinson drawing on international contacts from her period as a UN High Commissioner for Human Rights, and Higgins providing a lighter but equally dedicated touch. Producer Thimali Kodikara, of British-Sri Lankan background, is an artist and activist based in New York, where the production happens. *Mothers of Invention* highlights stories of women of colour and Indigenous women from around the world who are implementing initiatives, in line with its tagline that 'climate change is a man-made problem with a feminist solution'.

Leila Day and Hana Baba, African American hosts of *The Stoop*, launched their podcast in 2017 with an episode on 'blashion' (black fashion) and a discussion of cultural appropriation. They've since broadened their remit to tell stories from across the black diaspora that focus on race and identity. *Dear Joan and Jericha* features two British comic actor-writers as rude and ribald agony aunts; it brilliantly satirises the genre while delivering caustic commentary on sexism and power differentials, under the guise of life coaching and 'psycho-genital counselling'.

Less high-profile hosts abound. *The Wigs*, in which three Australian lawyers discuss legal issues in and out of the courtroom, claims to be the only podcast to feature practising barristers talking shop. Then there is the vast universe of fan culture podcasts, from Harry Potter love-ins and *Handmaid's Tale* take-downs to sports enthusiasts raving about football, basketball and cricket.

While the chumcast/chatcast thrives on banter and spontaneous chat, it needs some kind of underlying structure, too: at the very least, advance bullet points on where the conversation may go, with any requisite preparation done pre-show (checking out facts and figures, dates, names). Guests add variety and can stop hosts running out of steam. Basic production elements might include a musical theme to open and close, and the addition of jingles, sound effects or sonic IDs to highlight a show staple, such as 'goal of the week' or the Harry Potter 'quote of the day'. While the hosts can provide such things if necessary, a separate producer is helpful: they can note where the show drags as it is being recorded, and edit flagging or repetitious bits out before uploading the episode online. This does require either a generous friend with audio production knowledge or a small budget.

At the other end of the spectrum – editing and producing a major narrative podcast – the input of time and skills is stratospheric, as media organisations are only now beginning to understand. But the huge appetite for these podcasts continues to grow, and it's largely due to just one show: you know the one I mean. Podcasting's short history falls into two categories: pre- and post-*Serial*.

Serial: The accidental gamechanger from *This American Life*

Serial and its equally remarkable sibling, *S-Town*, were spawned by the legendary *This American Life*, a one-hour radio show (and later a podcast) created by Ira Glass in 1995 as a way of humanising and storifying news. Starting at NPR in the late 1970s as a 19-year-old intern, Glass worked his way through various roles and nearly every news show, as a tape-cutter, desk assistant, newscast writer, editor, producer, reporter and substitute host. The very first show he worked on was produced by one of the most inventive American producers of the day, Joe Frank: it seeded the idea that radio could tell stories in an original way. He also worked on *All Things Considered*, a current affairs show (still running) that allowed for a creative treatment of issues in the news. But mostly NPR applied formulaic constraints to news reportage: the classic inverted pyramid model, whereby the most salient information goes at the top and less important details come later, and the sacred journalistic tenet of objectivity, which required the reporter to withhold any indication of their reaction to the story.

Actually, radio news reports hadn't always been so formulaic. On 6 May 1937, when the German airship *Hindenburg* burst into flames over a New Jersey town with 97 people on board, Chicago reporter Herbert Morrison delivered a seminal report that totally abandoned any pretence of objectivity. In what was the first ever live news report for radio, Morrison graphically described the scene: 'It's smoke, and it's in flames now; and the frame is crashing to the ground ... Oh, the humanity!' Thirty-six people died in the incident. Morrison's torn cry, 'Oh, the humanity!', expressing his horror at the loss of life he was witnessing, became famous. It is still deeply moving to listen to his raw emotion.

More than 50 years after the *Hindenburg* incident, Ira Glass wanted to restore the personal, the emotional and the quirky to the reporting of the world around him. He experimented with various formats before launching what would become *This American Life* (*TAL*). Each episode of *TAL* delivers a true story themed around three acts, with a deceptively casual introduction by Ira. His script is written to sound spontaneous and conversational – 'So here's the thing ...' – without compromising substance, which at the time was a novel combination. On its website, *TAL* is described this way: 'Mostly we do journalism, but an entertaining kind of journalism that's built around plot. In other words, stories! ... Like little movies for radio'.

The *TAL* formula has been a huge success. The show reaches 2.2 million listeners each week via 500-plus US public radio stations. The podcast version is downloaded 3.1 million times per episode. It has won prestigious prizes, including more than half a dozen Peabody Awards and, in 2020, the first Pulitzer Prize for Audio Reporting. American radio academic Jason Loviglio summarises its strengths: 'The program's genius lies in its oscillating currents of empathy and interiority, emotional depth and disjunctive irony, journalistic precision and self-indulgent memoir'.

Ira built a strong team at *TAL*, who took to this new narrative journalism with zeal and panache. In 2005, journalist Sarah Koenig reported on a small town destroyed by Hurricane Katrina. Another producer who contributed stories on Katrina was Julie Snyder, who had joined *TAL* in the 1990s. In late 2013, Ira told Julie and Sarah they'd be off the *TAL* roster for a while, to give them a chance to come up with a new kind of show, intended for online distribution only – a podcast. It would be an experiment; they were not expecting great things. Julie recalls thinking that 300 000 downloads would be a decent outcome.

Koenig told the team about an incident in Baltimore from 1999: the death by strangling of a Korean American high-school student, Hae Min Lee, and the conviction of her former boyfriend, Pakistani American Adnan Syed, for murder. Syed was now serving a life sentence, found guilty largely on the word of a friend, Jay Wilds, who testified that he had helped Syed bury Lee's body. In 2001, when she was a crime reporter for the *Baltimore Sun*, Koenig had written about the disbarment of Syed's lawyer. Now another friend of Syed's had contacted Koenig, claiming Syed had been wrongly convicted, partly due to this lawyer's poor handling of his case. Fifteen years on, Koenig proposed that they reopen the investigation. Her breakthrough idea was that instead of doing it as one episode of this new podcast, the Adnan Syed/Hae Min Lee story would be the *entire* podcast: 'one story, told week by week', as the now immortalised opening sequence of *Serial* declares.

Serialising a story is not new: Koenig acknowledges Charles Dickens as one inspiration. But in an online audio world, having episodes drop weekly rather than all at once created an in-built anticipation that felt different. 'We weren't trying to be tease-y and build suspense in quite that way', Koenig told John Biewen in a new edition of *Reality Radio*. 'It was more like "we need another week to make the next one". We needed the time.' The sense of a live, unfolding investigation (did Syed do it or not?) was a huge factor in the buzz *Serial* generated. Subreddit groups and other social media chats proliferated online, their appetite whetted by the 'cliffhanger' moments that ended each episode. These, and the recaps played at the start over the signature pulsing music as Ira Glass intoned, 'Previously, on *Serial*', were a kind of homage to brilliant contemporary TV streaming series like *House of Cards* and *Breaking Bad*. The team wanted to make audio storytelling just as compulsive, and they certainly succeeded: *Serial* had five million downloads in the first six weeks after its October 2014 launch, breaking records on iTunes. By 8 January 2021, co-producer Dana Chivvis told me recently, that had grown to 250 million for the first season alone.

I met Dana when we were on a panel together at the Global Editors

Network (GEN) media summit in Barcelona in June 2015. *Serial*'s popularity had ignited interest in all things podcasting and audio, and suddenly everyone was trying to figure out how they could tap into the podcast 'revolution'. Hundreds of influential media players attended GEN and they put away their phones when Dana spoke, hoping to fathom *Serial*'s recipe for success. When it came to my turn, I played excerpts of beautifully crafted audio features we'd critiqued at *RadioDoc Review* (see chapter 2). But it was a throwaway line that got the most attention, on Twitter anyway. 'I've been thinking a lot about audio storytelling on the way here', I told the audience. 'And I've come to one clear conclusion.' There was an expectant silence, as they waited to hear some pearl of scholarly wisdom. 'Podcasting is God's gift to ironing!' I declared, to loud laughter.

Maybe if we'd never had *Serial*, someone else would have become the dominant shorthand of this rising industry. Maybe. But *Serial*'s late 2014 debut is nonetheless an important historical marker ... The number of monthly podcast listeners in America practically *doubled* in the five years after 2014, from around 39 million Americans to an estimated 90 million. In the five years preceding 2014, the same metric grew by only 35 percent.

In other words: There was podcasting before 2014, and there was podcasting after 2014.
– Nick Quah, 'We're Entering the Era of Big Podcasting', *Vulture*, 2019

Serial prompted an avalanche of analysis in the press. Influential columnist David Carr of the *New York Times* hailed it as podcasting's first breakout hit, 'aesthetic storytelling that feels like the best of public radio'. The *New Yorker* gave it three glowing reviews. August journalism institutions weighed in. 'For its innovations of form and its compelling, drilling account of how guilt, truth, and reality are decided, *Serial* is honored with a Peabody Award', noted the judges in 2015. 'Beautifully and intricately composed, utterly gripping, it's a damning attack on disturbing flaws in the justice system.'

The role of the host

Besides the 'live' serialised structure, people often commented on Sarah Koenig's role as host. In one sense, she was the standard reporter, sifting through a ton of research, trying to make sense of it all. What was different was that she acknowledged her doubts and shifting allegiances along the way. As one *New Yorker* review noted, the point of *Serial* 'was not so much to solve the mystery as to reveal the process of attempting to solve the mystery'. For example, in Episode Six, 'The Case Against Adnan Syed', Koenig reviews the evidence for and against Syed being the killer. She refers to 'a stray report in a police file' she's seen, which describes how a girl, Laura, had been told by a boy in the neighbourhood that he'd seen a dead 'oriental girl' in the boot of a car, and that the car belonged to a guy called Adnan. Koenig interviews Laura on tape and talks to the 'Neighbour Boy' as well. (Read the transcript aloud to understand how to write 'orally'.)

11.20 Ep 6 Serial: transcript.

This is what's weird: that original police report, about [Laura], it's dated April 28th. By that time, Adnan had already been in jail for nearly two months. But Laura was under the impression that whatever happened to her neighbour had *just* happened. She told her dad right away and he called the cops right away.

And I talked to friends of Jay who also knew the Neighbour Boy and they said, 'Oh *that* guy?' They gave the impression the Neighbour

> Boy was a bit of a gossip. A guy untalented at keeping secrets –
> which could play either way I guess, but they meant it like 'Nobody
> would tell *him* anything they wanted to stay quiet'.
>
> The Neighbour Boy never shows up at trial. He's never mentioned.
> So I let it go. But, you know, it is *weird*. And if Laura's story is true,
> then there's another witness to this murder. It's one of the things
> about this case that kind of bobs above the water for me, like a
> disturbing buoy.

This transparency was shocking. Nonfiction reportage was usually pre-packaged, definitive; the journalist dived into the story and told us unambiguously what happened. But Koenig took us along with her, swept us up in the thrill of the chase. It was a departure for Koenig too. 'I was a bit reluctant at first, because it's not a totally natural thing for me to do', she told John Biewen. But as executive producer Julie Snyder noted in *Reality Radio*, they needed to do it:

> The story really lived in the details [but] the details, a lot of the
> time, felt a little dull ... You didn't know why you were getting
> this information. And when Sarah told us what she was doing or
> thinking, and the significance of it, it was 'Oh, I see'. And then there
> were also other times when Sarah told us what she didn't know, and
> I thought it was kind of ballsy and ... emotional. She didn't pretend
> to always know what was solid, what was true.[2]

The companionable host, inviting you to share their quest, has now become almost a podcasting cliché. But Koenig points out that her ruminations were not just empty speculation. 'I don't think you can get away with it if you haven't done your homework. Even when it sounds like I'm kind of casual in my interpretations of things, I'm not. My observations were based not only on my reporting but on the documentation that exists in the case.'[3]

But the fans had no such principles. One of the most disturbing aspects for Snyder and Koenig was how folks on the internet treated their careful investigative journalism as pure entertainment. A mainstay of the show was the call Koenig would put through to Adnan Syed in prison each episode. More than 30 hours of this tape were whittled down to a tiny fraction for the show, but it was enough to have fans salivating over their relationship. Did Sarah fancy Adnan? Was Adnan trying to manipulate her, to get himself an appeal? Did Adnan really do it?

The reality behind the entertainment

A reminder that this was, in fact, true crime came with a heartbreaking subreddit post from the brother of Hae Min Lee, the murdered girl. In October 2014, just weeks after the podcast dropped online, he posted as 'brotherofhae' with the heading: 'I am Hae's brother – do not AMA'. ('AMA' means Ask Me Anything. The post below contains spelling and other errors as in original.)

> TO ME ITS REAL LIFE. To you listeners, its another murder
> mystery, crime drama, another episode of CSI. You weren't there
> to see your mom crying every night, having a heartattck when she
> got the new that the body was found, and going to court almost
> everyday for a year seeing your mom weeping, crying and fainting.
> You don't know what we went through. Especially to those who are
> demanding our family response and having a meetup ... you guys are
> disgusting. Shame on you. I pray that you don't have to go through
> what we went through and have your story blasted to 5mil listeners.

Sarah Koenig and Dana Chivvis replied to brotherofhae's post, seeking to be in contact, but he says he ignored it. He says he posted a screenshot of their chat. But he then took it down, saying he realised that doing so transgressed their privacy, by posting their personal info. It doesn't sound like the irony was intentional.

Team *Serial* eventually accepted that they could not control the reception of the podcast. The subreddit is still live today, nearly seven years on, with some 65 000 members. New listeners still debate whether Adnan is guilty.

Koenig kept researching until the final week, unearthing new material and checking out leads. As brotherofhae noted, she was certainly rigorous. 'Although I do not like the fact that SK pick our story to cover, she is an awesome narrator/writer/investigator. No wonder why this podcast is so popular.' By now the podcast was averaging 2.25 million downloads per episode and everyone was waiting for the denouement. Brotherofhae was one of many listeners anticipating a revelation. 'Being a media person that she is, she wants some big ending', he wrote.

But Koenig equivocated in the end. 'It would have been great to answer the question, solve the crime', she told John Biewen with a laugh. 'We would have loved it, and I think we held out hope for quite a while.' In the final episode, Koenig interrogates herself. 'As a juror, I have to acquit. But I am not a juror.' She continues: 'As a human being ... if you asked me to swear that Adnan Syed is innocent, I couldn't do it. I nurse doubt'. She ends the 12-episode immersion admitting that she still doesn't have all the facts. 'Based on the information we have before us, I don't believe any of us can say what happened to Hae.' Reflecting on this inconclusive outcome three years on, Koenig is philosophical. 'I'm OK with not knowing. I can live there, in the uncertainty, and it's been a good lesson.'[4]

The podcast did help Syed trigger a new trial, in 2016. *Serial* dropped a few plainly edited 'bonus' episodes as updates – a storytelling advantage the podcast format offers. After various legal processes, Syed's conviction was upheld, in 2019. At this point, Koenig informs us, she is bowing out and becoming a spectator, like the rest of us.

Serial as cultural phenomenon

Serial is now well established as a cultural phenomenon. It was lampooned on *Saturday Night Live*; Koenig was voted one of the 100 most influential people of the year by *Time* magazine; *Slate* made a recap podcast about it, *Slate's Serial Spoiler Specials*; and *The Onion* made a hilarious satirical show, *A Very Fatal Murder*, that mocked its true-crime tropes. Academic articles began to emerge, as did a whole new field of podcasting studies, energised by young PhD candidates keen to analyse podcasting as an exciting new medium. A 2017 book, *The Serial Podcast and Storytelling in the Digital Age*, contains essays that draw on analytical tools from narratology, media theory, critical race theory, post-structuralism, psychoanalysis and postmodernism.

In 2019, HBO aired a four-part documentary, *The Case Against Adnan Syed*. The show sought to humanise Hae Min Lee, showing video of her as a schoolgirl, and also featured footage of Syed. Watching the characters I'd got to know as voices or through Koenig's description felt weirdly out of kilter. I had formed images in my mind, as audio encourages you to do, and their actual faces seemed staged rather than real. The *Baltimore Sun* called it 'a skillfully crafted work – absorbing and entertaining'. I had to force myself to watch to the end.

The Case Against Adnan Syed was based on a book, *Adnan's Story: The Truth*, by Rabia Chaudry, the lawyer and friend of Adnan Syed who first tipped Sarah Koenig off about the case. Shortly after *Serial* ended, Chaudry created a 'competing' podcast, called *Undisclosed*. It was hosted by Chaudry and two other lawyers, Susan Simpson and Colin Miller, who sifted through the story, giving an alternative, pro-Syed view. Though the first season, *The State v. Adnan Syed*, sounded distinctly amateur, the team got their act together and have now made 17 seasons, each one investigating a purported miscarriage of justice. So, besides its own howling success, *Serial* spawned direct media offshoots.

But where does *Serial* sit now, in the podcasting pantheon? In 2021, more than six years after its release, Nick Quah invited *New Yorker* critic Sarah Larson onto his show, *Servant of Pod*, to reassess the 'long tail'. Larson anointed it as indeed a gamechanger. 'People were thrilled by it and they were thrilled to be thrilled by it', she observed. 'It just made everything explode into people's consciousness and I think the excitement and the nostalgia of that podcast moment is what its legacy is.' Quah agreed, noting how it still sounds better than most things being made today. He attributes this to its tight structure ('how it sounds – the flow'), the host's convincing narration ('most scripts are read, not performed') and, most of all, the 'sensational' writing, so direct and conversational in tone.

One major critique at the time was a piece in *The Awl*, a now defunct website created by Jay Caspian Kang, a Korean American who is now a writer-at-large for the *New York Times Magazine*. Called "'Serial' and White Reporter Privilege", it lambasted Sarah Koenig – a white Jewish American – for having a limited cultural understanding of the Asian communities that Hae Min Lee and Adnan Syed came from. An Asian American himself, Quah weighs this up. 'Maybe having a person of colour actively working on the story' might have helped, he offers.

Other critiques of *Serial*'s approach to ethics centred largely on the absence of victim Hae Min Lee from the story, and the voyeuristic treatment of true crime as entertainment. On the former, the *Serial* team did approach the family, and tried to construct a rounded picture of Lee from what second-hand artefacts they had: a diary, photos, interviews with friends. On the latter, such moral dilemmas pre-date *Serial*. Crime was being exploited as story almost from the beginning of the printing press, says scholar Joy Wiltenburg. Broadsheets and pamphlets circulated in Germany from the mid-16th century, recounting crime and the executions of the condemned, were written with an explicit appeal to emotion.[5] The genre would eventually give rise to the term 'sensationalist', coined in the 19th century.

The *Serial* team's approach peddled neither horror nor uplift. What Sarah Koenig and her colleagues did do was to uphold contemporary journalistic ethics around principles such as fairness and accuracy. In practice, this can involve behaviour that may not be nice or polite.

For instance, Koenig acknowledges that 'doorstepping' (showing up unannounced at his door) Syed's friend Jay Wilds was 'a dick move'. But as she told John Biewen in *Reality Radio*, she did not resile from it. 'I, as a reporter, have to do some aggressive things to get information. I guess what I'm saying is that two things can be true at once. I think it can be jarring and unpleasant for people, but I also think it's necessary.'

Beyond Season One

The *Serial* team would create further content. Season Two, a co-production with film director Mark Boal, examined whether a former prisoner of the Taliban, Bowe Bergdahl, was an American war hero or a US Army deserter who had selfishly put his comrades in danger. While the first episode packed a huge punch, overall it lacked the impact of Season One, mainly because Sarah Koenig never got to interview Bowe Bergdahl directly and everything felt second-hand.

But Season Three was another remarkable offering, a year spent as a fly-on-the-wall in a courtroom in Cleveland, Ohio. Averaging an impressive 5.23 million downloads per episode, it was a blistering insight into the hideously flawed 'justice' system in the US and the inequalities, racism and prejudice it supports. For this season, perhaps mindful of the 'white privilege' commentary, Koenig was joined by a co-host: Emmanuel Dzotsi, 'a young Black reporter with an Ohio pedigree and a British accent', wrote Jason Loviglio in *RadioDoc Review*. Loviglio pointed out that Dzotsi helped listeners *feel* the racial profiling practised by police, and that *Serial* Season Three had deep social impact, in a way that neither of the other seasons had – more as good literature does.

Serial's success saw it branch out of *This American Life* as its own entity, Serial Productions. In 2017 the company astonished the podcasting world with *S-Town* podcast, another instant classic (see chapter 6). In 2020, they had a more modest hit with *Nice White Parents*, a penetrating study of racial and cultural bigotry in the New York school system. Around the same time, the *New York Times* announced it had purchased Serial Productions, for a reputed US$25 million. Season Five launched in April 2021 with *The Improvement Association*, a timely investigation by reporter Zoe Chace into election fraud allegations in North Carolina.

On its website, *TAL* is not coy about its contribution to audio storytelling:

> Back in 1999, the *American Journalism Review* declared that the program was 'in the vanguard of a journalistic revolution' and since then, a generation of podcasts and radio shows have sprung up – *Radiolab, Invisibilia, StartUp, Reply All, Snap Judgment, Love + Radio, Heavyweight* – building on the lessons we learned about narrative journalism and inventing all sorts of things we never could've.

One further show was about to create a whole new podcast template: the narrative news podcast.

The Daily: The Death Star of news podcasts

In February 2017, the *New York Times* launched *The Daily*, and with it a new form of 'narrative news' that would reach two billion downloads by September 2020 and launch its own gaggle of imitations. Each episode of 25 minutes or so might feature one or two of the *Times'* 1700 journalists, who tell host Michael Barbaro not just the bare facts, but the way things happened, to whom and why – the *story* behind the news.

The Daily's impact derives from a combination of factors. First, it has a likeable host in Barbaro, a *Times* journalist who was in his thirties when the podcast launched. Barbaro is excellent at interviewing his colleagues, whose expert insight into their beat provide the show's 'special sauce'. Barbaro adds a few extra flourishes: he will pithily recap an interviewee's complex answer and ask them if that's what they meant

– and it invariably is. That makes the guest feel validated and inclined to continue with generous answers, while also bringing the listener up to speed, ready to stay the distance.

Barbaro's other noted characteristic is his punctuating of a conversation with an empathetic 'hmmmph', as he registers surprise or understanding. This became A Thing on the internet. One woman tweeted: 'whenever I tell my husband a story I imagine @mikiebarb grunting in appreciation at my profound insight'. As playful homage, the team even compiled a collage of diverse Barbaro 'hmmmph' interjections.

The Daily's final ingredient is the superlative sound design. Rather than just assign someone from the multimedia section, to which so many newspapers relegated their early audio stories, the *Times* recruited an actual Executive Producer of Audio. That became Lisa Tobin, a 30-year-old radio producer from WBUR public radio in Boston, who had worked on NPR's *Morning Edition* show. She, in turn, recruited public-radio producers Theo Balcomb (youngest ever supervising producer at NPR's flagship current affairs show *All Things Considered*) and Andy Mills (from the renowned *Radiolab*). From day one, this core team of four set high production standards: interviews were well recorded, closely miked; meta-scenes (e.g. the interview set-up parts that would normally be dropped) were included for texture and mood; and archival audio and actuality (in industry jargon, 'tape') were woven throughout.

Most telling of all, the podcast had a signature theme and music composition that immediately signalled that this was the opposite of a heavy-handed news show. Barbaro told the composers, Jim Brunberg and Ben Landsverk of Wonderly Music, that he was after a 'siren' sound: one that would seduce listeners into staying with him, as the beautiful mythical sirens of old had lured sailors to them on the rocks. So instead of the driving beats of a typical news headline sting, we hear luscious, swirling viola, piano, drums and guitar sounds at the top, and little pulsing syncopations through the show – an aural delight – while the ascending notes that end the theme are supposed to sound like an unanswered question.

Success builds

The huge success of *The Daily* was totally unanticipated. In fact, an almost 7000-word strategy report by *Times* journalists released in January 2017 (a month before *The Daily* launched) did not mention the word 'podcast' once! The report clearly identified a barrier to customer growth: 'Stories written in a dense, institutional language that fails to clarify important subjects and feels alien to younger readers'. But its solution was couched in visual terms, as it bemoaned 'A long string of text, when a photograph, video or chart would be more eloquent'. The word 'audio' had two mentions. Had the analysts studied narrative podcast formats, they would have realised that they are framed in precisely the sort of casual, conversational language that would appeal to younger people who are versed in the vernacular of online communications. The way forward was to get new digital subscribers, the report continued.

Luckily, *The Daily* – with its tagline 'how the news should sound' – was onto exactly that. By August 2021, *The Daily* would have *four million* downloads a day – more listeners than the paper had readers. The audio team by then had grown to an astonishing 50 and the podcast was being touted as the paper's new front page. Barbaro was nonplussed at his sudden celebrity. 'People who love the show really feel connected to my face, my voice. It's shocking!' he told the podcast *Longform*. Asked about an incident where he famously teared up while interviewing a coalminer whose ragged breathing brought home viscerally that he was dying from silicosis (dust disease), Barbaro pointed out that he got emotional when doing print interviews too – it was just that nobody could hear that. 'Audio is a very honest medium', he reflected. 'You're discovering how you feel as you feel it – and that is very powerful.' He had one other cautionary comparison between podcasting and print: the dirty secret known to audio producers who have listened in real time (as you must) through mix after mix of tape. 'Audio is *unspeakably* time-consuming to turn around!'

As *The Daily* took off, it became a launch pad for one-off theme-based shows by the *New York Times*, such as *Rabbit Hole*, about the murky world of YouTube fame; *1619*, about the 400th anniversary of the start of slavery in the US; and, in 2018, *Caliphate*, a deep dive inside the world of ISIS, which won a Peabody Award and was a finalist for a Pulitzer Prize – until things all went horribly wrong, and the kudos crumbled.

Caliphate

Caliphate, hosted by the *Times'* personable terrorism specialist, Rukmini Callimachi, was the *Times'* first narrative nonfiction podcast. In keeping with podcast conventions, it placed Callimachi-the-person in a central role: the first episode, called 'The Reporter', was about her getting trolled by ISIS followers and fearing for her life. Another episode, where she tracked down catatonic Yasidi girls who had been kept as sex slaves, was heartbreaking.

But much of the series relied on the testimony of a self-described former ISIS operative based in Canada, Shehroze Chaudhry, who went by the name Abu Huzayfah. Huzayfah told Callimachi in graphic detail how he had executed two men at an ISIS camp in Syria; his story featured in some six of the podcast's ten chapters, one of them actually documenting Callimachi's process of fact-checking Huzayfah's claims. The series was acclaimed for both its journalism and its 'cinematic' production style, credited to producer/reporter Andy Mills. But in September 2020, the Canadian Government arrested Huzayfah/Chaudhry for perpetrating a hoax.

A subsequent internal examination by the *New York Times* saw much of the podcast retracted, shortly before Christmas in 2020. *Times* executive editor Dean Baquet recorded an episode of *The Daily* with Michael Barbaro to explain how their famed editorial rigour was found wanting. '"Caliphate" should have had the regular participation of an editor experienced in the subject matter', states an editor's note now attached to the podcast. 'The Times should have pressed harder to verify Mr. Chaudhry's claims before deciding to place so much emphasis on one individual's account ... It is also clear that elements of the original fact-checking process were not sufficiently rigorous.'

Media discussions of the lapse in standards suggested that *Caliphate* had flown under the radar *because* it was a podcast, and therefore was not subjected to the same sort of editorial scrutiny as, say, a print article. *The Daily* had become so good at applying high audio narrative standards that the audio unit had almost evolved its own operational principles, divorced from the way the *Times'* other journalism was run. It turned out that *Times* staff with Middle Eastern expertise had indeed raised warning flags but had been ignored.

In a humiliating about-face, the *New York Times* returned the coveted Peabody Award and transferred Callimachi to a lowlier beat (higher education). To the surprise and anger of many watching on social media, co-producer Andy Mills was not publicly censored. In fact, the week after the debacle became public, he was elevated to the role of co-host of *The Daily* for a special episode about a popular radio personality, Delilah.

Mills then became the subject of another hot topic on social media: men treating women badly. In Mills' case, he was accused of harassing and belittling female colleagues at his former job, as a producer with *Radiolab* at WNYC. One woman said that at after-work drinks, when she mildly derided as 'hipster' his karaoke preference, Mills poured the remainder of his beer over her head. She also alleged he had told her she had only been hired because of her gender, not her ability. A former *This American Life* reporter tweeted that Mills had said women would not be hired at *Radiolab* because they 'were bad at Pro Tools' (top-end audio-editing software). Other allegations related to harassment of female colleagues.

In January 2021, *Radiolab* responded by publishing 'A Note' apologising 'to those we failed'. The following month, Mills resigned from the *Times*, acknowledging his bad behaviour. 'I look back at those actions with extraordinary regret and embarrassment', he wrote, noting that he had been issued a warning by WNYC's HR department. But he also claimed to have been scapegoated: 'I have been transformed into a symbol of larger societal evils'.

Mills is far from the first person to suffer from being vilified on social media. Whether it went too far is not for me to say. What I can report is that there was indeed a movement afoot to address 'larger societal evils' – a collective howl demanding an end to the racism, sexism and general sense of entitlement so long the supposed birthright of straight white men. The rest of us were over it – and in podcastland, too, a reckoning was on the way (see chapter 9).

Despite the *Caliphate* imbroglio, podcasts continue to thrive at the *New York Times*. In July 2021, the paper announced it had appointed a new Director of Audio, Paula Szuchman. Szuchman will oversee the *Times'* two distinct audio branches: News, with flagship *The Daily*; and Opinion, with prominent shows *Sway* (with Kara Swisher), *The Ezra Klein Show* and *The Argument*. Also in the mix are pop-culture chumcast *Still Processing*, quirky relationship tales in *Modern Love*, music show *Popcast*, *The Book Review* and narrated newspaper articles, plus the separate offerings from Serial Productions. From the four people who launched *The Daily* in early 2017, the *New York Times'* audio team has grown to almost 100.

The Daily's success has spawned numerous other daily news podcasts, making the form 'one of the fastest growing areas of media consumption', according to a Reuters Institute report in November 2020.[6] The report tracked news podcasts in six countries (the US, the UK, Australia, France, Sweden and Denmark) and found '102 daily news podcasts, of which 37 were launched in the last year'. They punched well above their weight. Although they make up less than 1 per cent of all podcasts, they account for more than 10 per cent of the overall downloads in the US and 9 per cent in France and Australia. The report identified several formats: 14 per cent were an extended chat (e.g. *Newscast* by the BBC; *The NPR Politics Podcast*; *The Ben Shapiro Show* produced by The Daily Wire), 24 per cent offered a concise news round-up (e.g. *FT News Briefing* from the *Financial Times*; *Omni Pod* from Omni, Sweden; the BBC's

Global News Podcast; and *From the Newsroom* produced by Australia's news.com.au), and 20 per cent produced a microbulletin aimed at smart speakers and streaming apps (*BBC Minute*; *NPR News Now*; *Ekot* from Sveriges Radio, Sweden). But remarkably, almost half of all daily news podcasts (43 per cent) followed *The Daily*'s 'deep-dive' narrative, sound-rich format: exemplars include *Today in Focus* from the *Guardian* UK and *7am* from Schwartz Media in Australia. Listeners skew younger and highly educated, and numbers are substantial: France's *La Story* from *Les Echos* had 70 000 downloads a month, while the *FT News Briefing* had more than two million.

The Daily has unquestionably made its mark on podcasting and journalism. But just a month after *The Daily* launched, another narrative journalism podcast radically extended audio storytelling aesthetics and set new download records. The *S-Town* podcast clocked up ten million downloads in the first four days after its release, in March 2017. The next chapter examines what made it so special.

 ## Monetising podcasts

How do people earn money from their podcasts?
There are four main ways.

1   Subscription: listeners pay

2   Advertisers/sponsors

3   Commission: find a publisher

4   Grants and funding

Podcast income can range from extremely modest (just covering expenses) to stratospheric (for breakout hits), but there is one common principle: to be marketable, your podcast needs to have a particular *audience*. The more data you can gather on the audience – numbers, demographics, listening habits – the more likely you will be to find advertisers, sponsors and/or publishers. The most popular podcasts run a hybrid model: for instance, avid listeners might pay for 'bonus' content, while advertisers will pay for an ad spot during the show.

1 Subscription model: listeners pay

This is the most likely model for passion projects, and indie and non-commercial podcasts. It basically means crowdsourcing funds from listeners who like your podcast enough to support you, at a rate they choose. **Patreon** <patreon.com> is a platform designed expressly for content creators; it provides a private RSS feed so that you can share bonus episodes with your 'patrons' and also allows you to contact them directly. Patreon takes a commission to cover administration and pays you either monthly or per episode created. **Ko-fi** <ko-fi.com> is an alternative model, where you get paid directly by fans. Creators pay a platform fee, or upgrade to a premium package for a monthly fee. **Apple Podcasts** introduced an in-built subscription model in 2021, which allows show creators to set a cost for listeners; this can range from zero to a set amount, with Apple taking a percentage of any earnings.

2 Advertising and sponsorship

Data shows that podcast ads get better results than ads in other media. Listeners not only tend to listen through the promotion, they report higher engagement with the product.

Podcast advertising relies on a CPM rate: the 'cost per mille' (per thousand) listens of a podcast episode, measured over a one-month period. Average US CPM rates in 2021 were US$18 for a 30-second ad and $25 for 60 seconds. Therefore, if you can prove you have 50 000 listeners, you could charge US$1250 for a 60-second ad. If you can get two such ads per show, you've earned US$2500 for one episode. Prices also vary according to position: an ad at the start of the show is worth more than a 'mid-roll', by which time the listener may have turned off.

Ads come in two varieties: 'baked-in', meaning they are a permanent part of the episode and won't change over time; and 'dynamic', which can be retrofitted, perhaps to suit various geographic audiences, or to promote a new product that was not around when the podcast first dropped.

The 'baked-in' ads are increasingly read by the host. This was seen as heresy early on, particularly in traditional public radio circles. Ira Glass of *This American Life* stunned the sector when he announced in 2015 that public radio was 'ready for capitalism'. He later clarified that he did not mean that public radio and podcasts of that ilk should abandon their mission, but was simply suggesting that podcasters take advantage of the post-*Serial* boom in podcasting (which he had helped create) to generate money that would underwrite their production costs.

Soon more and more podcasters were happy to trade dignity for dollars: I recall being bemused the first time I heard Nick van der Kolk of the subversive show *Love + Radio* expounding the virtues of his new underpants brand. But listeners got used to it. The only thing that grates now is when the host segues straight from a plot point to a promotion, without a 'We'll be right back' or a recognisable musical sting to separate ads from show.

The point is, host-read ads have a huge influence on listeners, who have built a relationship with the host through their voice. Advertising agencies such as AdvertiseCast in the US can tailor this demand to the show's demographic, linking directly to would-be advertisers. The importance of data is evident when you see the results. According to AdvertiseCast, the controversial Canadian academic,

Jordan B Peterson gets 360 000 downloads per episode of the show he hosts with his daughter, Mikhaila. His demographics skew 78 per cent male, 74 per cent tertiary-educated, with a median income of US$77 000 and a median age of 42. Mikhaila reads ads targeted at this demographic, even mentioning her father's serious illness as an incentive to buy life insurance. A true-crime chumcast, *Moms and Murder*, gets 85 000 downloads an episode and its listeners skew 90 per cent female, median age 39. Hosts Mandy and Melissa read ads for an online counselling service and 'the perfect-fit bra', among other things.

A sponsor is the acme of advertising – one organisation that will bankroll perhaps the full cost of producing your podcast in return for mentions both in the show and the show notes. Be bold and reach out to whoever might chime with your audience – think laterally. They can only say no!

3 Publisher/commission

Sometimes podcasters take a sophisticated pitch to a publisher that includes the podcast focus, format, production team, schedule, budget and anticipated audience. They might approach big corporates on the lookout for the next hit: Spotify, Audible, Wondery, iHeartRadio. Or they might respond to invited rounds at organisations such as the BBC, ABC or CBC.

There are pros and cons to these deals. If you get a sizeable lump sum to make an entire podcast season for a network, you have a guaranteed income throughout production. You will also be heavily promoted; both factors might set up your career. But if you underestimated your budget or schedule, you still have to deliver the agreed product and might end up subsidising it yourself. With only seed funding, you may not have enough to make a show to the standard you want. But if you do, you will probably have more control over intellectual property and rights than if you have signed up to a big corporate.

4 Grants and funding

More and more organisations now offer competitive funding to make a podcast. The annual Google Podcasts creator program offers training and financial support to encourage diverse voices in podcasting. The Whickers, established in 2015 to commemorate the great British broadcaster Alan Whicker, offer an annual Radio and Audio Funding Award of up to £6000 to an emerging audio producer based anywhere in the world to create an original radio or audio documentary of 28–45 minutes. Arts organisations, media institutes and philanthropic groups in many countries also have funding rounds for which podcasts would be eligible.

Then there are prizes (see box on pages 44–46, chapter 2). Cash awards can help develop a new project, and a prestigious gong can strengthen a CV to improve your chances of getting funded in the future. The Podcasting, Seriously Awards Fund was established in 2021 'to encourage more BIPOC, Queer, and Trans audio creators to submit their work for consideration into awards competition and media/journalism awards by reimbursing them the cost of the submission'.

TIP: Know your audience

Cultivating your audience is critical, whatever the model. Maintain active accounts on social media, and be sure to interact with listener feedback. Large social media followings impress advertisers. If your podcast is about parenting or sustainable fashion or mountain climbing, consider compiling a newsletter along this theme. It can be a mix of your own activities and broader developments you come across.

If listeners sign up for it, that provides tailored reach to your community, which shows a committed, measurable audience – gold for advertisers and sponsors. The platform where you place your podcast will provide data on download numbers and more: some drill deeper than others, so choose according to your needs.

6

Podcasting as literary journalism: *S-Town*

Warning: The theme of suicide is discussed in this chapter.

In all media, there are classics. Think of films like *Casablanca* and *Star Wars*, and TV series like *Game of Thrones* and *Breaking Bad*. Narrative podcasting has its hits, but in podcasting there are really only a couple of classics. The first is, of course, *Serial*, because it changed everything (see chapter 5). The second? *S-Town*, a seven-part narrative nonfiction podcast that redefined the possibilities of the medium. As of May 2020, it had been downloaded 92 million times.

    S-Town, a podcast from *This American Life* and *Serial* released in 2017, has attracted plenty of media attention and the odd academic article. But nobody to my knowledge has viewed it closely through the lens of 'literary journalism', that sharp reinvention of journalism that happened in the 1960s and '70s through writers like Tom Wolfe, Joan Didion, Truman Capote and Hunter S Thompson, and continues today in the hands of long-form feature writers at outlets such as the *Atlantic* and the *New Yorker*, as well as in the slow zine movement and dedicated online sites such as Longreads and Narratively. Noted contemporary narrative nonfiction authors include a new wave of writers of colour in the US, such as Isabel Wilkerson (*Caste*), Nikole Hannah-Jones (*The 1619 Project*), Rachel Kaadzi Ghansah, Henry Louis Gates Jr, Wesley Yang and Jay Caspian Kang. Important book-length literary journalism has also been published by writers including Katherine Boo, Rebecca Solnit, Leon Dash, James McBride, Ted Conover and Jon Krakauer in the US, and Helen Garner, Anna Funder, Chloe Hooper and Anna Krien in Australia, along with the travel reportage of Pico Iyer, based in Japan, and Miguel Sousa Tavares, from Portugal.

The term 'aural literature' has been bandied about in relation to *S-Town* but in a generalised way. So, in order to give us fresh insights into how and why *S-Town* broke new ground, I've gone back to the literary journalism playbook. In this chapter, I discuss how the principles of literary journalism map directly to this remarkable podcast, which I binged over two days when it first dropped online. Do please listen first – and enjoy!

What is literary journalism?

In 1995, American writer and academic Mark Kramer defended literary journalism in an essay called 'Breakable Rules for Literary Journalists':

> As a practitioner, I find the 'literary' part self-congratulating and the 'journalism' part masking the form's inventiveness. But 'literary journalism' is roughly accurate. The paired words cancel each other's vices and describe the sort of nonfiction in which arts of style and narrative construction long associated with fiction help pierce to the quick of what's happening – the essence of journalism.[1]

The year Kramer wrote those words, coincidentally, broadcaster Ira Glass quit his job at NPR to launch *This American Life* (*TAL*). Though he rejected the term 'literary nonfiction' ('It's pretentious, for one thing, and it's a bore'), Glass loved the kind of writing it espoused – so much so that in 2007 he published an anthology, *The New Kings of Nonfiction*, in which he brought together iconic literary journalism figures such as David Foster Wallace, Malcolm Gladwell, Michael Lewis and Susan

Orlean, alongside emerging writers in the genre. In his introduction, Glass explained what drew him to their work: 'They try to get inside their protagonists' heads with a degree of empathy that's unusual. Theirs is a ministry of love, in a way we don't usually discuss reporters' feelings towards their subjects. Or at least, they're willing to see what is lovable in the people they're interviewing'. The empathy Glass admired is also very evident in *TAL*'s two spin-off shows: in *Serial*, Sarah Koenig demonstrates conflicted feelings about convicted murderer Adnan Syed (see chapter 5), and in *S-Town*, host Brian Reed openly shares with the listener his fascination with the podcast's protagonist John B McLemore.

Glass further recognised that, for all their diversity, his nonfiction 'kings' were using two basic building blocks: the plot, and the ideas lurking behind the plot. 'Usually the plot is the easy part', he wrote in the introduction to his book. 'You do whatever research you can, you talk to lots of people, and you figure out what happened. It's the ideas that kill you. What's the story mean? What bigger truth about all of us does it point to?'

What is perhaps remarkable is the audaciously plain way podcasts can get big truths across. Just a few years before *Serial* and *S-Town* dropped, innovative online narrative journalism was headed down a complex multimedia path. It had reached new heights in 2012 with 'Snow Fall', a *New York Times* online production that created a riveting account of an avalanche, complete with animations and video clips embedded in a classic long-form print framework. The story attracted 3.2 million visitors, won a Pulitzer Prize and literally entered the lexicon: as media scholar David O Dowling noted, journalists began to ask, 'Can we "Snow Fall" this?'[2]

The following year, writer Jon Henley collaborated with a team of 22 at the *Guardian* UK and *Guardian* Australia to publish 'Firestorm'. This compelling work combined video, audio, photography and emergency rescue operation recordings, anchored by Henley's narrative spine, to tell the extraordinary story of how an Australian family escaped a terrible bushfire. The lead photo shows Tammy Holmes and her five grandchildren cowering under a jetty in waist-deep water in their small Tasmanian town, against a blood-red sky. Taken by Tammy's husband, Tim Holmes, the photo inspired a bigger investigation of how climate change was affecting fires and communities. Other notable multimedia works followed. In 2014, Ta-Nehisi Coates's 'The Case for Reparations', a masterful 16 000-word essay published in the *Atlantic*, interwove photographs, video and interactive infographics as Coates set out his convincing argument for why African Americans deserve to be compensated for the discriminatory outcomes of slavery.

These digital narrative works suggested that storytelling was getting technically very sophisticated. But *Serial* demonstrated that website wizardry was not a necessary part of popular long-form journalism – a linear audio story alone could attract a huge audience. *Serial*'s success spurred the *TAL* stable to experiment again. And so in March 2017, the world woke up to *S-Town*, a seven-hour, 66 000-word podcast that is a deep immersion in the life of one mordant genius, John B McLemore, who lived in the small Alabama town of Woodstock, which he called 'Shittown'.

S-Town host Brian Reed and producer Julie Snyder wanted their podcast to be as riveting as a great novel, which they signalled by calling each episode a 'chapter' (a descriptor *Caliphate* would later adopt). Brian Reed would be its first-person author, demonstrating the sort of meta-reportage, subjectivity and self-reflexivity that literary journalists have long claimed. Ira Glass noted this quality approvingly in the work of his nonfiction kings: 'a lot of the power of these stories comes from the writers telling you step by step what they're feeling and thinking, as they do their reporting'.

Media scholars David O Dowling and Kyle Miller propose that immersive and subjective long-form audio storytelling such as *S-Town* borrows from techniques associated with documentary cinema as well as the novel, creating a genre that is 'adept and multifaceted in providing serious reportage, cultural critique and probing psychological intrigue'.[3]

Does that make it literary journalism? 'Literary journalism draws on immersion, voice, accuracy, and symbolism as essential forces', wrote Norman Sims in his 1984 book *The Literary Journalists*. Sims later observed that literary journalists 'triangulate different stories, sort through participants' memories, make judgement calls, calculate the structure of the story, adopt a point of view and decipher the symbolism of details'. Mark Kramer offered further pertinent concepts in his 1995 essay quoted earlier, and a decade later Robert Boynton's book *The New New Journalism* summarised literary journalism as 'rigorously reported, psychologically astute, sociologically sophisticated and politically aware'.

Language is also a key part of literary journalism: the ability to write descriptively, and to capture authentic-sounding dialogue. Tom Wolfe, the iconoclastic journalist who conjured the psychedelic Zeitgeist of the 1960s in books such as *The Electric Kool-Aid Acid Test*, was a master of this. In *The New Journalism*, the 1973 anthology he co-edited, Wolfe outlined his own preferred approach: scene-by-scene construction, use of dialogue, point of view and what he called 'status life' – 'everyday gestures, habits, manners, customs, styles of furniture' that reveal a character's way of being in the world. The 'gonzo' journalist Hunter S Thompson went further, charting his own drug- and alcohol-induced befuddlement, acutely observed reactions to political events and wild journeys in influential books such as *Fear and Loathing in Las Vegas*, *Hell's Angels* and *The Great Shark Hunt*.

I believe Reed and Snyder absorbed some of these elements of literary journalism, perhaps without even realising it, and turned *S-Town* into a contender for aural nonfiction royalty.

The genesis of *S-Town*

On 28 March 2017, *S-Town* dropped online as a complete series – an unprecedented move, which obviated the need for 'trailer' grabs at the end of each episode that are designed to make you come back a week later.

Instead, the chapters flowed seamlessly, as in a book. It was downloaded a record-breaking ten million times in the first four days; by early May, download numbers had passed 40 million. But the podcast, which had been three years in the making, almost didn't happen. It all began with an email to *TAL* from John B McLemore, with the subject line: 'John B McLemore lives in Shittown, Alabama'. As *TAL* routinely received many attention-seeking emails, staff thought McLemore could be either a narcissist or a nut. Still, his email asked Brian Reed to investigate a murder, and a subsequent email provided a link to a related news story. Eventually, a year on, Reed rang him.

That phone call, relayed in edited form in the first episode, immediately revealed that McLemore was a remarkable character. Although he lived in 'a crummy little shittown in Alabama, called Woodstock', his interests had always been ambitious and wide-ranging: 'Even when I was a kid in school, I didn't want to hang around other kids', McLemore tells Brian Reed in Chapter One. 'Because kids are talking about getting girls, or deer hunting, or football. Whereas I was interested in the astrolabe, sundials, projective geometry, new age music, climate change, and how to solve Rubik's cube.'

Reed informs us that when McLemore is not obsessively research-ing climate change, he is looking after his aged mother, caring for numerous stray dogs on his 128-acre property, tending a huge rose garden (displaying extensive botanical knowledge in the process), fixing antiquarian clocks and building a vast maze. McLemore's use of language is arresting. In a deep Southern US drawl, he mentions a visit by the 'Praetorian class' (the police) and laments the 'proleptic decay and decrepitude' of the area. Reed reassures listeners he had to look up the meaning of 'proleptic' (using a word or phrase in anticipation of it becoming true), but succumbs to McLemore's powerful personality and agrees to visit him. 'It felt as if, by sheer force of will, John was opening this portal between us and calling out through it, calling from his world.'

> I felt like this was something I wished were a type of podcast that existed, so that's what we were trying to do. This is the type of podcast I'd be interested in hearing more of. Something that had the feel and form of *S-Town* ... We made what we were wanting to be out there.
>
> – Brian Reed, in Meg Watson, 'The Journalist and the Clock Maker', *Junkee*, 2017

Listeners embark, with Reed as companion/guide, on a story as tortuous as McLemore's maze. In *S-Town*'s first episode, Reed introduces McLemore via this scene:

> He's a redhead, with red goatee and glasses, looks a bit younger than his 48 years, in ratty jeans and ratty sneakers, and a Sherwin-Williams T-shirt that he probably got for buying a can of paint at the hardware store ... He's naming the plants all around us as we move – goldenrod, Russian sage, a climbing Lady Banks' rose ...

In its evocation of place and attention to detail, this is not unlike that first, famous 'nonfiction novel' – Truman Capote's *In Cold Blood*. On his first page, Capote describes the denizens of Holcomb, Kansas, where his multiple-murder story takes place: 'The local accent is barbed with prairie twang, a ranch-hand nasalness and the men, many of them, wear narrow frontier trousers, Stetsons, and high-heeled boots with pointed toes'.

When Reed moves on, we meet McLemore's young sidekick, Tyler Goodson, who is in the workshop sharpening a chainsaw 'tooth by tooth'. This is another image redolent with symbolism, whose potency is amplified by the steady click-click sound we hear as Tyler wields the tool.

Still in Chapter One, we encounter Reed's overtly novelistic technique, one he has said he borrowed from Edward P Jones's book on American slavery, *The Known World*. 'If Tyler has his shirt on, you know he must be going to court. At least that's what his mom will tell me one day.' This simple device of inserting future tense sets up a narrative tension and foreshadows what lies ahead: a shape-shifting tale that takes us deep inside a Southern Gothic landscape of tattoos and nipple rings, bigotry and beauty, love and loss – the world of Shittown, Alabama, abbreviated as *S-Town*. To quote the podcast blurb:

> John despises his Alabama town and decides to do something about it. He asks a reporter to investigate the son of a wealthy family who's allegedly been bragging that he got away with murder. But then someone else ends up dead, sparking a nasty feud, a hunt for hidden treasure, and an unearthing of the mysteries of one man's life.

In one sense, this is an admirably concise summation of *S-Town*. But it gives no idea of the emotional roller-coaster and deep cultural exploration of a community on which we are about to embark. To paraphrase former Australian prime minister Paul Keating, it's all tip and no iceberg.

One key to getting the whole of the iceberg in view is to parse *S-Town* via these characteristics of literary journalism: voice and subjectivity; immersion and rigorous reporting; symbolism; structure; psychological awareness; and sociological astuteness. Next, I'll unpack them, using excerpts from the podcast transcript, which is available on the *S-Town* website.

Voice and subjectivity

As Mark Kramer notes, the 'defining mark' of literary journalism is 'the personality of the writer, the individual and intimate voice of a whole, candid person ... someone who has illuminated experience with private reflection, but who has not transcended crankiness, wryness, doubtfulness, and who doesn't blank out emotional realities of sadness, glee, excitement, fury, love'. In just this manner, the voice of narrator/host/author Brian Reed anchors *S-Town*, literally and figuratively. In Chapter One, he shares his doubts about McLemore's credibility:

> I'd say it's about this point that I ask myself, is John fucking with me? Is he just a bored guy who contacted me on a lark and never expected me to actually follow through? Is this murder not real and he knows it? It's not only the fact that he is right now pouring potassium cyanide into a bucket in front of me that makes me wonder this.

In Chapter Two, it is through hearing Reed's stricken reaction to a phone call that we learn the awful news that McLemore has committed suicide – by drinking potassium cyanide. This violent means of procuring death is not as bizarre as it may sound. We already know John uses potassium cyanide as a chemical agent in his clock-repairing process.

In Chapter Three, Reed attends McLemore's funeral, where McLemore's mother, Mary Grace, is chief mourner. Revealing how closely attached he is by now to the Goodson family, Reed says: 'As Mary Grace speaks, Tyler's mom clutches my arm'. When a cousin, Reta, appears and seems to be taking over McLemore's affairs, leaving Tyler in the lurch, Reed is shocked. 'I don't think this was the clockmaker's intention', he tells us.

Tyler starts taking matters into his own hands, challenging Reta's authority by appropriating items on McLemore's estate that he claims are his own, and searching for gold McLemore is believed to have hidden, taking Reed increasingly into his confidence ('We got to find it, Brian'). But in Chapter Five, when Tyler gets rough with a man who has stolen a valued heirloom and intends to 'snip fingers' as punishment, Reed is rattled. This is a response 'which I find unsettling', he tells us. Likewise, when Reta seeks to acquire some gold nipple rings McLemore had, Reed recoils: 'Ugh, I'm sorry, I'm just reeling from you saying they should cut his nipples off'.

Reed steers listeners through shifting sympathies as he reveals further twists to the story, everything mediated through his deeply personal voice. He uses a colloquial style, an approach that is less available to print journalists but standard for audio folk, and which generates enormous intimacy. Not only are we privy to Reed's interpretations and conjecture, we gain an extra layer of understanding through his tone – his laughter, his disgust, his sadness. It's a huge narrator role to occupy, and he mostly carries it well.

Towards the end, Reed tells us about a new aspect of McLemore's life – that he had an intense though unconsummated relationship with a man named Olin Long. An email from Long leads Reed to investigate McLemore's sexuality, which is a matter of some ambiguity. In his first email to Reed, McLemore declares: 'Me, I am 47, unmarried, sort of, ahem, like ahem – let's just say I might be a fan of David Sedaris, or in other words, I might know who Audre Lorde and Ann Bannon is, if you get the idea. Of course, that could get you killed around here'.

Reed observes casually: 'I took that to mean John was gay, though when we talked about it after, he told me that he'd gone both ways in his life'. Reed's subsequent 11-hour interview with Olin sheds considerable light on McLemore's repressed sexuality. In Chapter Six, making what Norman Sims calls 'a judgment call', Reed reveals that McLemore had a sexual relationship with a married man, something McLemore had told him off the record. 'It wasn't the fact that he had been with men that he didn't want recorded, but that he had been with this particular guy', Reed explains. In the podcast, Reed justifies including the information on the anonymised man as follows:

First, since John died, two other people who knew him well have told me the same information on the record. Also, John was very clear that he did not believe in God or an afterlife. So John, in his own view, is worm dirt now, unaffected by this. And lastly, what John disclosed, and where it led me after he died, helped me understand him so much more. And I think trying to understand another person is a worthwhile thing to do.

But in a small community like Bibb County, this breach of confidence is problematic, because Reed mentioned the man had worked briefly for McLemore. Locals will probably be able to identify anyone who worked at McLemore's and the man may therefore have been involuntarily outed. In other ethical concerns, some commentators wondered whether Reed had the right to make the podcast at all, given that McLemore had died without explicitly consenting to the podcast being about him, rather than about the murder he first wrote to *TAL* about.

The question was made more complex because McLemore was known to suffer from depression. Did mental illness affect McLemore's ability to consent? Julie Snyder was adamant that McLemore was aware the focus of the podcast had shifted. 'He knew that the story we were interested in was going to be about him and his community and his relationship with that community', she told the *New York Times* in 2018. Her comments came as the executor of McLemore's estate launched legal action on the grounds that the podcast revealed personal aspects of McLemore's life without his permission and violated Alabama's Right of Publicity Act. Lawyers representing *S-Town* contended that the work was journalism and was not covered by the Act. In May 2020, the *S-Town* team settled the case, on undisclosed terms. The executor, Craig Cargile, subsequently made this statement: 'As the administrator of the Estate of John B. McLemore, I declare that the estate has no objection or claim to the podcast, nor does the estate have any objection or claim to any future uses of the podcast or the journalistic and creative work relating to John B. McLemore by the defendants or their designee'.

As for the question of whether journalists should only describe the life experiences to which their subjects have explicitly consented to make public, the field of biography would be greatly impoverished, indeed reduced to mere public relations, if that edict were followed.

Mark Kramer offers insight on the responsibility of the journalist in interpreting a life: 'Literary journalism couples cold fact and personal event, in the author's humane company'. While Reed is clearly partisan, as he warms to the Goodson family and remains wary of other residents of Bibb County, he is never less than humane.

Immersion/rigorous reporting

S-Town is rich in details that deepen the storytelling and lead us closer to an appreciation of the complex reality of McLemore-the-man and his love–hate relationship with his community. Chapter Four delves into McLemore's career as a horologist, as Reed tracks down the antique-clock enthusiasts, clients and colleagues who were on McLemore's self-penned funeral list. One, his old college professor, tears up as he shows Reed a personalised sundial McLemore had made for him. It had taken McLemore more than 20 years to complete.

Among the unsavoury types we meet in Tyler's tattoo bar in Chapter Two is a 6-foot, 350-pound, bearded man in a John Deere hat 'whose name I never do catch, who tells me, quote, "I'm so fucking fat, I don't care no more", and lifts up his shirt to show me the giant words he has tattooed on his stomach – Feed Me'. In showing us that these 'rednecks' (a term McLemore used, with some affection) and racists accepted McLemore, Reed deliberately complicates our view of his subject early on. The ambiguities will only deepen.

In Reed's longitudinal reportage and intensive interviewing, his characters take real shape. His conversations with Olin Long, for example, trace the former air-force linguist's 12-year relationship with McLemore and its sublimated sexuality. The edited interview is the spine of Chapter Six, introducing us to a little-known aspect of McLemore's life, crucial to understanding the denouement in Chapter Seven.

Reed here employs in-depth interviewing of the type practised by many journalists, including Svetlana Alexievich, the first full-time journalist to win the Nobel Prize for Literature. Her work includes an extraordinary oral history-based account of the aftermath of the nuclear meltdown at Chernobyl, *Voices From Chernobyl*. As the scholar John Hartsock has noted, 'Hers is very much an immersion journalism. In her case it is an immersion into other people's emotional lives'.[4] Similarly, with Olin, we learn about the unfulfilled yearning of one encounter with McLemore, when he delivered Olin flowers from his nursery:

> I'm sitting there in a truck with John B McLemore outside a
> doctor's office picking up my azaleas … I wanted to pull his shirt up,
> expose his belly, and just kiss all over his belly around that red hair,
> just to that extent. And I wanted to do it slowly and sensuously …
> It was the hair, the skin, the intelligence, the – he was in a jolly
> mood that day.

Svetlana Alexievich's subjects grew to trust her, and the same gradual uncovering happens with the characters we meet in *S-Town* over Reed's numerous visits and phone interviews. Tyler's portrayal begins to blur from tattoo entrepreneur, dedicated young father and loyal defender of Mary Grace (his 'mama'), to troubled ne'er-do-well who, burdened by the legacy of a violent, predatory father, struggles to accommodate the special place he holds in McLemore's affections. McLemore committed suicide the day after Father's Day, when Tyler and McLemore had gone fishing. It was an idyllic outing:

> **Tyler Goodson**: He said, Tyler, you've just got to learn to just stop
> and take some time for yourself, and try to enjoy life … And hell,
> John can't swim. I mean, hell, we wasn't in no deeper water than
> about waist deep, and he wouldn't go nowhere without me holding
> his damn hand like a kid. [Reed laughs] We waded up and down the
> river and stuff, and I was slipping over rocks finding some crawfish
> and hellgrammites and stuff, showing him. And he never done stuff
> like that before …

Brian Reed: Did it seem like he was saying goodbye?

Tyler Goodson: I don't know. Hell, we spray-painted our damn names up there on the damn bridge.

But our perspective constantly shifts. One minute we are on Tyler's side, seeing Cousin Reta as a gold digger. But later, we start to see that Tyler is crossing a line and that maybe Mary Grace would be better off with Reta.

John Hartsock identifies a 'visceral emotionalism' in the voices that come through Alexievich's interviews, and this is evident in Reed's distillation of McLemore himself. He captures McLemore's ringing self-assessment: 'I don't just look at myself as a 49-year-old semi-homosexual atheist living in a Shittown full of Baptists in Buttfucksville, Alabama. I look at myself as a citizen of the world'.

He records McLemore's blistering view of the townsfolk: 'A bunch of fussing and fighting, snaggletooth, stolen trucks, meth labs, stabbing, hooping, hollering, and going to jail'. And he gains McLemore's disarming admission that while on a recorded phone call to Reed, he has 'pissed in the sink' as an act of environmental awareness:

> Instead of wasting three or four gallons to flush the commode, I just peed here in the kitchen sink and used about one cupful of water to flush the sink. And I got a little short dick, but I got a pretty good aim, so I can usually aim right for the centre of that damn thing without splashing everywhere.

This descriptive scene acquires additional force because it is followed almost immediately by music and the brrr-brrr of a dial tone. That sound has an in-built expectancy, as the listener naturally tries to anticipate who will pick up. Reed is returning a call from Tyler's sister-in-law, Skyler. Tension ratchets upward until, finally, Skyler delivers tragic news: McLemore has taken his own life. The chapter's cliffhanger ending on this point marks an utterly unforeseen narrative twist – a true jaw-dropper.

The next chapter opens with sombre music, then a reprise of the call. Skyler's response this time is artfully broken up by Reed's introduction to the show, carefully spaced over the ominous music. It fades out as Skyler repeats the ending of the last episode: 'John B killed his self Monday night'. The removal of the music here emphasises that we are on new ground, about to hear what was cut off before. First, Reed's reflex reaction: 'Are you kidding me?' Then his gathering horror, as the news sinks in.

MUSIC

Skyler: Has anybody called you?
Brian Reed: No, not that I know. I have a few missed calls, but don't think that they're from anybody down there. Why?

MUSIC

Brian Reed: From *Serial* and *This American Life*, I'm Brian Reed. This is Shittown.

MUSIC

Skyler: Well, we have some bad news to tell you.
Brian Reed: OK.
Skyler: John B killed his self Monday night.

MUSIC FADED OUT

Brian Reed: Are you kidding me?
Skyler: No.
Brian Reed: Oh my gosh.

There is a certain artifice in how Reed has, as the reporter, recorded the sound of his own distress at the news: as an audio journalist, he would understandably have pressed 'record' before he made a phone call to the community, but there is still a cool self-awareness in the technique, as he records his faltering voice and expression of sympathy.[5] The effect is to position the listener as almost an eavesdropper on the scene, compelled to imagine what has happened.

The juxtaposition of these scenes – the joking McLemore peeing in the sink and the terrible reality of his suicide – delivers a savage gut punch. That, and the use of music to mete out meaning, as in the opening of Chapter Three just described, comes down to the deliberate structuring of audio elements, which we will examine next.

Structure

Mark Kramer emphasises that, in literary journalism, 'structure counts' and *S-Town*'s Julie Snyder told me, in a 2016 interview, that she concurs: 'We map out pretty detailed structures for every episode ... *When* do you want to know something? ... *Where* are the places that you are going to have a feeling or a realisation?'[6] Accordingly, each of *S-Town*'s seven chapters has an individually delineated theme and a title that comes from interview quotes. But Kramer also advises literary journalists to mix 'primary narrative with tales and digressions to amplify and reframe events'. This, too, is abundantly clear in *S-Town*. In Chapter Five, for instance, Reed rings Tyler Goodson's mother but instead finds his grandmother, Miss Irene Hicks, on the end of the phone. This leads to an entirely new perspective on Tyler's situation, as Miss Hicks details nine felony charges against Tyler, then describes her troubled extended family's situation. Besides supporting Tyler, she looks after a son named Jimmy who suffered brain damage after being shot. She also supports Tyler's mother, who finds it hard to hold down a job because of health problems. There are extended family members living with her and a dog about to have a litter of puppies, while Tyler and his children and pregnant girlfriend are living in their half-finished house. Reed wonders how she copes. 'I just take my medicine and take my Bocelli', she replies. That's Andrea Bocelli, the opera singer, soon to become a player in the story.

As veteran *New Yorker* writer John McPhee has observed, 'Structure is the juxtaposition of parts, the way in which two parts of a piece of writing, merely by lying side-by-side, can comment on each other without a word spoken. The way in which the thing is assembled, you can get much said'. By harnessing the nature of the audio medium, this juxtaposition is amplified in *S-Town*. Reed and Snyder layer voice with sound – in this case music – in order to create a heightened meaning.

Take, for instance, when Miss Hicks muses again on Tyler's erratic behaviour: 'I can't make up my mind whether to scold him or love him or something'. To underline this observation, it is followed immediately by the exhilarating opening bars of 'La donna è mobile', the famous Verdi aria sung by, of course, Bocelli. With careful phrasing, the music lowers and Reed's narration comes over it, reflecting on the conundrum of Tyler's character, before Bocelli returns in full throttle and Miss Hicks 'responds' to him with delight: 'Oh, that man's got a voice like an angel'.

This clever placement of music adds texture and pace, embellishing Miss Hicks' conflicted feelings for Tyler. But it becomes masterful when Reed returns to the piece later in the chapter. This time, Tyler has been doubting his own moral character and concludes: 'I wish I had a little bit better guidance' – an allusion to his father being a convicted sex offender. This segues back to the same Verdi aria where, over the opening phrase, Reed informs us that Tyler's behaviour has inspired some of McLemore's most virtuosic rants. The music level dips and the soulful opera counterpoints McLemore's baleful brilliance:

> We ain't nothing but a nation of goddamn, chicken-shit, horse-
> shit, tattle-tale, pissy-ass, whiny, fat, flabby, out of shape Facebook-
> looking damn twerp-fest, peeking out the windows and slipping

around, listening in on the cell phones and spying in the peephole and peeping in the crack of the goddamned door, and listening in the fucking sheet rock. You know, Mr. Putin, please, show some fucking mercy! I mean, come on, drop the fucking bomb, won't you?

With exquisite choreography, the music ends in a crashing coda that adds dramatic resolution. There is an audible sigh from McLemore, exhausted by his own tirade, then, in a starkly contrasting tone, he mutters: 'I gotta have me some tea'.

In this section of *S-Town*'s Chapter Five, we can find numerous resonances between audio's renowned ability to create pictures in the mind (with the listener as co-creator) and Mark Kramer's vision of what the literary journalist sets out to achieve for readers. 'The writer paints sensory scenes, confides on a level of intimacy that stirs readers' own experiences and sensations, and sets up alchemical interplay between constructed text and readers' psyches', Kramer notes. 'The readers' realizations are what the author and readers have made together.'

Other structural aspects emerge organically, when the producers combine actuality snippets with a well-matched interview excerpt. For instance, Tyler's Uncle Jimmy, who has a brain injury, is present at some gatherings. He expresses his understanding of what is said in the form of verbal affirmations. They provide sometimes sharp commentary on the unfolding events, as when Tyler is describing how McLemore promised he would leave him some gold. 'Beaucoups and beaucoups of stuff', intones Uncle Jimmy. It adds a degree of aural symbolism to the already deep symbology of *S-Town*.

Symbolism

Reed and his cast of characters are forever trying to decipher what Norman Sims calls 'the symbolism of details'. In Chapter One, Reed and McLemore are briefly lost in the latter's own maze – a telling start.

'It actually has 64 possible solutions, depending on how you swap the gates around', he tells Reed, foreshadowing the labyrinthine possibilities of this story. We also hear about the 'witness marks' on the old clocks McLemore fixes: the imperfections put there by the horologists who have repaired the antique timepieces through the ages. It is a beautiful metaphor for the flaws we will uncover in those we meet in *S-Town* and the ways in which those flaws provide insight into the messy reality of human beings.

The clocks and their long history also invoke McLemore's troubled past. For all his brilliance, his life has been full of missteps – dropping out of university, closeted sexuality, ambiguous social attitudes and a sense of doom about impending climate change. In the opening moments of the podcast, Reed cleverly intertwines clocks and mazes as symbols: 'I'm told fixing an old clock can be maddening. You're constantly wondering if you've just spent hours going down a path that will likely take you nowhere'. The clocks and sundials – to which McLemore devoted so much of his time and skill – bear plangent mottos that further build the symbolic meaning. One, 'tedious and brief', provides McLemore's epitaph. The potassium cyanide that will kill McLemore is introduced in Chapter One as McLemore drunkenly foments a chemical reaction on a coin, which will see it emerge as a gold-plated souvenir – a powerful allusion to transformation.

Tattoos take on increasing symbology through the series. In Chapter Two, we find ourselves in Tyler's tattoo bar with the punny name Black Sheep Ink. He considers this place his 'church'. The co-owner, Bubba, thinks of their tattooing service as providing a form of therapeutic expression for the bar's outlier clientele. 'Maybe it's a meditation, a milestone, an excuse to get out of the house, a new girlfriend, a death', Reed muses. 'John's motivation was especially bewildering to Bubba, because John had made it clear almost every time he came in the shop how deeply he despised tattoos.' Bubba tells Reed he came to believe John got them as a form of charity, a financial subsidy. 'We're in a rut … we need some money … He sacrificed his skin to help us out.'

By the final chapter, though, we are in much darker territory. McLemore has started offering himself as 'a little bit of practice material' for Tyler. He has descended into a terrible depression and the pain of extreme tattooing has become something between a BDSM ritual and an expression of his thwarted, perhaps fatherly, perhaps sexual feelings for Tyler. With heavy irony, McLemore now calls his compulsive, masochistic tattooing sessions 'church'. He declaims the links: 'Wild Turkey is the holy water. The little filthy-ass room is the sanctuary ... the tattoo needles are the reliquaries'.

The marks McLemore acquires are also symbolic. He has taken a switch from the woods, had others beat him with it and then tattooed over the welts. The shocking, flayed imagery of his back is supposed to resemble the floggings found on a freed slave. Given Alabama's ardent pro-slavery history, the image is particularly loaded, reinforcing the many references to racial bigotry throughout the podcast, such as the name of the local lumber mill, KyKenKee, which uses the proprietor family initials to suggest KKK.

Above this landscape, hovering none too subtly, is the ghost of William Faulkner, famed denizen of this Southern Gothic landscape. His short story, 'A Rose for Emily', features a psychologically damaged woman who holes up in a decaying mansion with her father and struggles against an oppressive society. On Reed's first visit, McLemore presents him with a copy, making an obvious connection to his own situation. He also gives him the Guy de Maupassant story, 'The Necklace', and 'The Renegade' by Shirley Jackson. Reed observes drily: 'I notice a unifying theme to all these stories, a creeping sense of foreboding – in these places that are allegedly home to polite society, an undercurrent of depravity'. The podcast takes up the Faulkner link directly, resurrecting a 1968 musical adaptation of the story by the British rock group The Zombies as its theme song, to close each episode in haunting harmony.

Sociological awareness and psychological astuteness

S-Town displays a keen awareness of where McLemore's life and activities fit within the prism of Alabama and broader American life. The tattoo bar doubles as a drinking club for 'a collection of misfits, of self-proclaimed criminals and runaways and hillbillies'. Bibb County is 95 per cent white, 'and that is no accident', Reed tells us. It was the last place in the state to allow desegregation of schools. Reed marvels at the openness of the bigotry, proclaimed right into his microphone.

The more Reed investigates and explores, the more nuanced his depictions of the people he meets become. As Mark Kramer says, the whole point of literary journalism's long immersions is to comprehend subjects at a 'frank, unidealized level' that 'leaves quirks and self-deceptions, hypocrisies and graces intact and exposed; in fact, it uses them to deepen understanding'. By the final chapter, Reed is clear-eyed about McLemore: 'So much of the stuff John said he hated about Shittown – Harleys, tattoos, misogyny and homophobia, racism, he said he despised it. But that stuff was part of him, too'.

When Reta's husband dismisses Tyler as a criminal, Reed observes: 'That's what Tyler's been reduced to in their eyes. But this is what conflicts like this do to the participants – reduce them'. Tyler has his own crisis of conscience. Reed has been pressing him on his plan to mutilate the man who stole his grandfather's gun. 'I kept questioning Tyler, trying to understand why he thought this was OK, but nothing he said did quite make me understand. And I realized it was probably going to stay that way'. As he's about to hang up, Tyler suddenly asks Reed, 'Do you see me being a bad person?' Reed replies, 'No, man, I see you as a complicated, normal person. You know, I disagree with some of your decisions. But you also – you've had a very different life experience than I've had'.

Rather than offer simplistic truths, *S-Town* honours the unknow-ability of real life. Because of McLemore's horological practice of fire gilding, he may have suffered from mercury poisoning, which would have affected his mental acuity. Perhaps his repressed sexuality added to the pressure he felt. And it is possible that he needed more of an outlet for his amazing intellect than could be found in the dedicated fellow horologists and friends who had held him dear over many years, before he withdrew from them.

McLemore's suicide note, which with typical outrageousness he emailed to the town clerk, provides a deeply moving finale to the podcast. I cried as Reed read it, as I'm sure many listeners did.

> I have not lived a spectacular life. But within my four dozen plus years, I've had many more hours to pursue that which I chose, instead of moiling over that which I detested. I have coaxed many infirm clocks back to mellifluous life, studied projective geometry and built astrolabes, sundials, taught myself nineteenth century electroplating, bronzing, patination, micro machining, horology, learned piano ...
>
> But the best times of my life, I realize, were the times I spent in the forest and field ... I have audited the discourse of the hickories, oaks, and pines, even when no wind was present.

This epic depiction of one man ends with a description of how McLemore's great-grandfather, a notorious gangster, obtained the family estate by extortion and murder. His mother, Mary Grace, took to sitting on the land while pregnant with McLemore, rubbing her stomach and begging God to make her child a genius. As listeners now know, she got her wish. And in delivering the story of this charismatic, self-destructive prodigy, Reed has elevated the art of audio storytelling to new heights.

Ultimately, *S-Town* delivers what Kramer describes as the epitome of what literary journalism can offer: 'the process moves readers and writers towards realization, compassion, and in the best of cases, wisdom'. Brian Reed put it plainly: 'I think a good story sucks you in and makes you re-evaluate your own life, your own attitudes and your own preconceptions', he said. 'It's funny, it's emotional, it makes you feel things.'

Reed was speaking to a reporter from the *Tuscaloosa News*, a local Alabama paper that examined the impact of *S-Town* on Woodstock a year after the podcast dropped. By then, fans were making pilgrimages to the town, visiting McLemore's grave, whose headstone bears a sundial and is inscribed 'Life is tedious and brief'. One friend of McLemore's interviewed in the show, former town clerk Cheryl Dodson, had been moved by his death to develop a suicide prevention group.

Sadly, Tyler Goodson, in whose welfare McLemore was so invested, felt adversely impacted by the podcast. He was charged with repossessing goods belonging to McLemore, which he had claimed to Reed were his. 'It's caused a lot of stress in my life, and my life's been pretty stressful as it is and it hadn't really helped much', Tyler told a local TV station after the podcast's debut. 'Sometimes, I regret ever speaking into that microphone because I was probably upset or wasn't thinking clearly.' Tyler pleaded guilty to burglary and eventually got a ten-year suspended sentence and five years probation. He has been contacted on social media by fans of the podcast around the world, but is unimpressed with *S-Town*'s wide acclaim. 'It's hell being famous without the rich part', he told an *Esquire* journalist in 2018. 'If money came along with it, I wouldn't feel near as bad about it.'

Ethics and impact

Tyler Goodson's response is an important reminder of the responsibility a podcast producer bears towards the real people they represent. Journalists have long been mindful of the line they walk between advocacy, intimacy and truth telling, especially in immersive storytelling that might see them embedded in a community for months or even years. They naturally become close to some of their subjects, as Reed did with McLemore and, to a lesser degree, with Tyler.

Janet Malcolm, with characteristic bluntness, called this longitudinal reportage the art of seduction and betrayal. You get the interviewee on side, then when they've spilled their guts, you write/create what you like, sometimes stitching someone up in the process. Malcolm opened her 1990 book, *The Journalist and the Murder*, with these now classic lines, often cited in journalism ethics courses: 'Every journalist who is not too stupid or too full of himself to notice what is going on knows that what he does is morally indefensible. He is a kind of confidence man, preying on people's vanity, ignorance or loneliness, gaining their trust and betraying them without remorse'. The book refers to one specific case, when a journalist, Joe McGinniss, made an accused murderer believe he was writing a book to clear his name, when in fact McGinniss would use their relationship to make a case for his guilt.

Gay Alcorn, Melbourne-based editor of the *Guardian*, echoed these sentiments in a piece called '*S-Town* Never Justifies Its Voyeurism, and that Makes It Morally Indefensible'. She decried Reed's ethics in going further with the podcast's focus than the murder investigation McLemore originally contacted Reed about. She says the team assumes 'with a degree of arrogance that this is Reed's story, not McLemore's, whose agonies are laid out for our voyeuristic entertainment. Not in a cheap, tabloid TV way, but in a sophisticated, subtle way'. She criticises Reed for recording his distress at the news of McLemore's death. But as noted, it is within audio production parameters to set record for calls you make to highly germane contributors. Indeed, it would have been remiss of him not to have done so.

Alcorn further alleges that Reed unjustifiably publishes 'the most personal and sordid details of a man's life' and does not come clean to listeners about his purpose. Actually, he does. Even before Reed meets McLemore, it is clear that the 'murder' is less important to McLemore than having the ear of a national radio reporter. Reed confirmed this focus to *Junkee* three months after the podcast dropped. 'The story became about what John asked me to do, which is, "This is such a shit town. You need to blow the lid off this shit town". And it became clear that what that meant was John's *experience of it*, he told *Junkee* reporter Meg Watson.

Reed felt that covering this broad frame of McLemore's life in Woodstock also meant he needed to delve into personal topics such as his sexuality. 'To not discuss his sexuality as part of that – of why his experience of this place in rural Alabama was such a "shit town" – would be unfair to reality', he said to Watson. This coverage generated mixed feelings in the gay community. One prominent critique in *Slate* summed it up: '*S-Town* Was Great –Until It Forced a Messy Queer Experience into a Tidy Straight Frame'. Reporter Daniel Schroeder disputes Reed's 'predetermined thesis of McLemore's need for a traditional romance' and laments his lack of understanding of alternative gay models for sex and relationships. Schroeder interprets the nipple-tattooing scenes between Tyler and McLemore as having 'a decidedly queer aspect to it [Reed] doesn't seem to get ... one of the few moments of safe physical intimacy he could share with Goodson'.

But Alice Lesperance, a gay writer who grew up three hours south of Woodstock, declares *S-Town* to be 'so lively and so honest that it feels almost intrusive' in a very personal way. 'It feels like *S-Town* knows my own memories too well', she writes. '[For] the first time in nearly three decades on this earth, I had a real-life representation of someone who – minus a few eccentricities – seemed to match up with my own life.' Lesperance describes how she and her girlfriend listened together to the part in Chapter Six where Olin and McLemore commune over *Brokeback Mountain*, the film that the men called their 'grief manual'. She cried, but not just because of the movie:

> I was also crying for Olan [*sic*], and for John B. and all the other
> people like me who grew up in places like Alabama or Montana and
> had no reflections of themselves in the movies they watched or the
> books they read. I was crying because *S-Town* sounds like home to

me, and because it did its own small little part in helping repair the damage done in two decades of feeling like I couldn't exist in that place.[7]

But if some gay listeners felt included, other marginalised groups felt very much the opposite. Writing in *BuzzFeed*, Wesley Jenkins denounced *S-Town*'s avoidance of tackling head-on the racism that Reed so clearly detects. In a piece titled 'The Empathy of *S-Town* Doesn't Extend to Black People', he expresses his torn feelings, as 'a queer, black, Southern man'. Jenkins accepts that the podcast is 'a portrait of John B. McLemore's complex place in society and a deep dive into his troubled humanity, not a dissection of racial issues in the South. The storyteller and the main character are both white men and they, like anyone, should be allowed the space to tell stories about themselves'. Reed told *Junkee* that he wished he had been 'able to address race more head on' but that it was difficult to do because 'the world that John lived in was super white'. But as Jenkins points out, the story is still permeated with overt and latent white-supremacy themes, which affects how black listeners hear folk such as the denizens of the Black Sheep Ink tattoo parlour. 'I don't think most black listeners will (or should) be able to look past the racism of those "characters", because their real sentiments endanger our real lives.'

Jenkins' charge that *S-Town*'s generation of empathy works largely through a white lens had been reflected in an earlier review by white *New Yorker* critic Sarah Larson. 'In the end, we empathize with almost every character, and find commonalities between them and ourselves', Larson wrote. She perceptively summarised its groundbreaking role, but cautions where the line should be drawn on personal privacy. '*S-Town* helps advance the art of audio storytelling, daringly, thoughtfully, and with a journalist's love of good details and fascinating material – but it also edges us closer to a discomfiting realm of well-intentioned voyeurism on a scale we haven't quite experienced before.'

This issue – how much to reveal of what you know of a protagonist in your story – creates ethical dilemmas for any serious investigative journalist. Tiny personal moments can build a bridge, help others see the full humanity of someone, along with their failings or even crimes. But gratuitous inclusion of salacious or invasive material can be needlessly demeaning or even harmful.

These are hard choices for us to make. Every cell in our storytelling DNA is avid for those 'wow' elements, the bits that make eyebrows raise and pulses quicken when we hear them. But sometimes they have to be left on the cutting room floor. I've done it – a woman who'd worked in Vietnam during the Vietnam War told me on tape the vivid details of how she'd once killed a man. Afterwards, she signed a release allowing me to use it for a radio series and a book, but the next day rang me and asked me not to use that bit. The killing was done in self-defence during a firefight, she told me, but it might get taken out of context so many years later and could cost her her job. She made a good case. I (sadly) deleted the anecdote from the tape. The *S-Town* team made similar cuts, leaving out a lot of material. 'Everything is a decision about "what does this add, what does this show?"', Reed told *Junkee*. It's one model to adopt when making a tough editorial call.

Besides honouring the sad, brilliant life of John B McLemore, *S-Town* pushed out the parameters of what podcasting could be. As the prestigious Peabody Award judges' citation noted: 'If *Serial* launched the podcast as mass entertainment through a police procedural, its sibling successor, *S-Town*, breaks new ground for the medium by creating the first true audio novel, a nonfiction biography constructed in the style and form of a seven-chapter novel'.

But for some listeners, as Wesley Jenkins noted, it would never be something they could truly take to heart. 'Black audiences are used to this – a certain sense of deadness, a distance from the work of white creators, even when that work displays undeniable power or genius', he wrote. In the next chapter, I look at how a team of mostly white creators dealt with tropes of gender, race and diversity in three acclaimed podcasts I worked on with Australian newspaper *The Age*. I also take you inside the production process and show you how a complex narrative podcast evolves.

((●)) **Ethical practice in audio storytelling**

1   Do not edit in a way that misrepresents the interviewee's views.

2   Make interviewees aware of your podcast's focus.

3   If somebody does not want to talk to you, leave them alone.

4   Do not cherry-pick evidence and thereby distort the truth.

7

Creating a hit narrative podcast, Part 1: Finding the story

Award-winning Australian journalist Richard Baker was one of many reporters who dreamed of emulating *Serial*'s enticing storytelling format. In 2016, he acquired a team for his first venture into podcasting, on which I was fortunate enough to be a consulting producer. Over the next two chapters, I'll share how we went from unlistenable audio stodge to making three hit podcasts that all won gold at the New York Festivals Radio Awards, among many other accolades. I'll show you before-and-after scripts and describe the many moving parts that go into creating a long-form narrative podcast. You can hear all three podcasts – *Phoebe's Fall*, *Wrong Skin* and *The Last Voyage of the Pong Su* – on any podcast platform, and check out the websites for lots of extras and explainers. In this chapter we will look at the overarching aspects of making a narrative podcast, and next chapter we get to drill into the minute-by-minute detail.

Phoebe's Fall

So how did we get there? Let's start at the very beginning. In 2016, Richard Baker was based at *The Age*, a venerable Melbourne masthead, and he had a particular podcast story in mind. Too sprawling for even a weekend magazine cover feature, it was about a young woman, Phoebe Handsjuk, who had died in 2010 after falling 12 floors down a garbage chute in a luxury apartment building. Covering the news in some depth a few years earlier, Richard had noted anomalies in the police investigation. Why did the police not interview Phoebe's boyfriend, a much older man with whom she'd had a troubled relationship? Why did the CCTV footage of the apartment building go missing? And how does a drunk woman put herself into a tiny chute, a metre off the ground, without leaving any handprints around it?

In early 2016, Richard suggested to *The Age*'s new Head of Digital Editorial Capability, Julie Posetti, that the story could best be told as a podcast, which would investigate if Phoebe died by accident, suicide or murder. A former radio reporter who understood audio, Julie enthusiastically backed what would become the newspaper's first podcast, *Phoebe's Fall*. A core team of six was assembled: Richard would be joined as host by Michael Bachelard, another lauded investigative journalist; producers Tom McKendrick and Tim Young would focus largely on technical elements; and consulting producers Julie and I would advise on script, structure and storytelling-through-sound, and generally assist the print journalists' transition to audio storytelling.

While it might sound simple, moving from a written medium to an aural format is not an easy process. Audio is first and foremost a temporal medium: it only exists in real time. Pacing affects how listeners engage and understand, while texture (the types of sound used) and placement of one sound in relation to another also play a key role in capturing the audience. Most crucially, voice – what John Biewen calls 'humanity's oldest and best storytelling tool' – is central to audio journalism. The voice of an interviewee or host can provoke a visceral connection with the listener that print simply cannot emulate. But to be effectively produced as a serialised podcast, an audio *story* has to deploy excellent audio production techniques (high-quality sound recordings, well-judged speech edits, careful use of music and ambient sound, a script adapted to spoken-word delivery) as well as conventions of narrative structure: strong plot, fully fledged characters, narrative twists, inviting language and a flowing episodic format.

Shaping *Phoebe's Fall*

At a preliminary production meeting in July 2016, the team heard a 37-minute audio draft of a first episode, based on Richard's early interviews with Phoebe Handsjuk's family and friends. To anyone with an attuned ear for audio narrative, listening to it was a dismaying experience. Though it contained gems of interview quotes, and some moving and even funny stories, the overall impression was of a dreary lecture. It was dense with expository narration that could not be absorbed in one hearing; turgid, due to relentless swathes of interview excerpts with no non-verbal relief; and at times it sounded unnatural, because edit points had been set via transcript rather than by ear and intonations did not match. The learning for the print journalists was quick and brutal: to make an audio story, you have to edit for *how* something is said, as much as for *what* is said. As host, in a conversational medium like podcasting, you have to write like you talk. And the spaces *between* the words matter too.

 Moving from print to audio story

1   Edit for *how* something is said as much as for *what* is said.

2   As host, write like you talk.

3   The spaces between the words matter too.

Our main task that first day was to devise the episodic structure. I suggested we adopt a thematic rather than a chronological approach – a concept that came naturally to me, but that Richard found 'a breakthrough moment'. Using a whiteboard, we batted around themes. The first was obvious: getting to know Phoebe as a three-dimensional person, not a police statistic. This would draw on the moving interviews conducted with family and friends. The second episode should be around the event of her death, but how to approach it without being morbid or voyeuristic?

In a sudden epiphany, I suggested, to quizzical looks from the print journalists, that we focus it on the garbage chute that killed her, making the chute a physical presence, almost a character. We would find a man who made similar garbage compactors, who showed Michael their grisly mechanics, amid loud, lacerating sound. We would add scenes recorded by Phoebe's family, who in trying to understand what had happened, conducted careful reconstructions with a friend of the same build entering a similar chute. As the chute clanks, we imagine poor Phoebe hurtling inexorably downwards. The episode, though grim listening, would find a balance between exploring Phoebe's humanity and the forensic detail of her injuries, delivered through a montage dramatisation of excerpts from the coroner's report.

The third episode would return to Phoebe and her often turbulent relationships. It features a secret recording Phoebe's mother, Natalie, had made at the apartment of Phoebe's boyfriend, Anthony (Ant) Hampel, soon after her death. Undercover recordings are not illegal in Victoria and can be justified by public interest. We were mindful of the boundary between respecting Ant's privacy and satisfying our listeners' desire to fully understand Phoebe's situation when she died – the same dilemma the producers of *Serial* and countless other true-crime podcasts have faced.

Award-winning Australian producer Sharon Davis sums up such quandaries well. Writing in *RadioDoc Review*, Sharon asks: 'As journalists and storytellers, how do we balance the pursuit of justice and our responsibility to the victims with the demand to tell a gripping tale? As listeners, are we using the pain of others for our own entertainment?' Given that Ant had curtly (via legal letter) rejected Richard's request for a meeting, let alone an interview, and that he was such a central part of Phoebe's last days, we felt that it was vital to include this recording, which provided important insights into Ant's feelings and character.

The botched police investigation warranted its own episode next, and the inquest and surrounding legal issues made an obvious sixth and final episode. That just left the fifth episode to fill. Phoebe had had two funerals, one held by her family, the other by Ant: they would make an emotional penultimate episode, called 'Saying Goodbye'. Phoebe's beloved grandmother, Jeanette, gave the eulogy at a lakeside Viking-style funeral that acknowledged her Norwegian heritage. Jeanette's tone was celebratory, not sad: 'You were Xena, Warrior Princess! Today you will be honoured with a warrior's funeral, and as Phoebe Phoenix. While *we* live, Phoebe lives'.

Some listeners wondered on social media if we weren't playing into fetishising the 'Dead White Woman' that was becoming a common trope of true-crime podcasts and TV programs by including descriptions of Phoebe's beauty. My response: everyone we interviewed who knew Phoebe well mentioned her remarkable good looks. For better or worse, her beauty had shaped her life and how people responded to her. If we were to omit that, it would be distorting the truth, just as it would be to omit any quality that was universally described, such as kindness or a sense of humour, or their opposites.

Scripts and sound

An intensive three-month production period followed, during which Richard and Michael gathered more interviews, and the team refined scripts and honed the hosts' rather stiff early presentation. Tiny changes made a big difference: back-announcing speakers in the present tense, not past tense, conferred immediacy ('That's Natalie', not 'That was Natalie'). Julie helped Michael overcome a tendency for singsong delivery, where an over-emphasis on certain words risked trivialising their impact: '*Drugs* and *alcohol* are at the *heart* of Phoebe's story'. Richard, naturally animated in person, became wooden in front of the microphone. We mitigated this by having him improvise his response to the (scripted) questions Michael posed. This host-to-host Q&A and banter engaged listeners while advancing the unfolding narrative.

Cutting back interview grabs and deleting straggling phrases that undermined the 'oomph' of an ending point came next. For example, in Episode One, we first meet Phoebe's father, Len, as he tells us how he loves bodysurfing. In a powerful metaphor alluding to Phoebe's troubled mental state, he describes in the rough cut how he would cope with the occasional massive wave and avoid panicking. 'It's a matter of how we manage turbulence, not that it exists. That's how I see it.' The phrase 'That's how I see it' is flabby. It weakens the strong point being made – that we have to learn how to navigate turbulence. Losing just those five words gives emphasis, and leaving a space around it, via music or ocean effects, lets it sink in for the listener.

As we fleshed out each episode, we added more ideas for sound to relevant story beats. We are in Melbourne: cue its distinctive tram bells. It's a hot summer night: the tinny drum of cicadas instantly takes us to that. We included lots of this auditory punctuation. Sometimes we needed music to allow for a switch in direction; at other times, we achieved this via actuality. In Episode One, Michael narrates how Phoebe e-stalked her art teacher and was kicked out of art school. The next scene has her friend, an athlete called Sarah, describing Phoebe's prowess at karate, as we continue to build her character. I suggested recording the sound of a class in the gym. A few seconds of a chanting exercise layered over the 'thwack' of martial arts training provides the perfect transition (shown in the script excerpt on the next page) and subliminally extends the 'kick' metaphor ('kicked out of art school'). This sudden jump cut animates the narrative and the effects provide aural texture, which is always welcome.

Not surprisingly, mistakes were made. A long interview with Phoebe's mother, Natalie, was recorded as she and Richard walked along a cliff top at a place she loved. Richard was not thinking about technical issues and as Natalie spoke about Phoebe's short life and awful death, the interview acquired the toxic rumble of wind noise. Listening back, key sections were so inaudible they had to be discarded – it is impossible to 'clean up' wind. Also, Natalie started to pant from the exertion, which made most of the content sound incongruous. By a kind of aural serendipity, though, one grab used in the opening montage, 'I hope you're sitting down?', which recounts Natalie learning of Phoebe's death, had added poignancy, as she sounds as if she is hyperventilating from shock.

Richard re-recorded the interview months later, in a quiet, interior setting. It could have been traumatising for a bereaved mother to revisit such a painful topic, but over years of contact since he covered Phoebe's death in 2010, Natalie had developed a trusting relationship with Richard; this second interview reflected that, with Natalie opening up about her emotions in a deeply moving way that the strenuous cliff walk had not encouraged.

Script excerpt, Episode One, *Phoebe's Fall* (2016)

Audio source	Speaker
Michael	The year before she died, Phoebe was living with Ant Hampel when she became obsessed with another older man. This time, her art teacher.
Natalie	She would've admired him … he was probably really good at something. There was no sort of rhyme or reason … the people that she became obsessed with. And it was like an obsession.
Jeanette	It was an obsession, yeah.
Natalie	It could've been anyone.
Michael	Phoebe sent him emails demanding he have an affair with her. He accused her of stalking him and she was kicked out of art school.
GYM FX: chanting, kickboxing	TRANSITION SCENE
Sarah M	She was doing karate as well as kickboxing …

Impact of *Phoebe's Fall*

Phoebe's Fall launched in September 2016. It went straight to number 1 on iTunes Australia, and – a huge thrill – knocked *Serial* into number 2! Reviews showed marked interest from younger women – a demographic not previously closely associated with *The Age*, but actively fostered for the podcast by audience engagement leader Dewi Cooke. Soon *Phoebe's Fall* would achieve well over a million downloads. It did not conclusively determine whether Phoebe had died by accident, suicide or murder, an outcome Michael registered as showing our even-handedness. 'I felt it was a credit to us after *Phoebe's Fall* that some people believed one explanation for her death ... and others entirely the opposite', he notes.

Where the podcast *was* unequivocal, though, was in shining a light on the inadequacies of the police investigation. It triggered changes to the coronial process, including better support for families. 'Where there's been an apparent howler of a decision made, it's easier for a family to have that appealed or challenged', Richard explains. As someone who had had many front-page stories before, he was bowled over by the response. People who had never talked to him about his hard-hitting journalism were now bailing him up at school functions and barbecues, wanting to know more about Phoebe. Richard decided there and then he'd make another podcast – once he found the right story. It came, like so many aspects of his journalism, from an old contact.

Making *Wrong Skin*: Who owns the story?

In 2017, Richard got a call from a First Nations man about his relatives in Western Australia, in a sublimely beautiful part of the Kimberley, full of ancient red-rock formations and huge yellow termite edifices. Its Nyikina Mangala people are part of the oldest continuous culture in the world, dating back at least 60 000 years. The Kimberley is the size of France, but it's home to only 44 000 people. One of them was now telling Richard about a young couple, Julie Buck and Richard Milgin, who got together despite being 'wrong skin', meaning they came from families barred by traditional law from having a relationship. Fearing retribution, they ran away, back in 1994. Julie's body was found some months later; Richard Milgin is still missing, but he is presumed dead. Besides being about the collision of ancient culture and modern law, a sub-story was about power, corruption and greed, involving mining royalties potentially worth billions of dollars. It had emotion, intrigue and no clear outcome – the perfect ingredients for a podcast, but not an easy one to make, given the cultural sensitivities. Let me explain the background.

Respecting who owns the story

There has been a huge growth in recent years in awareness of Indigenous peoples' rights and respect for Indigenous cultures in Australia. 'The resurgence of self-determination and our right to manage how we are represented, which we refer to as Indigenous agency, is a worldwide movement', writes Margo Neale, in the acclaimed book *Songlines: The Power and Promise*. The term 'songlines' refers to a kind of 'Aboriginal archive of knowledge embedded in Country'; it is also the name of a stunning 2018 exhibition Margo co-created as Head of the Indigenous Knowledges Curatorial Centre at the National Museum of Australia, led by a community curatorium of senior custodians, who helped create artworks rooted in the lore of three Australian deserts.

Some aspects of Aboriginal cultures are highly stratified, with knowledge passed only to qualified community members. But the elders Margo worked with were clear that *all* Australians needed to know about the songlines. As she wrote, 'If you want to truly belong to this country, as Australians, you have to know your story about this place, this continent and its creation'.

Margo is of Aboriginal and Irish descent, from the Gumbayngirr and Kulin nations, and has been a prominent author and art curator for many decades. In 2015 I began working with her and an art historian, Ian McLean, to explore the relationships between Indigenous artists and white figures in the art world that underpin the production of contemporary Aboriginal art – a vitally important cultural and economic activity. It was a journey of understanding for me, a deep dive into the very different dimension in which Indigenous peoples live in remote communities, where ceremony and culture are still largely intact. It led to Margo and me co-hosting a podcast, *Heart of Artness*, which distilled some of the remarkable revelations we uncovered.

In one interview, I sat with Yolngu artists by the banks of a river in Arnhem Land, on Australia's tropical northern coast. A small plaque nearby informed visitors that some 30 people were massacred there in 1911. A white surveyor had been reported missing, presumed to have been killed by the local people, so police carried out a 'punitive expedition' – the chilling euphemism for a massacre. Two weeks after the mass killing, the surveyor showed up. Yinimala Gumana, the young chair of the local Buku-Larrnggay Mulka art centre, read out the inscription and described on tape how his grandfather, Birriktji Gumana, had returned from a hunting trip and found the bodies of his friends and family floating in the river. 'He only recognised them by their armbands', he said. We fell silent, subdued by this terrible image. Then the senior artist Garawan Wanambi said, 'Let's talk about the *gapan* [white ochre] and how we share our art with the world'. And for the next hour, he and fellow artist Gunybi Ganambarr generously shared their insight and philosophy.

Originally, when Ian asked me to get involved with this important research, I had rather piously demurred. 'I've never been to a remote Indigenous community', I told him. 'So I don't think I'd be an appropriate person.' Shortly afterwards, I met Margo for the first time. I mentioned that I'd declined to be involved, expecting a pat on the head for recognising cultural boundaries. To my surprise, she blasted me: 'They're human beings – they're not from bloody Mars!' She suggested in no uncertain terms that I get back on board. I did – and will be eternally grateful, because the project was one of the most rewarding of my life. Far better to sit and listen to people than to abandon any interaction.

The project ran for several years and, along the way, Margo became a friend. I grew fond of her energy, erudition and blunt honesty. But what of the school of thought that only Aboriginal people should tell Aboriginal stories? I would be editing and interpreting these inter-views, shaping them into story for the podcast. 'Certainly, it is not appropriate for a non-Indigenous person to tell an Indigenous story without permission of the Indigenous person whose story it is', Margo told me. '[But] it's all about relationships at the end of the day between people with goodwill and judgment on where the power lies and sharing it appropriately.' And so we pressed ahead, with Margo checking my first drafts for anything that might be inaccurate, or worse. I sent advance copies to the artists, to be approved, or revised, before we dropped online: this podcast was also an academic research project, and we followed formal ethical guidelines reviewed by a university board.

But journalism works to other principles – and deadlines – and editorial control is not usually shared with subjects. With regard to the coverage of people of colour, media organisations around the world are slowly realising they need to be more inclusive, both in terms of employing and empowering people from diverse backgrounds and, relatedly, in how they represent people from marginalised groups (see chapter 9). But while it is good to see strides being made at last at institutional levels, I think the most important tenet is one we can all observe: the desire to advance mutual understanding.

The Yolngu have always sought to engage with outsiders and live in a 'two-ways world', where both cultures can be accommodated. Margo likewise believes that if done with care, permission and respect, white Australians can seek to tell Indigenous stories. 'We are all Australians now. We share the continent, we share the history', she told me. 'So it's unrealistic to say that other voices can't be heard in this cross-cultural interaction because that's what it is; a cross-cultural interaction.'

Indigenous podcast voices: A brief introduction

In Australian podcasting, younger Indigenous voices are at the fore, with playwright Nakkiah Lui and actor Miranda Tapsell bringing a deeply satirical but also heartfelt perspective to issues of race and culture in the ironically titled *Pretty for an Aboriginal*, and a second production, *Debutante: Race, Resistance and Girl Power*, commissioned by Audible. Meanwhile, 20-something host Marlee Silva sets out to 'empower Indigenous women by helping them understand their worth and what they're capable of' in *Tiddas 4 Tiddas*, while *Search Engine Sex* is a sometimes serious, sometimes humorous analysis of the questions people ask on the internet about sex. Its host, Rowdie Walden, says the Spotify-sponsored show 'is all about breaking down the barrier of where a stereotypical Indigenous voice belongs'. *Curtain*, hosted by journalist Amy McQuire and lawyer Martin Hodgson, has a very different style and purpose. It sets out to interrogate systemic injustice in the legal system that affects Indigenous Australians. Its first season investigated anomalies in the 1992 conviction of an Aboriginal man, Kevin Henry, for murder. It has since explored topics such as the harmful effects of mandatory sentencing, which saw one man sentenced to life imprisonment for murder even though there was no evidence he took part. Apple Podcasts lists other shows on a curated collection called First Nations Stories.

In the US, mainstream podcasts are increasingly including First Nations voices. One episode of *This American Life*, 'Trail of Tears', sees two sisters retrace the route of the forced relocation from Georgia to Oklahoma of their Cherokee nation in the late 1830s. In contrast, *Coffee with an Indian* is hosted largely by First Nations man Brian 'BB' Melendez, in Nevada. This often pungent podcast covers issues related to politics and culture on a 'modern Indian

Reservation', from addiction and spirituality to dealing with a fractured cultural identity. In Canada, *Red Man Laughing* is hosted and written by Anishinaabe comedian Ryan McMahon, from the Couchiching First Nation in Ontario. McMahon, the first Indigenous comedian to have a full-length program on the CBC, explores arts, culture and society on the Indian & Cowboy podcast network. McMahon has also made the acclaimed *Thunder Bay*, about the ongoing impact of colonialism on Indigenous residents of a small city, and *Stories from the Land*. CBC's award-winning *Finding Cleo* investigates the disappearance of a young Cree girl who had been taken by welfare authorities in the 1970s and adopted out in the US.

Bringing *Wrong Skin* together

Back in Melbourne, I thought of Margo's words when I asked Richard about the thorny politics of parachuting him, a white journalist from the other side of the country, into the small Aboriginal community of Looma in the Kimberley, to investigate the missing couple. There was another, crucial aspect to their story: Julie had been 'promised', under traditional law, to an old man, Jimmy (Mawukura) Nerrimah, a well-known artist who was more than three times her age. The placement of young women with older men was a common cultural practice in the region – in her early teens Julie had been made a 'child bride' of another man, with whom she'd had a baby girl, Zaria. She did not want to repeat the experience with Jimmy and took off with her young boyfriend instead.

For Richard Baker, cultural ownership of the story was not the main issue. 'Fourteen-year-old girls being married to 70-year-old men against their will is child abuse, in modern times. So, I'm gonna report on it.' But there would clearly be a need for cultural mediation. The team approached several Indigenous academics to act as consultant. They eventually found someone who was prepared to help but who requested anonymity, due to the delicate politics. The consultant helped the team reframe their views on things such as child marriage. 'This person pointed out that at the time of [British] settlement, 12-year-old girls in England were being married, so get off your high horse and don't say it's all about us. And that was valid so we rescripted around that', executive producer Greg Muller recalls.

The other element of the story concerned land rights and mining royalties. The Kimberley landscape is redolent with rock paintings and sacred sites that contain precious cultural knowledge, handed down orally through countless generations via songlines. In 2020, mining giant Rio Tinto caused international outrage when it detonated two rock shelters in Juukan Gorge in the Kimberley, which were about 46 000 years old. The explosions were against the wishes of the traditional owners, the Puutu Kunti Kurrama and Pinikura (PKKP) people, but due to a complex and unequal negotiation process, Rio Tinto technically had permission to detonate. The company has since been ordered to pay compensation to the PKKP, but clearly no amount of money can make up for this cultural vandalism.

To try to avoid such predations, legislation had been introduced in the mid-1970s to award land rights to Indigenous peoples who could prove they were the traditional owners. If their claim was upheld, the traditional owners could then make deals, or not, with organisations such as mining or tourist enterprises, which would then award the traditional owners royalties for land use. These royalties could be massive, and bring much-needed funds into communities often deprived of basic infrastructure, health and educational resources. Nevertheless, the traditional owners sometimes rejected commercial approaches, valuing the physical and cultural integrity of the land more highly than its economic potential.

Given the enormous sums of money involved, the operation was rife for corruption. And some Aboriginal people in Looma and the region were telling Richard that this was what had happened: powerful families were directing the flow of money their own way, and cutting out some of the rightful traditional custodians, by intimidation and other nefarious means. The multiple layers of the story made Richard even more determined to tell it. 'It was a story about abuse of power, which is a story that transcends race and creed and all that sort of stuff. It's a classic human story ... that needed to be told.'

Getting to know the community

The landscape became a key element in the podcast. 'I really wanted to make the Kimberley a character', says Greg Muller. With a degree in music and sound engineering, as well as practical experience as a TV and radio journalist, Greg was hoping to head west with a binaural recording kit and create 3D scapes in stereo. 'You would hear the kids playing, the river roaring, and ... just the movement around those communities. The four-wheel drives, the troop carriers, the old women talking. That's such a unique sound.' But being 4000 kilometres from Melbourne made that too expensive an indulgence. Instead, producers Tim Young and Rachael Dexter gathered ambient sound on the hop as they recorded Richard's interviews.

A recent graduate, Rachael had to quickly adapt to the very different cultural world of a remote Kimberley community, where a typical journalistic schedule does not apply. Instead of slotting people in for interviews, you go with the flow and wait for acceptance. 'It was probably like 10 per cent field recording and 90 per cent hanging around and chatting to people and travelling', she recalls. 'We'd rock up in a hired four-wheel drive from the airport, pristine white Pajero in Looma – we knew we were going to stick out like a sore thumb, so I'm not going to jump out of the car with all of my kit and start recording. You just couldn't.'

Although they were operating largely on instinct, Richard and Rachael's gut feelings aligned with cultural protocols. They were prepared to take a back seat until given some sign of approval, and to make themselves useful in the meantime. 'Rich had already spent months and months and months talking to some of these people but even so we went in gently, gently, gently', explains Rachael:

> We brought lunch up for everybody, we spent a few hours just chatting to all of the women. Some wanted to speak to Richard but they didn't want to do it on tape and they didn't want to do it in front of the men. So we were a bit of a tag team. Rich went and spoke with some of the women, which was really important in order to get trust, even though it wasn't on tape. And I spent that two and a half hours making dozens and dozens and dozens of chicken sandwiches to feed all of the kids who came over from the school!

Word got round that the pair seemed OK and at the end of the day, a community leader called Joe Killer showed up and offered to drive them around the town his father had founded, back in the 1960s, after Aboriginal cattle hands were thrown off cattle stations due to the government's introduction of a minimum wage. By his second podcast, Richard had learnt to paint descriptions of the people he was talking to. This is how Joe came through:

> When you meet Joe for the first time, you soon learn he loves a laugh and is extremely fit for a man who's just turned 70. He wears a big cowboy hat, like lots of men in these parts, and his long-sleeved blue shirt covers a barrel chest. His only concession to age is a blue haze across his big brown eyes.

Joe Killer would turn out to be a key character. 'Joe was showing us where Julie had been chased out and the place where she died', Rachael recalls. While Richard listened, Rachael was preoccupied with trying to record good-quality sound:

I just had a little Zoom mic in my hand, I didn't have my headphones, it had all just happened very quickly. I remember kind of panicking and going, 'God I hope I'm capturing something OK'. It was an amazing experience, the Kimberley. A lot of stressing about the sound because these interviews happened in weird impromptu places. And not places where you can control the sound, you know, we're on the side of the road outside of somebody's house. I'd brought all this kit up there – I hardly used it.

Most of the people interviewed for *Wrong Skin* were Aboriginal, and not used to dealing with media – there were few media producers in the area. This presented both ethical and technical challenges. If someone was shy, or inarticulate, or perhaps not comfortable with English, they might mumble or move off-mic. Sometimes their English was hard to discern. Greg decided to float Richard's narration in and around the Aboriginal voices: 'So we did a lot of introducing, someone starting to tell a story, you get the sense that it's their voice, you get the key words out, Richard would do some of the heavy lifting in explaining it but you'd be weaving it in and out. It was tricky to get right'. The podcast features the voice of Julie's best friend, Lisa Skinner, so close they used to share clothes; tragically, Julie was identified because the denim skirt found on her body bore Lisa's name. We hear from other women, such as senior Nyikina woman Lucy Marshall, who saw the couple run away, and saddest of all, Julie's daughter, Zaria, who was only eight when her mother disappeared. Among the male characters, we meet Wayne Watson, a friend of Richard Milgin, who is caught up in power struggles between warring families. We also hear from Julie's brother Graham about the awful coincidence that saw him working in the very morgue where Julie's body was taken.

Among the non-Aboriginal voices are two detectives and a classic outback figure, Owen (Freddy) Fingers, a cattle station owner with an earthy turn of phrase. An Aussie expat friend of mine, listening in England, was flooded with nostalgia for Australian plain speaking when she heard this immortal line in Episode 3. 'They call it vision impaired – but you know, he's fuckin' *blind*!' Like all these printed excerpts, it's way better heard than read.

As Richard wrote his narration, almost unconsciously, he started to 'embrace the subjective', as John Biewen puts it:

> On the matter of promised brides, I'm torn between thinking 'Who am I to question cultural practices that have been going on in the Kimberley for thousands of years?' and wondering how any girl – my own ten-year-old daughter comes to mind – would feel about being promised out to a man two or three times her age?

Thanks to *Serial* and Sarah Koenig, the personalised host voice has become part and parcel of podcast journalism. Richard, who had almost never used the first-person voice in his print articles, found it uncomfortable at first but ultimately liberating. 'For the listener, you are a main character whether you think you are or not', he reflects. 'They want to know what you think or feel about crucial elements of the story. I think if you as a host are unable to show that you also are affected by the real life drama, then you risk alienating your audience and appearing inhuman.'

Reception and recognition

Audience reaction showed people were far from alienated. *Wrong Skin* got strongly positive reactions both domestically and from overseas listeners, with many reviews mentioning how little they knew of this part of Australia and how special it was to hear Aboriginal voices from such a remote area. More importantly, the feedback from the Aboriginal community was overwhelmingly positive. 'The women are pleased that somebody has cared enough to stick up for them and more than a few men have complimented me on having "the balls" to stand up to some pretty violent people', says Richard.

Wrong Skin won a slew of prizes, in Australia and the US, which confirmed its appeal. It also brought forth enough new evidence for police to push for an inquest into a case neglected since 1994. Not everyone was happy: in speaking truth to power, Richard exposed some unsavoury behaviour within the community and got perpetrators offside. But the majority supports him. 'I had a man from the Western Desert in Western Australia ring me to say that he and his other senior men were there to go to bat for me culturally and spiritually as they believed I'd come under attack in those senses from dark forces in the Kimberley. So as unnerving as that was to be told that, it was also reassuring. As the man said to me, "You're in our world now".'

But Richard was already sniffing out what would be his next podcast – an incredible drug-running story that brought together two unlikely locations: Victoria's famed Great Ocean Road and the mysterious and menacing Democratic People's Republic of North Korea.

Researching *The Last Voyage of the Pong Su*

By 2019, podcasting had become established at *The Age* as a commercial strategy. Tom McKendrick, the new Head of Audio and Video, viewed it as intrinsically linked to bringing subscribers on board: 'It all centres around the trust that people have in the masthead'. Richard Baker was becoming a 'brand' in his own right. But he was not operating to a formula. Far from it. 'I like to do things that haven't been done and do it differently', he explains.

Richard now wanted to explore how and why a North Korean cargo ship, the *Pong Su*, tried to land 150 kilograms of heroin on Australia's southern coast in 2003, and to examine the Australian Federal Police investigation that followed. Remarkably, the AFP would entrust him with 15 hours of their surveillance recordings, which tracked the drug mules waiting on shore for the drop. There was also audio archive of the huge military operation that ended with an Australian warship apprehending the *Pong Su* and having the elite Special Air Services board it via helicopter. It had all the ingredients of a cracking adventure story, but with 33 'characters' to present, some of them non-English speakers, the challenge as always was to deliver it as a compelling serialised audio narrative.

For Richard, the motivation to make this podcast was largely focused on the *people* involved in the drug heist, on both sides:

> I wanted to find out how guys on that ship ended up there
> and what happened to them, and potentially what were the
> consequences of getting caught and going back home. And same
> for the drug traffickers, waiting on shore; how does that work?
> How do they get there? What world do they come from? And
> what's the cost of all of this?

Humanising both sides of this story would be a key driver. Richard would be host and primary reporter; Rachael Dexter, field producer and executive producer; Kate Cole-Adams, author and a former senior feature writer at *The Age*, narrative consultant; and I would again advise on optimal storytelling through sound. On this third venture, the team's skill sets would work in thrilling harmony.

The first recordings

The earliest recordings for the podcast were made at Boggaley Creek, the lonely cove near Lorne, Victoria, where the heroin drop took place. As Richard told her the outline of the story, Rachael recorded relevant ambient sound: crashing surf, dragging kelp across rocks, the crunch of gravel in a car park. They also had a couple of locals to interview: surfing legend Barry 'Tubes' Langan in his ice-cream shop and carpenter Dicky Davies, who would utter the classic line that gave the first episode its pithy title, 'This Fucking Boat'.

Dicky was a grizzled Aussie battler, so well known in the local pub that he got his beer at a special price. He was a journalist's delight: outspoken, hilarious and with an opinion on everything, from the proliferation of craft beer ('all this Prickly Moses ... it shits me ... Not everybody's a bloody yuppie!') to the sight of the massive *Pong Su* close to shore one chilly April morning ('What the fuck, is he gunna get washed on the rocks?'). A carpenter who rose early, Dicky was also one of the few people who witnessed the raid by the AFP. He described it in earthy detail, which immediately takes the listener to the scene:

> I get the paper, I go round behind the pier to see if the swell had picked up ... Here's about 80 federal cops, just in the middle of the road. Got blokes hunched over the boot of cars ... There's Chinese blokes ... There's coppers just everywhere, and I'm just going, 'What the *fuck's* going on here?' ... So, I kept going around behind the pier, and there's cops all round there as well. Next thing there's cops with jet skis, towing jet skis. Cops with rubber duckies on the back of their cars. All federal, Australian Federal Police ... Straightaway I thought to meself, 'This is this fucking boat!'

Richard was a very experienced interviewer before he got into podcasting, but interviewing for audio needed new skills. The voice recording itself mattered as much as what was said. The hard-earned realisation that he should not talk over people (because you can't edit it later) gave rise to a slower exchange that brought its own rewards. 'It's really just letting people talk and letting the pauses remain, and let them follow up after they've had a thought of whether or not, "Should I say this?" And if they open their mouths, well, it's usually pretty good because they've had to put a bit of thought into it.'

Part of Richard's journalistic style that is a boon in making rich narrative podcasts is his ability to 'secure the talent'. When he meets someone – anyone – he connects with them on a human level first. This is what led Phoebe's mother, Natalie, and the rest of the family, to trust him with the story; and it's why someone from Looma contacted him about what happened to Julie Buck and Richard Milgin so long ago. This genuine relationship is increasingly rare in a world where so much interaction takes place online, and where most young people prefer to message someone rather than call them direct, let alone meet them IRL (in real life). Being open and transparent is also at the heart of Richard's journalism: 'People give more of themselves to you, when I guess you put your cards on the table. It doesn't mean you always see eye to eye on everything and there's not tension in those relationships!'

Shoe leather and face-to-face time ... is the most important skill in journalism. It isn't your writing, or your ability to craft a story, it's actually to get along with people and get people to *tell* you their stories. So, you've got to find ways to connect with people on different levels.

– Richard Baker, award-winning podcast host

This ability to relate well to people paid off hugely in getting the AFP – and their precious surveillance tape – on board the *Pong Su* podcast.

Access to police recordings

The set-up went back almost a decade. One Christmas, years after the *Pong Su* incident, Richard had been walking past AFP headquarters, when he saw a couple of guys he knew in a bar. They waved at him to come in. He ordered a beer, sat down – and was introduced to their buddy, Damien 'Des' Appleby. Des had been the AFP officer in charge of the *Pong Su* investigation.

Fast forward to February 2019. Richard was in Canberra on other business when he found himself with an hour to kill. He happened to be near the AFP office and decided to contact their media officer, to dip a toe in the water about the *Pong Su* podcast he was then planning. He knew the media officer and called her up. 'I know she's a fan of podcasts ... and I explained very briefly. She said, "Oh that sounds exciting!" And she came out and we talked shop. And a little while later she said, "Yeah, that's got full-on approval".'

It's easy to imagine how different the response might have been had Richard instead sent an official email requesting an interview about a drug bust that saw a large bag of heroin go missing. But a beer years before and a short chat in the sun opened all-important doors that would provide unprecedented insight not only into the workings of the AFP, but also into its members' human frailties. Who knew that senior police on an operation had to survive on Easter eggs and junk food and sleep five to a room?

The timing was also right. By 2019, 16 years after the heist, the legal aspects of the case were done and dusted. 'The appeal avenues have been exhausted so, for all the people in that legal process, there was nothing riding on it', Richard reflects. 'And Des has probably reached a stage in his career where he's comfortable in his own skin and his own seniority – he was able to give a frank and full account. And I think they were proud of the job they did.'

Richard also met those he interviewed more than halfway. He gave them a transcript of their interview – something he would not have done for a print article. For a newspaper article, if it was on a sensitive topic or featuring someone who was not used to being in the media, he would ring them and run past them any quotes he intended to use. 'I find that safe, I mean, why would I want to put a story out that someone's gonna come out and go, "I never said that!" I'd rather have that argument [earlier].' With a podcast, there is the additional aspect of people being self-conscious about hearing their own voice. 'It's a nervous thing, "How am I gonna sound? Am I gonna sound like an idiot? Will they splice together different parts of my stuff to change my meaning?" So, I just think it's a comforting thing for people to have.'

This approach also allows interviewees to correct any inadvertent errors, such as a misremembered date. As to whether it might compromise editorial integrity: Richard makes the interviewees no promises about how he will respond to any requests for changes. In reality, it has never happened. 'No one's ever contacted me to say change anything.'

But the podcast was still looking one-sided: an Us vs Them story of heroic Aussies pursuing dastardly North Korean drug dealers. Then came a breakthrough. Some time back, Richard had followed the case of one Chris Koch. As he says of him in Episode Ten:

> He's a smart and engaging guy. Chris was a high-profile motivational speaker who became caught up in a murky international finance scheme in the 1990s ... He was convicted of obtaining a financial advantage by deception in 2010 and served seven years in jail.

When Chris Koch was released, he wanted aspects of the shonky world he had got caught up in investigated. So he called a journalist he trusted – Richard – and asked to meet for coffee. Richard mentioned he was working on the *Pong Su* podcast. And 'by the longest of long shots', he asked Chris if, while he was inside, he'd ever come across the four North Korean men who'd been put away for the operation. To his astonishment, Chris turned out to have been close friends with two of them: Ta Sa Wong, the man who got the drugs to shore, and Yau Kim Lam, who took possession of them. Chris had literally lived next door to them in a low-security prison and while they plied him with excellent homemade curry, he advised them on their legal options.

This revelation was dynamite, Rachael Dexter remembers. Before that, they did not even know if anyone from the *Pong Su* remained in Australia. Now they had two real human beings who made a mean chicken curry, liked to grow vegetables and were mad about soccer.

One other factor saw the podcast move from backburner project to urgent reality. Richard and Rachael went to Hong Kong to interview Des Appleby in his new role there. After recording a long interview, they all went out for a meal and several beers. So many, in fact, that while recording the second half next day, Richard had to suddenly bolt for the bathroom where, to Des's amusement, he threw up. The hangover was worth it, Richard reckoned: whether out of solidarity or sympathy, Des opened up in an unusually candid manner. And back in Australia, the AFP now facilitated access to the surveillance recordings made in the week prior to the bust – they had bugged the car of the Asian 'shore party' they suspected would intercept the haul. 'Essentially, we got the keys to the castle', Rachael recalls. 'And that's when it all started to really flesh itself out.'

Rachael handled the translation and voicing of the Chinese-language surveillance tape brilliantly. First, she identified via a Mandarin-speaking intern that the transcripts were 'primitive' and had them redone; then, instead of the usual procedure of hauling in a colleague to voice a script, as had been done with *Phoebe's Fall*, she negotiated a budget and sourced three Asian Australian community actors. 'There's no point of even using the tapes and their translations if you're not going to show what kind of energy and tone was in that', she explains. These actors fully inhabit the rounded transcripts, bringing the drug mules alive: arch, enigmatic Yau Kim Lam; poor, exploited Kiam Fah Teng; and confident, angry Chim Kwang Lee, product of a posh boarding school education in Singapore.

Script and structure

With all the raw material in, we were now set to devise structure and script – you can see the actual before, after and to-and-fro scripts in chapter 8. We knew that we would need to be nimble, too. A podcast that drops weekly rather than all at once can accrue new leads, which can deepen the reporting. 'People were contacting us throughout the [*Wrong Skin*] series with more information', Greg Muller recalls. It meant that episodes had to be restructured on the run: 'This story was actually evolving as we were telling it'. For Richard, this was very different from his print investigative journalism, which was anchored in immutable evidence. It meant he had to keep an open perspective at all times – probably a good thing. 'You can't afford to get concreted into a single-focus view of things. With print investigations that are document based, you know the material you have to play with and its opportunities and limitations from the get-go.'

This investment of serious production time can be justified by how long a listener stays with the show – a deep immersion in a 'brand' is highly valued by podcast publishers and advertisers alike. 'There's a lot of pluses in being associated with a good podcast because of the devotion and the high engagement with the audience', explains Richard. 'And subliminally, that message, whatever you're trying to get through your ad will seep in because people are generally in the zone, you know, they're really concentrating deeply while they're listening to a podcast.'

Most big podcast producers have separate marketing teams who chase sponsorship or ads. But with *Pong Su*, Richard personally pitched to the Transport Accident Commission (TAC), an organisation in Victoria that handles compulsory motor insurance and promotes road safety. With the *Pong Su* podcast set along the scenic Great Ocean Road, the connection seemed obvious: 'The Great Ocean Road is absolutely chock-a-block over summer and stressed with examples of really bad driving', Richard explains. TAC bought the pitch and invested a substantial sum to be sole sponsor. Richard wasn't surprised: 'Because that product's gonna reach an audience they want to reach'. That reasoning didn't work with the next organisation he approached, Tourism Victoria. Strangely, they had no interest in promoting a podcast about smuggling heroin onto their beaches!

You can increase listener engagement with good artwork and helpful show notes, and by providing metadata: with *The Age* podcasts, listeners could delve into the corners of the story via beautifully designed websites that featured, for instance, videos of the Special Air Service boarding the *Pong Su*, a 'Who's Who' summary of characters in *Wrong Skin*, and a summary of loose ends in Phoebe's case and the full coroner's report.

Social media is invaluable for building interest in the podcast as it unfolds. It also allows listeners to talk to each other as a community, and share ideas, reactions and opinions. And the conversations can continue long after the last episode drops. 'There's infinite time for people to buy in and maybe shape the direction', says Richard. 'And just because you've put a full stop on something doesn't mean you've closed the book. You can always do another episode if there's something valid to do.' Lots of podcasts provide updates on major breakthroughs. It shows how remarkably fluid podcasts are, compared to, say, books or TV shows.

With *Phoebe's Fall*, we added four 'mini-episodes' as events unfolded: two dropped midway through the season, focusing on a mystery phone number and on political developments triggered by the podcast; two later ones reported that a review of the *Coroners Act 2008* (Vic) had been announced (after the podcast was mentioned in the Victorian parliament), and finally, in June 2018, we reported the reforms to be implemented.

With *Wrong Skin*, we had two extra episodes: one to report that four months on, police seized a vehicle registered to one of the powerful men in the community who had declined to speak to us. Another, six months later, informed listeners that police had completed their investigation and handed the results to the coroner. With *Pong Su*, two 'prequel' episodes filled in the backstory to the drug shipment's origins in Thailand, as Richard got new leads.

In this chapter I've shown you how we prepped the podcasts and introduced you to some production decisions. But now let's go right under the hood and take you line by line, beat by beat, into *The Last Voyage of the Pong Su*.

8

Creating a hit narrative podcast, Part 2: Under the hood of *The Last Voyage of the Pong Su*

In July 2019, the core *Pong Su* production team met for the first time at *The Age* in Melbourne. Aside from contributing informally to an early planning discussion about *Wrong Skin*, narrative consultant Kate Cole-Adams had never worked on a podcast before – and indeed had never even listened much to podcasts. Her first impression of the project was of 'an extraordinarily "plotty" drama with enormous amounts happening'. But other aspects appealed even more:

> The thing that really, really got me in was the kind of intimacies of the relationships that it had access to and that it could build up ... the lived thing that underpins that whole *Pong Su* narrative, which is about all the little people, and the little fish. That sense of these parallel lives that all intersect for this period in this process. And to me that's where the emotion comes from. I think it's a very poignant story, as well as a very powerful story about lived experience under different political and social regimes and circumstances.

That uniting theme – whether you were a North Korean ship's hand or an Australian SAS officer, you were 'little fish' subject to 'hidden forces' beyond your control – was articulated by Richard in the first episode. I append our comments from the draft of that episode, as Kate and I tweaked the wording for clarity and emphasis.

NARRATION SCRIPT

To hit on that deeper truth, what happened and why, we've got to get to know and understand the people, the little fish, at the centre of the Pong Su drama:

What drove the master of the Pong Su to risk his ship and the lives of his men?

Why did two men do the unthinkable and jump into a tiny dinghy in huge seas and in the middle of the night?

Why did the men waiting ashore to receive the heroin risk 20 years in jail and never seeing their parents ~~alive~~ again or their children grow up?

And why are some of them still lying about their names and nationality?

Who are they protecting?

The answers to all those questions lie in accepting a universal truth: that the lives of every one of us are shaped by hidden forces that we rarely see and may never know.

Kate Cole-Adams

Emphasis sounds a bit odd here (needs to be on 'hit' rather than 'on' – but maybe that sounds a bit ambiguous?). Might be simpler to just say 'to find that deeper truth' (which means changing previous reference to 'finding').

Siobhán McHugh

Need equal emphasis on '*know* and *understand*' the people.

Kate Cole-Adams

Again, having listened, I'd suggest cutting this to: 'Why did two men jump into a tiny dinghy in huge seas and in the middle of the night?' Rhythm is better.

Kate Cole-Adams

Not convinced you actually need to state this, given that rest of sentence makes it clear. I think it's cleaner and has more force without 'hidden': 'The answers to all those questions lie in accepting a universal truth: that the lives of every one of us are shaped by forces that we rarely see and may never know.'

Kate hit on those twin themes – hidden forces and 'little fish' – on one 'astonishingly productive and instructive day' that also saw a ten-episode framework emerge from Richard's bare outline, arranged along one whole wall of the office. 'Richard stuck up ten sheets of white paper and started jotting plot notes on them, and Rachael kept whipping out bits of coloured paper and adding scenes/quotes. I was trying to come up with episode titles and juggle/weave themes. I felt as if we were on a film set!' Kate recalls.

I joined them the next day, adding suggestions for sound, rather than just interview or narration. A second layer of pink Post-it notes for audio elements joined the yellow plot points. Sometimes these were fairly obvious: for example, in Episode Two, when Richard lists the food reserves the *Pong Su* held (rice, pork, vegetables, etc.), I suggest stir-fry effects such as sizzling oil, banging a pan. Later, when he mentions the huge Crown Melbourne casino where the *Pong Su* drug mules hung out, I suggest creating a montage of recent news reports of Chinese gangsters detected there.

Sometimes my ideas for sound are more abstract, such as at the end of Episode One, where I added this comment:

[SCRIPT] For now, all Wong could do was take cover, watch and hope the *Pong Su* wouldn't leave without him.

[COMMENT] A big blast of a ship's horn might articulate this fear? And make a nice ending punctuation before trailer? It also foreshadows the *Pong Su*'s flight.

Richard kindly calls these suggestions my 'sprinkles of magic', but after four decades of storytelling through sound, and deep, critical listening, these have become second nature to me. On hearing a raw interview, I am mentally filleting it, discerning natural 'paragraphs' in the intonation or the emphasis. But Richard acknowledges that 'knowing when to stop off a grab and just to leave it there' is not always clear to him. For example, towards the end of Episode One, Dicky Davies reappears to tell us that the police spent years searching the area for the missing bag of heroin. He laughs as he recalls how he was often out in the same waters:

> People reckoned I wasn't going gar fishing, I was looking for the dope, which would've been nice to find! I wouldn't still be a carpenter if I found it, anyhow. **Anyway, that's about as much as I know, but you can ask me questions. That's without a word of a lie.**

I deleted those last two sentences – not only are they superfluous, they rob the effect of the sly joke Dicky makes about how rich he'd be if he could find the drugs. Now, the line 'I wouldn't still be a carpenter if I found it, anyhow' and his chortle make for a satisfying out.

Scripting

With Kate's nuanced advice on storytelling stakes, and Rachael's remarkable capacity to source and keep track of the voluminous amounts of raw data and recordings, soon we were all set. Richard would go first, 'blocking out' (writing up) a draft script for each episode – something he delivered with extraordinary speed, thanks partly to Rachael's organisation of the materials on Google Drive. Folders were clearly labelled (archive, news footage, interviews, actors, episodes) and the interview transcripts were hyperlinked to the actual audio recordings, a major time saver (Otter.ai and Trint are two good providers of this). Richard can't speak highly enough of Rachael. 'She's a great all-rounder. She's got great ideas with the sound, she's really tight on structure and just super organised so it's really easy for me to go away and write a script because I know where everything is, and if I have a question, I know she knows where it is.'

Then aged 26, Rachael had a degree in journalism from RMIT, majoring in philosophy and literature. 'But to be honest, I didn't get into the industry from my degree. I got it because I spent all of my uni time volunteering at SYN, which is Student Youth Network, a community youth radio station that's based at RMIT.' From there she got an internship at ABC Radio, and another at Al Jazeera television in Malaysia, working on a flagship documentary show. Back in Melbourne, she juggled breakfast radio production and a night shift doing video production at *The Age*. Then came *Wrong Skin*, and eventually a full-time position as a multimedia producer at *The Age*.

Richard, who is in many ways a classic blokey Australian with a passion for sports, beer and nature, is also a graduate in English literature. He unexpectedly came up with the idea of starting each episode with a short literary quote, beautifully voiced by actor Jason Chong, that spoke to the deeper metaphorical meanings of the podcast. These quotes came from a range of sources: Shakespeare's *The Merchant of Venice*, Samuel Coleridge's poem 'The Rime of the Ancient Mariner', TS Eliot's 'The Waste Land', South Korean poet Cho Oh-hyun, and American poets Mary Oliver and Anne Sexton.

Now it was down to nutting out each episode. I've appended examples below.

Episode One: The opening

The opening of the first draft production script is on the next page. The left-hand column notes the audio source; the right-hand charts the word content. There is salty language from Yau Kim Lam, the North Korean shore interceptor caught in a crisis, and from Dicky, resident pub icon.

Strong sound design in the opening minutes sets the focus clearly on the boat and the ocean, and indeed the old rust bucket *Pong Su* remains a physical presence and a virtual character throughout the series. For years, large cargo ships used to berth at the bottom of my street on Sydney Harbour and I have always thrilled to the primal bellow of a ship's horn. Vicki Hansen, the series composer, would recreate this using what she called 'a repetitive, electronic sound reminiscent of a ship fog

Episode One draft production script: BEFORE

SFX: WIND BUILDS, HEAVY SEAS, LISTING OF SHIP, CHAINS. OUTBOARD MOTOR STARTS. BREATHING, THEN HUGE WAVE WIPES OUT.	[Re-creation]
\<ep1_tape2_scene1_ onedead_extreme> NEEDS PHONE FX	LAM: *I exhausted. Fuck!* *They won't carry them together. Y'know,* *one is dead, you know? Hello? Hello? One* *is dead, you know? The stuffs are heavy.* *No one dares to take them. Too heavy to* *pull up the hill, you know.* *OK, OK, OK, speak slowly, speak slowly.* *Hey! One is dead on the beach. We, we* *just carry as much as we can.*
RICHARD VO	That's the voice of a man called Lam, seconds after one of the craziest, most brazen drug trafficking operations ever, turned to shit. I'm Richard Baker, a journalist with *The Age* and *The Sydney Morning Herald* newsrooms in Australia. This is *The Last Voyage of the Pong Su*.

horn to symbolise the *Pong Su* itself – it was a big, dark, hulking sound that formed the basis of the theme music for the podcast'.

We used this potent sound at different points. At the end of Episode One, it's a metaphorical allusion, signalling the distance between the stranded smuggler Ta Sa Wong and the ship. In Episode Two, over music, the horn blast near the top has the ship on the move, heading from

North Korea to Jakarta and the Western Australian coast. That episode introduces us to the totalitarian state, and for Vicki that tonal placement is also 'eerily reminiscent of the hidden, repressive and militaristic nature of North Korea – overbearing, monstrous and frightening'. The episode ends with the *Pong Su* bearing down on Lorne, the police still blissfully unaware of what is about to unfold, so the double blast of the *Pong Su* becomes a galvanising wake-up call. In Episode Five, it signals the chase, the belligerent ship trying to outpace Australian police and navy vessels.

But to start the whole series, to recreate that fateful stormy night when the drug drop took place, the ship's horn just has to be the first sound we hear. It puts the *Pong Su* itself front and centre in our minds. The blast also symbolises the pandemonium on board as Ta Sa Wong and his unnamed friend were lowered into the roiling waters of the dark ocean with 150 kilos of tightly wrapped heroin on board their tiny dinghy. 'Go well', it seemed to shout after them. 'We'll be here for you.'

The soundscape in the left column was imagined by Richard, mocked up by Rachael and, later, fully realised in all its evocative heft by sound engineer John Greenfield in the mix phase.

Timing, and relative levels of each sound, all had to be carefully judged. We hear the clanking of ship chains, then the sputtering motor of the outboard, mixed with the ocean noise. Music seeps through, but the focus is on that dinghy ... and then, someone's heavy panting. Sombre music builds, then a burst of radio static, 'Yeah yeah', more static, a voice crackling through in a foreign language. 'I exhausted', he gasps, in English voiceover. 'Fuck!' We struggle to take in this panicked call. 'They won't carry them together. Y'know, one is dead, you know? Hello? Hello? ... ' The desperate voice continues.

Then, our first glimmer of understanding, as Richard says, 'That's the voice of a man called Lam, seconds after one of the craziest, most brazen drug trafficking operations ever, turned to shit ...' He finishes his introduction. A beat, and we jump to the series trailer, a montage of compelling grabs, starting with a startling PA announcement, 'This is Australian warship, I intend to board you ...'

The changes between that first rough draft and the final script and audio mix (below) were various. In that first iteration, the breathless message from Lam is placed all in one chunk. It looks fine on the page. But listening to it in real time, it felt too long and disjointed, monotonal. We'd already had more than a minute of watery, somewhat ambiguous sounds. We needed to know what was going on. So I suggest bringing Richard's first line in halfway through Lam's report, as you hear it in the finished podcast. That instantly puts everything we've heard in context and sets up expectation for what comes next. It also adds much-needed texture, as we break Richard's narration into two. We also cut some of the voiceover of Lam's content, paring back to the essence.

The original phrase 'turned to shit' jars. In the interests of giving Richard gravitas as the teller of this tale, we changed it – first to 'went pear-shaped' and then, even more plainly, 'went horribly wrong'. 'Pear-shaped' seems flippant when we are first learning that one man is dead.

The final script looks like this:

Episode One draft production script: AFTER

SFX/MUSIC: WIND BUILDS, HEAVY SEAS. SHIP'S HORN BELLOWS. LISTING OF SHIP, CHAINS.	[Re-creation]
SEA. OUTBOARD MOTOR STARTS. BREATHING, THEN HUGE WAVE WIPES OUT. MUSIC.	

`<ep1_tape2_scene1_`
`onedead_extreme>`
 	
PHONE FX
	Yeah yeah.
	
	[Foreign language]
	
	LAM: *I exhausted. Fuck!*
	They won't carry them together.
	Y'know, one is dead, you know? Hello?
	Hello? One is dead, you know?

RICHARD VO SFX under	That's the voice of a man called Lam, seconds after one of the craziest, most brazen drug trafficking operations ever went horribly wrong.
	LAM: *OK, OK, OK, speak slowly, speak* *slowly. Hey! One is dead on the* *beach. We, we just carry as much as* *we can.*
RICHARD VO	I'm Richard Baker, a journalist with *The Age* and *The Sydney Morning Herald* newsrooms in Australia. <u>This</u> is *The Last Voyage of the Pong* *Su.*
TRAILER	*This is Australian warship …*

Episode One: Refining the script

Further in, I spot fresh places where use of sound can both animate and act as a bridge, allowing us to change narrative direction while telescoping a story element. For example, about halfway through, we're coming to the end of a powerful section, where Barry 'Tubes' Langan recounts how he nearly died in the region's huge surf. We have already cut his long-winded set-up back severely. Richard then suggests a silent pause, to transition to a completely new scene, where we meet the real estate agent, Donna, who is remembering how the drug mules tried to rent a house from her.

Episode One script excerpt: BEFORE

TUBES 12:26 and 13:41	Then the wave whacked and it was a double-up, really heavy. Held me under and I thought, I was saying to myself, 'Hang on, Hang on'. I was out of air right from the start … and the hold under was long and I'm squeaking and sort of letting out whatever other I had … I managed to get to the top and just got one mouthful and then the next big set came and bombed me and I was totally worked. Well, I've really thought I was going to drown. Like I thought I was had it … and this is what would have happened to those guys, possibly even hit them inadvertently, unawares that a giant wave would have been behind, just smashed on them. Even at dawn they would have been instantly thinking about losing all the drugs, of getting in trouble with getting in trouble with … what's his name?
RICHARD 14:14	The Mister Big.
TUBES 14:15	Yeah, yeah.
RICHARD	Tubes understands full well the concept of hidden forces. Those within an ocean that he cannot master despite a lifetime's effort, and those in faraway places directing the fate of the little fish like Wong and the dead man crunched in the surf in their dinghy in the dead of night back in 2003.
Silence to jump scene	
DONNA 1:03	It would be dead, nothing happening.

RICHARD	Donna Venables was working at Smyth Real Estate in Lorne back in 2003.
DONNA 1:22 and 1:41 and 1:54	Yeah, so a standard day in holiday rentals in April would be very quiet. And not much would be happening and we certainly wouldn't get any walk-in inquiries which I did on one particular day. I remember a Tarago van pulling up out the front of the office … and I remember an Asian man coming into reception who was quite shaky, or a little bit on edge. He was requesting a holiday rental fairly urgently.

While silence can be a potent intervention indeed, it works better around one voice than moving between scenes as here. Instead I suggest a common but effective device: go back and record Donna answering the phone in the office, saying who she is.

But also, the flow would be better with a strong 'out' from Tubes as well as this expeditious new 'in' from Donna. Tubes' story is dramatic, but it's still way too rambling. It needs to be trimmed of waffle and repetition. The story's punchline is: I really thought I was going to drown, which is what would have happened to those guys.

We cut out the intervening phrase, which drags, and we delete the dithering section about Mr Big. Now that things are clearer, Richard's narration seems expendable too: it's over-expository, and it impedes the lovely 'jump cut' we can achieve by crossfading straight from the ocean to the interior sound of the phone ringing.

The revised script is much cleaner and more economic: listen to the podcast to get the full effect.

Episode One script excerpt: AFTER

TUBES	I really thought I was going to drown. And this is what would have happened to those guys.
WATERY SEA FX. CROSSFADE INTO PHONE RINGING.	
DONNA	Smyth Real Estate, Lorne. Donna speaking.
RICHARD	Donna Venables was working at the real estate agency in Lorne's main street back in 2003.
DONNA 1:22 and 1:41 and 1:54	I remember a Tarago van pulling up out the front of the office … and I remember an Asian man coming into reception who was quite shaky, or a little bit on edge. He was requesting a holiday rental fairly urgently.

Line by line, we chip away. I see a clumsy phrase: the drug mules 'hurriedly loading' the heroin into the car. Who would really talk like that? I change it to 'shoving' the drugs in. Kate sees a tiny glitch in this line: 'That left the survivor, the fifth man we'll come to know as Ta Sa Wong', stranded alone on an isolated beach'. She changes 'an' to 'this': 'That left the survivor, the fifth man … stranded alone on *this* isolated beach'. It subtly shifts our perspective: now we, the listeners, are positioned on that same beach. Everything feels more real.

On it goes, down through the 30-minute episode. Kate works steadily on 'paring back some of the language, simplifying, and not overstating the big themes'. But there are micro changes, too. She picks up on Richard's early phrase, 'But to confine it to just that, a simple tale of good versus evil where dedicated white cops chase down Asian crooks, ensures the real story of what went down, and why, will remain submerged'. It's a false binary; the cops may not all be white. Kate replaces 'white' with 'Australian'. Not only is it more accurate and symmetric, it's got alliteration.

Episode One: Honing the narrative structure

Meanwhile, the bigger narrative structure needs attention. Richard had written this draft end of the first episode, mentioning his admiration for Wong. Buckle in: it's a long section!

> When I think about everything that happened that night and how everything went wrong with the drug delivery from the *Pong Su* to the men waiting at Boggaley Creek, the person I think about most is Wong.
>
> I know what he was doing was illegal. But I admire his toughness and wonder, given the way things work in North Korea, if he ever had a choice?
>
> He's the guy who had the balls to get into the rubber dinghy from the *Pong Su* and, along with his mate, take 150 kilograms of heroin ashore in darkness and fierce swells.
>
> He's the one who survived the dumping wave when his mate died. He's the one who brought his dead mate ashore and buried him. He's the one who helped find five out of the six heroin packages and delivered them to Lam, Lee and Teng.
>
> Wong watched the trio drive off into the night and then it was just him, his dead mate and the ocean. He had no way of getting back to the *Pong Su* and had no passport or identity documents on him. He was left with a GPS device, alcohol and cigarettes.
>
> He would have known the shore party had been arrested when dozens of police swarmed Boggaley Creek after daybreak.
>
> All Wong could do was take cover, watch and hope the ship would not leave without him.

This narration segues to policeman Des informing us:

> It was clear that he was up there communicating back to
> the vessel. So essentially they're trying to work out a
> way, well, this is my view. And what we know, from our
> examination of all the items found, is that they were
> waiting to try and get him back. So they're trying to pick
> him up. So to their credit, they were trying to recover
> the man. They hadn't immediately abandoned him, they were
> trying to work it out, how to do that.

Then Richard:

> Federal Police team leader Des Appleby is talking about
> how the *Pong Su* ran a zigzag course off Boggaley Creek
> for hours after it would have become obvious to those on
> board that the drug importation had been compromised.
> Remember how I said a kind of respect emerged between the
> two sides in this case? Well, I reckon Des is showing some
> there. When things got to court, the *Pong Su* crew said
> it was sheer coincidence that the ship had broken down off
> Boggaley Creek, and that no one had ever seen Wong and the
> dead guy before.

Des again:

> We didn't know he was there and he just stayed there
> observing us. So he was within maybe 50 to 70 metres from
> us at the scene. So he was observing what we were doing
> and we actually moved a couple of different sites. When we
> located the GPS, it was quite a huge win. But we could see
> that he'd been up in the hinterland behind Boggaley Creek
> observing the police and Customs and Victoria Police the
> whole time. So he was sitting there watching us. We didn't
> know he was there, but he was certainly observing us. But
> he has to stay put.

Richard tells us more:

> Wong never found his way back to the *Pong Su* and had to
> watch while his only pathway home disappeared in front of
> him.

> He was discovered a day later, and later on in this series we'll go into the incredible story of his capture.
>
> But when Wong was taken into custody police noticed two things.

Des takes over:

> He was very, very wet, tired. He'd obviously had a rough time. You could see he was bending over, obviously very fatigued, distressed.
>
> When we tried to interview him with an interpreter, because he said he was Chinese, so we brought in a person that could speak those languages and they said, 'He's not Chinese, he can't understand us, but he needs to go to hospital'.

Richard concludes:

> Sixteen years on from the night at Boggaley Creek, Wong's still in Australian custody. Same goes for Lam and Lee. The dead guy, well, the Victorian coroner is still trying to identify him and he's in a pauper's grave. He's someone's son or brother. Wong has applied to repatriate his friend's remains if he ever gets to leave Australia.
>
> As ever, the fate of these men is still entwined with the hidden forces that had them come to Australia in the first place.

The episode ends with Des hammering the point:

> And particularly as an organised crime figure here, they actually don't care about the people involved on the ground. They're disposable. So they're very hard-of-heart people. They actually have quite a contempt for countries like Australia because of the drug issues. So no one would care. They just send them, essentially, to their fate.

If we had delivered that episode as above, dear reader, would you have listened on?

I doubt it, because we'd told you pretty well everything you wanted to know. There are plot points here that could form a climax for a whole other episode!

For Richard, who had to mine vast amounts of material and synthesise a storyline, it was a valiant first run. There are infinite story choices to make, as he points out: 'Do you take the bend just here or do you keep going straight for a while?'

Kate reviews the rough episode structure. She reminds Richard that we had foreseen Wong ending this episode, alone, in hiding, on this beach, with no papers, no protection – watching the *Pong Su* so tantalisingly close, but unable to get back to it in those huge seas.

And that's all we need to know at this point. We can end it right there: 'All Wong could do was take cover, watch, and hope the ship would not leave without him'. Underline that with the blast of the ship's horn.

Now you will definitely want to go on to Episode Two!

Some of the scripting conversations develop on the Google Doc, and some happen by group email. We work gingerly at first, trying to get the measure of how comments are being received. But Richard is remarkably sanguine about our suggested alterations. Then, with the final story, script content and sound ideas in place for an episode, Rachael pulls together an audio cut. This will bring further adjustments, as we gauge the very different impact of listening in real time.

Crafting the audio: Sound and music

That gut-punching power of sound will be further enhanced now, with Vicki's musical scoring. Vicki is an accomplished composer with broad experience in film and screen, and she plays a wide range of instruments. The *Pong Su* was, however, her first podcast, so she was a little apprehensive at first.

I did find that scoring for an audio project was quite different to film as sometimes pictures can limit your imagination – the visual tending to dominate our senses. With that in mind I felt a lot more creative freedom to explore sound and to use some more experimental tones to help convey emotion and carry the story. As with my scoring for film, I'm of the 'less is more' approach, having heard podcasts where music was overused and thus losing its potency. I didn't want that to happen to *Pong Su* – to turn it into melodrama with an overwrought soundtrack.

At times one of us would specifically note in the script that a music pause/beat was needed. I put one, for instance, in Episode Six. Detective Celeste Johnston has just told Richard that their intelligence was that the drugs' ultimate destination was to be Sydney. Richard asks her why, then, did they choose the Great Ocean Road for the offload, a spot closer to Melbourne? 'I have no idea', Celeste says. 'And it still surprises me to this day why they would choose the Shipwreck Coast to stop their ship.'

This stopped me in my tracks when I heard it. It seemed an odd glitch in the planning and one we needed to flag. But the script went off immediately on a new tangent, so Celeste's very pertinent observation risked getting lost – hence the direction to add music to let it sink in.

Sometimes, it's a generalised guide: 'music builds tension' or 'music bridge, scene break'. Far from feeling intruded upon, Vicki found these suggestions useful: 'It allowed me to hear the story that the producers and writers were wanting to tell and what particular hit points they felt were important'. In general, she paid close attention to the script. 'Much more closely than with a film, as the whole story is built on words, and of course, in the case of *PS* [Pong Su], supported by a really great soundscape. I was conscious of the music blending with and enhancing the sound effects.'

A schedule starts to form. The audio mix signed off by the Team of Four (Richard, Rachael, Kate and me) goes to Vicki, who has a week to score it. She thinks first about a 'tone' for the series. It is a story about a North Korean ship and would involve 'Asian' sounds, without them being too overt. She decides on a varied palette: 'gongs, gamelan, guzheng, taiko drums, Pipa (Chinese lute), bells and various percussion instruments'.

Vicki then listens intently to the mix, working through the script in a linear way, identifying where music is needed and what it's there for. 'You're using the music to depict emotions that are either overtly, or covertly, inherent in the story ... I'm ultimately there to serve the story and really make it "sing", as opposed to creating musical masterpieces that draw attention away from the story.'

Vicki's mix is mastered by engineer John Greenfield, who had been working in television. But as a former musician, John has a deep audio sensibility that adds a polished sound design.

Out into the world:
The release schedule

Next, Rachael mocks up two trailers – one is action-packed, the other more focused on character and quirks. They go up on the *Phoebe's Fall*, *Wrong Skin* and related podcast sites, to drop quietly into subscriber feeds. Matthew Absalom-Wong, who devised the stunning artwork for *Phoebe's Fall* and *Wrong Skin*, again excels. The image he creates of the *Pong Su* ship, with its black-and-red bulk and its yellow derricks and cranes atop an infinite blue ocean, is arresting. The tagline is pretty inviting too: 'A North Korean dictator, bags of heroin, drug lords, spooks, sailors, Australian cops and a web of lies: Come aboard The Last Voyage of the Pong Su'. This is starting to feel real.

Finally, on 7 October 2019, Episode One goes live.

Every Monday for the next three months, as an episode drops online, two *Age* staffers unleash extensive social media and online promotion, some targeted specifically at Asia. There are YouTube videos and

Instagram, Twitter, Snapchat and Facebook posts. Digital subscribers to *The Age* and *The Sydney Morning Herald* find a teaser in their daily newsletter.

Using a totally different writerly voice, Richard delivers a news article to accompany each episode, dropping nuggets of the investigation without compromising the whole series. They form part of the newspaper, but also sit on the dedicated podcast website, itself a thing of beauty and a source of compelling metadata: a who's who, with thumbnail sketches of the 33 people we feature, and a mesmerising collection of archival footage, mostly supplied by the Australian Federal Police, placed online as short video excerpts.

That first week, we go straight to number 1 on iTunes in Australia, sailing past *The Mysterious Mr. Epstein* from Wondery at number 2 and *The Joe Rogan Experience* (typically the highest rating podcast in the US) at number 3. I know iTunes is not really a chart of top downloads, it's more about measuring the rate of download of new content – but I screenshot it just the same!

Now it's rinse and repeat. We are juggling several episodes each week, all at differing stages of production, as Rachael sets out in this dazzling schedule excerpt. This will continue until 10 December, when the tenth and final episode drops: four and a half months of absolute full-time commitment for herself and Richard, and many many hours for Kate, myself, Vicki, John and the rest of the team.

As beautiful as it looked, the original schedule had to be modified. Rachael eventually needed an assistant to help edit the rough audio mix, as besides her own supervisory input into the scripts, she was also handling legal and rights issues (use of excerpts of films, archive, etc.) and was busy recording new interviews that emerged as the podcast was published. For instance, a prominent lawyer who acted for refugees came forward to volunteer her memories of the imprisoned *Pong Su* crew, making it into Episode Eight.

Podcast production schedule, Weeks 7–9

PROD WEEK 7: SEP 23 — SEP 27	Episode 1 • Vicki sends MASTER MUSIC to Rach (Friday) • Rach send MASTER CUT to John at CH 9 (Friday) Episode 2 • Send rough cut to group (Tuesday) • Rach send FINE cut to Vicki (Friday) Episode 3 • Rough cut complete (Friday) Trailer 1 • Release on iTunes
PROD WEEK 8: SEP 30 — OCT 4	Episode 1 • John to send MASTERED episode to Rach (Wednesday) Episode 2 • Vicki sends MASTER MUSIC to Rach (Friday) • Rach send MASTER CUT to John at CH 9 (Friday) Episode 3 • Fine cut complete (Friday) & send to Kate & Siobhán Episode 4 • Rough cut complete (Friday) & send to Kate & Siobhán Trailer 2 • Release on iTunes
PROD WEEK 9: OCT 7 - 11 LAUNCH WEEK	Episode 1 • RELEASE ON ITUNES (Monday) Episode 2 • John to send MASTERED episode to Rach (Wednesday) Episode 3 • Add in music (Rach) (by Friday) • Rach send MASTER CUT to John at CH 9 (Friday) Episode 4 • Fine cut complete (Friday) & send to Kate & Siobhán Episode 5 • Rough cut complete (Friday)

Production highlights

Week by week, each episode takes shape. Below are some of the highlights of their evolution.

Episode Two: Master Sun's Big Gamble

This episode introduces us to North Korea as a mysterious polity and to the Kim family as dictators. The characters need fleshing out. Physical descriptions help; so do little details. Master Sun, for instance, has dozens of grandchildren. We include that he spends time ashore in Singapore buying dresses for the girls – something so disarming the defence lawyers will adduce this at his trial. These small insights scaffold our bigger theme – that beyond the whodunnit factor, this podcast seeks to chart our common humanity.

Episode Three: Going Fishing

One of the first exchanges we hear is laden with irony. Drug mule Teng asks Lee if he thinks their car could be bugged. Lee scoffs. If that were the case, you'd be in jail by now, he tells Teng: 'That is an international issue and only the FBI can do it'. Des tells Richard the listening police found that conversation most entertaining.

At the end, Richard had included Des's recount of the police getting word of the sting operation. Des says: 'Next thing it was stand by, stand by, from our surveillance! And they're on the move, and they were motoring, and they did a series of turns and lost surveillance'. On paper, 'they're on the move' looks a good out, but the intonation wasn't strong. Ending with 'they did a series of turns and lost surveillance' is weak. So I went back to Des's original interview and found a ringing clarifier: 'We knew they were going to do something; we just didn't know when, or where'. The episode now ends on a cliffhanger.

Episode Five: Hot Pursuit

This episode delivers in spades on the action-packed adventure Richard promised in Episode One. Narratively, the episode had a natural chronological arc, which Kate establishes as a timeline for the script. With lots going on, it is vital to avoid confusion. Here's how we worked to achieve this.

Episode Five draft script: BEFORE

DES 1:34:54 SFX: SHIP THROTTLE	But in seeing that military aircraft, the *Pong Su* just hit it. It just got out of there. So it pointed to Bass Strait and just throttled down.
RICHARD VO	Des was going to have to find another way to keep track of the ship ~~her~~. And quickly.
MUSIC POINT	For one thing, even though police now had ~~With~~ Lee and Teng in custody ~~and Wong and Lam soon to be~~, they ~~police~~ hadn't recovered as much heroin as they were expecting.
	This made Des think that the remainder could still be on board the fleeing *Pong Su*.

Rachel Dexter
To keep the dramatic part to the end of Des's bit.

Rachel Dexter
Nice pace!

Kate Cole-Adams
You can't say this yet because, in relation to the scene you're building right now, that hasn't happened yet.

Kate Cole-Adams
This might be a good spot to mention the pursuits by the *Van Diemen* and the *Fearless* (letting us know if they come before or after the cray fisherman scene) and setting up the idea of hot pursuit. Also might help to signal if the pursuit vessels were working together (i.e. communicating with each other) and at the same time (or in a relay).

	Over and above that, important people in <u>the Australian capital of</u> Canberra — and as far away as Washington DC — were demanding the *Pong Su* be kept in sight, now that her true origin was known.	**Rachel Dexter** This has been resolved since you made this comment right, Kate?
DES Hong Kong tape 2 0:7:47 \<Des_04_N_ Korean_ vessle>	It was a North Korean vessel off our coast and it'd been involved in a major drug matter and that just lit up ~~essentially~~ government.	**Kate Cole-Adams** Hmmm. I'm not sure. I'll have to check back (or forward – can't remember) but will keep going here for now. Can we hold the thought for now? **Rachel Dexter** Yep! Pop a pin in it
RICHARD VO	With Des's crayfisher plan no longer an option, the job of chasing down the fleeing *Pong Su* fell firstly to ~~a Tasmanian~~ police <u>boats from other states.</u> ~~on board the Van Diemen police boat and then a NSW Police crew aboard the Fearless.~~	**Rachel Dexter** Do we want to avoid using 'Des's' because it sounds awkward? **Rachel Dexter** Why don't we introduce their names when start talking about them specifically, because we're just about to jump into a diff. topic with Greaves for a bit.
SCENE BREAK		**Kate Cole-Adams** Yes good plan. Drip-feed details as we need them.

Kate's change to Richard's text, above, is helpful:

> Des was going to have to find another way to keep track of **the ship. And quickly. For one thing, even though police now had** Lee and Teng in custody, the police hadn't recovered as much heroin as they were expecting.

Adding 'and quickly' builds pace. More crucially, she deletes 'and Wong and Lam soon to be', noting that the police at that point in the story couldn't have known they would soon have the other two in custody. The additional clause, 'For one thing', clarifies further. And clarity is vital in spoken-word writing!

Episode Seven: You Need a Lawyer

At 45 minutes, this is our longest episode. It's also surprising – and a lot of that is down to Jack Dalziel, the small-time lawyer who ended up representing some 30 North Koreans on charges of smuggling a vast amount of heroin into Australia. Recording Jack uttering little gems, like how he faxed the North Korean embassy to offer his services, was like hitting paydirt, Tom McKendrick recalls. 'You almost want to high-five someone as they say it.'

Most of the script changes are micro – tighter wording, avoiding a repetitious phrase, stripping out superfluity. We wrap up the fate of the captured shore party in this episode. Teng, conscripted as a drug mule to pay off a gambling debt, got 22 years and would miss seeing his six-year-old son grow up. In one heartbreaking detail, included to build emotional connection, he told his lawyer he was too ashamed to tell his elderly parents in Malaysia what had happened. He wanted them to think that the reason he didn't visit anymore was because he was too busy working in Australia.

Episode Eight: The Defector's Choice

Kate suggests making the personal story of defector Thae Yong-ho the emotional linchpin for what would otherwise be an overly dry story about pre-trial preparations. We open with Thae describing his urge to defect from North Korea to South Korea, to give his sons a better life. The episode pursues varied twists and turns, including a visit to Seoul by the prosecutors. It is clear that we will finish with Thae but, structurally, we need a 'pitstop' in the middle. I return to his raw interview, and suggest including this:

> My family belonged to the core class, which meant that we enjoy political privileges and economic benefits ... School for an elite group was special so I even was able to watch British films like *Mary Poppins*, or American films, like *Sound of Music*.

Not only does it afford a better understanding of the system, it allows me to conjure an unlikely musical element in a story about a North Korean gulag – enter Julie Andrews' yodelling goatherd from *The Sound of Music*!

Next comes a re-sequencing. In a first draft, we included early on the gentle story of how lawyer Susan Armour noticed the crew had all gone grey in detention – they had been dying their hair black and had run out of supplies. Kate suggests moving this down to follow a section about how the North Korean men were held incommunicado. Not only does it flow better, it starts an emotional build, as Susan wonders how the men fared on their return to North Korea. This sets up the powerful climax: Thae tells of his 'Sophie's Choice' moment. If he does not defect, his sons will have a miserably constrained life. If he does, his siblings will be punished, maybe even executed.

Episode Nine: The Most Free
They'd Ever Be

The penultimate episode details the trial. The court denied access to the audio of proceedings, and there were no transcripts, but there was still plenty to work from. The trial was heard in the Supreme Court of Victoria, where Greg Muller, the executive producer of *Wrong Skin*, was now making a new podcast, *Gertie's Law*, about the workings of the court. In a bit of podcast mateship, he provided us with a transcript of the opening of a trial – the usher saying 'All rise' and so on. Voiced by

Rachael over sound effects of shuffling chairs, it works well to establish the formalities.

Richard set out the macro story as usual as a draft. Kate polished sentences until they shone.

Episode Nine script excerpt

Before	After
Right from the start, there was an unusual feeling among the lawyers about this case.	Right from the **outset,** there was **a strange atmosphere** among the lawyers **prosecuting** the case. **Almost an ambivalence.**
Kim Jong Il's regime was so unpredictable and brutal that Susan and others believed Master Sun and company may have been better off being found guilty and kept in Australia, albeit in a jail cell.	Kim Jong Il's regime was so unpredictable, **so brutal,** that Susan and others believed Master Sun and company **could be** better off being found guilty and kept in Australia, albeit in a jail cell.

The trial outcome is announced via a montage of archival news grabs – and it is astonishing. After a seven-month trial, the suburban lawyer Jack Dalziel and his team have beaten the might of the state! Like the rest of the crew, the four North Korean officers will return home.

We've all gotten quite fond of Master Sun by now, and of his old rust bucket cargo ship – so much so that when Rachael went to assemble the audio for the episode and located the actuality of the Australian Air Force blowing up the ship with a laser-guided missile, she was overcome. The whole team became quite emotional at this point.

But we still had one final episode to create – one that would really unleash pent-up feelings.

Episode Ten: Reckoning

We wanted to end the series with a personal take on the North Korean men, who had evolved from evil, two-dimensional stereotypes to living, breathing human beings.

Richard's draft script opens with a precious phone conversation he had with Wong, the surviving smuggler. It happened courtesy of Chris Koch, the man who had befriended Wong and Lam in jail. Long after Chris got out, he kept in contact. On one of those calls, he handed the phone to Richard. It's an amazing moment, to hear Wong, jovial and hearty. He sounds quite unlike the voice briefly heard in Episode Six in a police interrogation. Wong now speaks excellent English and laughs as Chris compliments him on his curry-making skills. He sounds lovely.

Chris is a wholly new character and likeable, too. I listen back to the original tape and add choice grabs about his relationship with Wong and Lam. They thicken the story. Chris describes how Wong and Lam were 'like brothers' and each would take a bullet for the other, how Lam has a child, and how Lam grew all the vegetables they ate.

The script leaves Chris to wrap up loose ends, including the fate of the 26 crew. Shockingly, Des thinks they were executed in North Korea.

The ending is in sight. Pumping with adrenaline, I comb the phone conversation between Chris and Wong for any new details. I find an ominous section from Chris: 'Anytime you get any information, you know, just ring me please or send me text, so I know everything is alright. Because you never know – they might put you on a plane and just disappear'.

That will work beautifully to maintain ambiguity and raise the stakes.

But before that, I think, Richard has to get personal. He has steered us on this journey for ten whole episodes that took up months of his life.

So I write in unanswered questions and reflections Richard might have. Kate hones it to reiterate our key themes.

As for me, I still have lots of unanswered questions about the *Pong Su* incident.

Why would the crew, and not the captain, be executed, if in fact that's what happened?

Why did the crew display such adulation for a regime that they must have known was cruel in the extreme?

And why did they choose one of the roughest coasts in Australia to make the drop, especially if the gear was destined for Sydney?

But I'm pretty certain of one thing. Whatever your job – cop, sailor, spy, crim, lawyer or reporter – we've all got more in common than we might think.

No matter where we come from, all of us are vulnerable to forces beyond our grasp. And much of the time, we've no choice but to play the cards we've been dealt.

I like to imagine that, as I speak, Wong, Lam and the rest of the North Koreans are at home and with their families.

I hope so.

Vicki's spare closing music picked up beautifully on the mixed feelings, as she describes:

The music there reflects the dark undertones of their possible fate upon returning home, then changes again for the last phone call with their friend Chris Koch, a poignant, bittersweet moment, a distant memory. It then morphs again into a mysterious drone that trails off into the distance, reflecting the disturbing uncertainty of their future.

The closing moment, between Chris and Wong, symbolises the rapprochement between Australians and North Koreans throughout. And so the series ends, the music adding a lovely, dreamy feel to the reprised and re-sequenced phone call. This ending made the team emotional again. For Kate, that conversation was 'perfect' storytelling. 'It changes us from the inside', she wrote. 'Now I will go and have a little cry.'

The wrap

I come down to Melbourne for the wrap party. It's been too big a part of my life to miss this! Over margaritas I meet Vicki and John in person for the first time and laugh as Mikkayla Mossop, who voiced the road safety ads for our sponsor, the Transport Accident Commission, tells us how she was too chirpy and upbeat at first and had to work hard to sound intimidating. '150 000! That's how many drug tests we'll do this summer.'

Reflecting on making her first podcast, Kate is amazed at how complex audio narratives are. 'It's nothing like as free-flowing and organic and natural as it sounds. It's quite an elaborate construction.' And that is both the joy and the frustration of making quality storytelling podcasts. If you do it right, it sounds, well, simple.

Kate is now drawn to the possibilities audio's 'lovely playfulness' offers to blur the boundaries between fiction and nonfiction. 'There's something about the format, the open-endedness of it, the fact that you can keep changing as you go along – you can digress and choose rabbit holes all over the place so long as you can get back out, and even if you don't get back out you can say, "Oh I'm stuck down a rabbit hole." That's freedom!'

For all of us, there is a sense of elation about how the individual contributions of a tight team created something much larger than the sum of its parts. Instead of the big listening focus groups used on

Phoebe's Fall and particularly *Wrong Skin*, we relied on our own expertise and internal debates. 'There's a danger in having too many cooks', Richard now realises. Rachael also felt happy to go with the flow. 'I'm much more Zen about the stoushes now ... because it's just so obvious that with a tight little team of people with different kinds of strengths, whose opinions we respected even if we all didn't agree, it would come out shit hot!'

For Tom McKendrick, *Pong Su* has helped consolidate the podcast-as-business terrain. He has commissioned journalists to do a range of chatcasts that help build the brand, and in 2021 at time of writing, the combined *Age* and *Sydney Morning Herald* mastheads have advertised nine new roles in audio production, social media distribution and digital storytelling, including a senior position, Head of Premium Content. Things have changed a lot since the ragtag days of grabbing studio time from the video people to make *Phoebe's Fall*. As Tom observes of the studio where I am interviewing him:

> We're sitting in a newly built, custom-made audio recording room, and that's very much a validation of what the company now thinks of the importance of podcasting. And we've a great workflow and skill set, which is ever expanding. It holds a very important position within our editorial strategy, which is to prove to our audience that we create content that's worthy of their subscription.

Other newspapers are now having major impacts in the investigative long-form field. The *Telegraph* in the UK made a moving podcast, *Bed of Lies*, about a scandalous infiltration by police of left-wing women's personal lives over many years. The *Washington Post* spent three years making *Canary*, a nuanced exploration of sexual assault experiences and challenging power differentials. *The Teacher's Pet* was an unexpected blockbuster for *The Australian* in 2018, garnering some 29 million downloads. The podcast explored the cold case disappearance of a young mother, Lynette Dawson, from Sydney's Northern Beaches, and accused her then husband Chris Dawson of her murder. It had poor execution, a rambling narration and an emphasis on salacious details, but it had the positive effect of triggering a police investigation into a suspected sex ring targeting schoolgirls.

The podcast has since had to be removed, for fear of prejudicing Chris Dawson's trial. For a time it looked as if it might even make it impossible to put Dawson on trial at all. As Justice Elizabeth Fullerton of the New South Wales Supreme Court scathingly remarked, 'the unrestrained and uncensored public commentary about Lynette Dawson's suspected murder' was 'the most egregious example of media interference with a criminal trial process which this court has had to consider in deciding whether to take the extraordinary step of permanently staying a criminal prosecution'. Eventually, Justice Fullerton refused a permanent stay of prosecution and in June 2021, a court ruled that Dawson could get a fair trial if a jury was given careful direction by a judge to remedy the pre-trial publicity.

Investigative or true-crime podcasts require huge investments of time and resources and should not be lightly undertaken. But if done well, a narrative podcast treatment can afford depth and emotional connection that newspapers can't emulate. After making three such hit podcasts, Richard Baker views the medium as a valuable chance to do 'extreme feature writing' – 'extreme' because 'it's very easy for people to lose focus or attention so you want to keep people with you the whole way. You gotta know how much backfill to give without being boring and how to keep your momentum up'.

But a final word of advice from Rachael: don't forget that finding the right *story* for a podcast format is crucial. 'I'm always wary of people who say, "I want to do a podcast", like the podcast comes before the actual idea itself', she notes. 'If you're gonna sink resources into it, say, "I'm doing this podcast because this is the best possible way to tell this story".'

**Platforms: publishing your podcast –
Q&A with James Cridland**

Audio 'futurologist' James Cridland edits the free
newsletter *Podnews*, an excellent source of information on
the podcast industry. He also co-hosts the podcast *Podland
News*.

Q. What is the difference between a podcast app, a podcast directory and a podcast hosting company?

A podcast app, like Apple Podcasts, Google Podcasts,
Spotify or Pocket Casts, is software that your listeners can
download to their mobile phone to listen to podcasts. Apple
Podcasts is on every new iPhone, and Google Podcasts is
an option on most Android phones. Apple Podcasts is the
most popular app in countries like the US, Australia and
the UK, where the iPhone is popular, but in many countries
in Europe and Latin America, Spotify has overtaken it.
Adelaide's Pocket Casts is a well-regarded and competent
alternative.

A podcast directory is the list of shows available on those
apps. Apple's directory is used by many other podcast apps;
both Google and Spotify maintain their own directories, and
there are more than 20 other directories that you may wish
to make sure that your podcast is listed in, from Indian app
JioSaavn to Samsung Podcasts, or Adam Curry's Podcast
Index that supplies the directory to a number of upcoming
podcast apps.

All these podcast directories tell podcast apps where to
find the audio for your podcast. You upload your audio to a
podcast hosting company.

Q. How many podcast hosting companies are there and what features do the most popular ones offer?

There are almost a hundred commercial podcast hosting companies: from heritage podcast hosts like Libsyn or Blubrry to newer companies like Captivate, Transistor or Buzzsprout.

All offer statistics like the number of total downloads: look for certification with the IAB (Interactive Advertising Bureau) to make sure they're calculating the data accurately.

Some offer additional features, such as selling adverts for you, giving you tools to organise your podcast and find guests, adding dynamic ad insertion features, or access to software to edit or polish your podcast.

Some companies, like Omny Studio, are designed for larger enterprise users; while others, like Anchor or RedCircle, have free options to allow anyone to podcast with them without cost, designed for those just starting out.

Q. What role does an RSS feed play in podcasting?

An RSS feed contains all the information about your podcast: from its name to each individual episode and where to find the audio. Your podcast hosting company will give you an RSS feed, and you'll normally give it to each podcast directory to make sure you're listed.

9

Inclusion, diversity and equality: Pushing the boundaries of podcasting

In 1930, German playwright and poet Bertolt Brecht observed: 'Radio could be the most wonderful communication system imaginable ... could be, that is, if it were capable not only of transmitting, but of receiving, of making the listener hear but also speak, not of isolating him but connecting him'. The day I speak to Radiotopia executive Julie Shapiro, she's just seen an email from a listener to *Ear Hustle*, the podcast from San Quentin prison (discussed later in this chapter) of which she is executive producer. 'Someone saying, "I've listened to every episode. So I just feel like you're my friends. And I could reach out and ask you for this."' The person was asking for a favour for a prison program. But it was the sense of connection that struck Julie:

> Podcast has opened up this accessibility. And a lot of hosts and
> producers are responsive ... So it's not so one-way. It feels like you
> can talk back or think back or share back. And I feel like that is
> still a very strong component of the whole of the medium, of the
> culture of it.

This 'parasocial' relationship between host and listener helps develop a strong sense of community among fans of a particular podcast – and it is being harnessed in many different settings around the world. It also plays well for niche voices, conferring a sense of belonging on listeners who feel marginalised by mainstream media. This chapter explores cultural diversity in the international podcast environment and examines the push to have more representative and inclusive voices heard in the Western podsphere.

International voices

Culture plays an important role in determining podcast preferences. In Denmark, for instance, four out of five indie podcasts are interview/chat, and of these, a huge amount are about football, a national obsession. In northern Germany, newspaper *Nordwest Zeitung* discovered their obituaries were a hit in audio format. According to a 2020 survey, Germans' listening platform also influenced content choice: those who found podcasts via Spotify mostly chose comedy (24 per cent) and sport (16 per cent), while those listening via Apple preferred news (23 per cent) or society and culture (16 per cent).[1] In the US, by contrast, about half of all podcast users listen to news podcasts, of which there are more than 50 of a professional standard, according to a Reuters digital news report in 2020. The report noted that listeners believed that the podcast news format 'gives greater depth and understanding of complex issues' and 'a wider range of perspectives' than other types of news media.

Away from the news, fictional storytelling is being reborn through podcasting. In Sweden, home of Spotify, fiction podcasts grew more than threefold between mid-2020 and mid-2021.[2] In the US, fiction podcasts made by filmmakers have come full circle: the dramas *Homecoming* and *Limetown* were turned into TV shows following their success as podcasts. Younger audiences are being targeted in this space, too. A multilingual, multicultural initiative called *Cultureverse* launched mid-2021, described as 'an immersive audio drama that celebrates our collective cultural past'. This podcast, aimed at 9–13-year-olds and supported by PRX, takes myths and legends from around the world and packages them as dramas involving 'ordinary kids'. It's co-hosted by actors Kelly Marie Tran and Yara Shahidi, and produced by the Paris-based Studio Ochenta network, which produces programs in more than 19 languages 'to build bridges across cultures'. The stories on *Cultureverse* derive from folk tales and legends from Mexico, India, China, Nigeria, Vietnam, Puerto Rico, the Cherokee Nation and more. They can be heard in various languages, including Spanish, Cantonese, Vietnamese and Korean.

Koreans are renowned for their love of elaborately costumed historical film dramas, but in the podsphere, they go for politics. These podcasts outstrip lifestyle, economics, science and sport in popularity, probably because they examine topics of public interest that the traditional news media have either suppressed or ignored. One podcast, translated as *The Petty-Minded Creep*, is even credited with helping to overthrow a government. Hosted by a journalist, a former opposition lawmaker, a sound engineer and one of Korea's first online satirists, it exposed the corrupt activities of former presidents Lee Myung-bak and Park Geun-hye. *The Petty-Minded Creep* launched in 2011 and mostly avoided charges of defamation because podcasting, unlike broadcasting, was an unregulated space, and because their reports were couched as comedy. One live broadcast of the podcast attracted an audience of half a million people and the podcast was estimated to have about 11 million listeners by 2018. That year, former president Park was sentenced to 24 years in prison after being impeached, while investigative journalist and podcast host Kim Ou-joon received an award.[3]

In China, things look very different. The environment is changing rapidly, but let's get some historical perspective.

A cultural revolution:
China and podcasting

In China, podcasts that tell personal stories are taking off – and that is a hugely significant development in a nation where first-person storytelling has been stymied by decades of living under a highly controlling communist government. As the Chinese satirical novelist Yan Lianke described it in a *New Yorker* interview: 'People's sense of themselves as individuals atrophied'.[4]

I got a taste of that in 2018, when I ran a podcasting workshop at the University of Wollongong for Asian broadcasters. The workshop arose from a talk I'd given the year before to the General Assembly of the Asia-Pacific Broadcasting Union (ABU) in Chengdu, China, home of giant pandas and Sichuan cooking. There was huge interest from Asian broadcasters, most of whom barely knew the term 'podcasting' – they were still dealing with radio as a live medium, used for news and entertainment, with a few shows also streamed online. The ABU covers a massive constituency. Its members in over 70 countries broadcast to over three and a half billion people – almost half the world!

Eight ABU people came to Australia for the course, from Vietnam, Malaysia and China. The three young Chinese broadcasters, who had impeccable English and polished delivery, hosted English-language shows for the state-run China Radio International (CRI). As an icebreaker exercise in personal audio storytelling, I asked everyone to wander about the university campus, record whatever took their fancy and make a one-minute audio postcard. One Chinese participant looked perplexed at the instructions. 'There is no right or wrong way to do this', I reassured her. 'It's a creative exercise.' She laughed: 'You can't tell me there is no right way to do it – I'm Chinese!' Her colleague took a less competitive approach. She scripted her piece as a moving note to her young daughter, something she said she would never have felt able to do for radio purposes: 'Radio would not have the tolerance for you to do such family-bound things ... you're taking advantage of a public platform to express your personal feeling. That is not OK'.

The third participant, a suave 32-year-old I will call L, devised a polished blend of philosophical reflection and personal commentary, which included the line, 'The University of Wollongong has the most beautiful campus I've ever seen'. It sounds unremarkable, but to my astonishment, L said it was the first time he'd ever used the word 'I' in an audio narration. Normally, on radio, he would use the third person, 'one', instead. 'I hide behind the narrative', he explained.[5] Chinese-Australian academic Louisa Lim, host of the award-winning *Little Red Podcast*, told me that Chinese broadcasters are trained to write content in a formulaic way, often opening a report with a rhetorical question and ending with a statement about the merits of the state and the public good, familiar references in an authoritarian society. But such conventions are being cast aside by a new wave of podcasters, including young Chinese who have lived overseas and embraced the much less formal approach podcasting prefers.

By the end of the week, having listened to lots of the podcasting canon, the three CRI broadcasters agreed with my proposition that podcasting created 'enhanced intimacy' compared to radio. But it would take a bit of research for me to understand how charged the whole notion of expressing intimacy in China was.

Ideas of intimacy: Chinese podcasting in context

I found that with recent globalisation and economic growth, many Chinese are reclaiming personal space, a development that scholars Wanning Sun and Wei Lei call the 'privatisation of the self'. Wei did her PhD, 'Radio and Social Transformation in China', at the University of Technology Sydney under Sun's supervision. I stumbled across it in a Google search (it has since been published as a book) and got sucked down a fascinating rabbit hole, as she described how market-driven transformation post-Mao has changed perceptions of intimacy and class, and how this was directly mediated by radio and proto-podcast formats. It may be the first time I addictively read a PhD and I was delighted to meet Wei Lei at a radio conference in 2018. Wei is young and outgoing, based back in Beijing after her studies in Australia, and so keen to spread the love of audio that she translated some of my articles into Mandarin (a first!).

Let me give you a brief peek into Wei's historical analysis. With the economic reforms that began in China in 1978, radio moved from being an instrument of propaganda, collectively listened to on loudspeakers, to focusing on what Wei calls 'the mass production of intimacy'. From the 1990s, people in China started to find intimacy and connection by sharing personal stories with the hosts of purposely created late-night talkback shows, listened to in private. This was a hugely novel experience in a country where, as Yan Lianke asserts, communism had for decades 'made it impossible to express true feelings in conscious life'. The radio host dispenses advice, sometimes chidingly. Most importantly, the host provides a listening ear, knowing that the community of listeners is developing its own intimacy just by being present.[6]

New 'drive' formats also evolved to service wealthier listeners, who increasingly have cars. This was not a time-based slot, as in the West, but a whole radio channel earmarked for privileged in-car listening. One show, *Car World*, moved from discussing car models and performance to catering to the well-heeled demographic's broader interests, featuring tourism and travel slots, and a discussion of public issues such as governance and infrastructure to which only these middle-class listeners were deemed worthy of making a contribution. Another show aimed squarely at a poorer group of car owners: taxi drivers. *Ordinary Folks Taxi* dispensed everything from medical advice to matchmaking. Other carefully controlled content on Chinese radio into the new millennium has included news, a health infomercial show, children's shows, drama and music.

Mao's Cultural Revolution (1966–76) annihilated the concept of sentimental value in China, Yan asserts. But with the help of the internet, it is coming back, via access to local versions of social media (the platform Weibo combines elements of Twitter, Facebook and *Medium*, while WeChat (weixin), a mobile messaging app founded by Tencent in 2011, is also widespread), popular culture memes and online audio formats. Wei Lei describes two main categories of popular audio products distributed via apps and online platforms. The first, 'healing' content, offers support on personal and relationship issues and resonates strongly with women, including university students and lonely rural workers transplanted to the city. The second, 'knowledge products', includes audio books, business, education and finance shows, playing to those hoping to gain an edge in a highly competitive society. One popular product is Get it (dedao).

Behind the picture of a booming Chinese economy that we see in the West, and within the constraints that govern China-based academics, Wei excavates the human complexities and tensions that drive all this listening. It is far from rosy. China's new class of white-collar workers are called 'mind-driven labour'; they commonly use words like 'anxiety', 'challenge' and 'hopelessness' in describing themselves. Young students and rural workers transplanted to the booming city economies feel vulnerable and isolated. Sophisticated city-dwellers sometimes listen in to the popular talkback shows on love and family, mocking as mere entertainment the heartfelt experiences that poorer or regional people relate. Even the accomplished broadcaster L told me that although he'd love to create a passion podcast on Chinese mythologies, he wouldn't feel comfortable presenting it in his own language, because his accent would reveal his humble village origins, which his smooth English conceals. Indeed, one of the most popular self-improvement podcasts teaches people – for a fee – how to disguise regional accents.

The podcast market in China:
Education and personal stories

A core characteristic Yan ascribes to China is pragmatism, and that too is being manifested via the many Chinese seeking this 'pay-for-knowledge' self-improvement content. Offerings tend to be short (under ten minutes) and simple, constructed of voice and music, without fancy production. The numbers for these 'meta-podcasts' are staggering: Ximalaya FM, China's biggest platform for shared audio content, reported 600 million downloads of its app by 2019. It has invested in an American podcasting distribution start-up, Himalaya Media, which can monetise content by having listeners 'tip' small amounts.

In 2018, *Marketplace* estimated China's commercial podcast market to be worth over US$7 billion a year, based largely on subscribers who pay to access self-help and educational content. Another podcasting company, Lizhi (Lychee), allows listeners to also post content; it was listed on Nasdaq in January 2020. As of June 2020, *Tech Crunch* reported, 56 million people used Lizhi monthly and six million of those created content. Dragonfly FM (Qingting FM), which offers a mix of audio books, music, advice, dramas, educational and children's content, is the third big Chinese audio platform. Interestingly, Xiaoyuzhou FM, a podcasting app launched in March 2020, has adopted a more indie-led approach, enabling manual subscriptions through RSS feeds, and encouraging users to leave feedback, thereby building a sense of a listener community.

Perhaps most interesting of all are the plethora of podcasts that have emerged organically in the last few years and have thus far largely managed to sidestep the constraints applied to more high-profile media such as reality TV. It is much harder for the state to track and monitor audio content: a side-benefit of audio existing only in real time. AI can do facial recognition and detect 'offensive' images such as the recently banned 'sissy men', but who is able to listen to every word of every new podcast that pops up, in order to discern subversive material?

Podcasting, therefore, offers a way of exploring the more nuanced aspects of life, and the vulnerable sides of Chinese society are being aired in *Gushi FM*, a long-form storytelling show founded in 2017 by host Kou Aizhe, modelled on *This American Life* and *Snap Judgment*. With an estimated audience of 1.2 million, *Gushi FM* (also known as *Story FM*) tells gritty human stories, in the first person, which mostly manage to get past the censors. Topics have included a lesbian who married a gay man, a teacher describing how she was molested in a village, and a sex worker who was duped into the industry. Only two of some 500 episodes have been removed, 38-year-old Kou told Agence France Presse (AFP): one on peer-to-peer lending and another about job losses during the pandemic.

In 2020, *The Economist* reported on other controversial niche podcasts. *The Weirdo*, hosted by three former journalists, discussed in one episode 'the challenges that Chinese men face if they identify as feminists, and the problem of racism in China towards black people'. AFP published a photo of the three hosts at a packed-out live show, recorded in a Beijing bookshop in 2021. The 'counternarrative' they provide is directed at young, university-educated urban listeners, who appreciate podcasting as a space to at least push back at orthodoxy. *The Unemployable* podcast caters to listeners who reject the 996 model (work 9 am to 9 pm, six days a week) advocated by Chinese employers and instead pursue travel, gap years and freelance options. But some podcasts have crossed the unwritten line. In 2021, AFP reported that an episode of *SurplusValue* vanished from Chinese apps – the cultural podcast's interview with a professor about the pandemic's impact involved some critical anti-government views. The show was cancelled.

The Chinese diaspora is tapping into the podcast boom. *Loud Murmurs* is a feminist Mandarin-language chatcast produced since 2018 by four bi-cultural Chinese women in New York. Host Afra Wang left China in 2012 and completed a master's degree in international history at Columbia University and the London School of Economics. As a girl, she wrote, she dutifully 'performed the weekly speech under the National Flag on Mondays and delivered high-scoring essays praising

Chinese writer Lu Xun as the patriotic force in anti-dictatorship and anti-imperialist struggles'. But she also imbibed US movies and TV shows, from *Star Wars* to *Home Alone*, trying to devine the broader political and social context. 'I learned the basics of bipartisanship from the comedian Jon Stewart, and I learned about racial problems and religious tension through the nihilistic humour of *South Park*', she notes. As an expat, in the wake of the #MeToo movement, Wang began to detect the more toxic aspects of US movie culture, and co-established *Loud Murmurs* to deconstruct for other Chinese women, how the industry contributed 'to the systematic devaluation, dismissal and suppression of women's voices'.[7]

AFP estimates that around 7000 new podcasts launched in 2020, with a combined audience of ten million. Yi Yang, a Shanghai-based producer, edits the Chinese-language *JustPod* newsletter, modelled on the popular *Hot Pod*. Yang organises an industry gathering called PodFest China, and is developing his JustPod company based on networks such as Wondery and Gimlet Media in the US. With car makers starting to build livestream podcasts into new electric car entertainment systems, the potential for expansion in China is massive.

But few Chinese are conversant with the US podcasting scene. Back in 2018, I ran another podcasting session in Sydney for a delegation of cosmopolitan CRI broadcasters. I hesitated before showing a slide about *Serial.* It was by then hitting almost 500 million downloads – surely it was old hat? 'What do you know about *Serial*?' I asked, before hitting play. There was a perplexed pause. 'Isn't it something Westerners like to eat for breakfast?' one man politely ventured. He wasn't trying to be funny.

That showed me just how powerful cultural silos are, internet or no internet. It also points to the importance of diversity in podcasting: representing diverse cultural and minority perspectives in the content, and having people of diverse and marginalised backgrounds among the content makers. That is one of the hottest topics in podcasting today, canvassed in the next section.

Equality, diversity and inclusion:
A reckoning

About ten years ago – yes, as late as that – I began to realise that my beloved audio community had a whiteness issue. Until then, I guess, I had never really seen or thought much about the *faces* behind the audio I listened to – I just communed with their voices. Then, agog with anticipation, I attended my first Third Coast audio festival in Chicago in 2011. My husband, Chris, and I started our six-week road trip in New Orleans, where we stayed in Treme, the oldest African American neighbourhood in the US. We picked that location deliberately as a homage to the HBO series *Treme*, which honoured the area's galvanising music and culture. One night we went to see the Treme Brass Band from the series play in a local venue, an evening made all the more special when a friendly waitress arranged a ride home for us – with none other than the illustrious bandleader and snare drummer, Benny Jones Senior. We were only staying a few blocks away but the waitress deemed it unsafe for two ignorant white folk to be wandering round there at night, so a genial Benny put us in the front seat of his pick-up. A hopeless groupie, I remember being so overwhelmed I could barely speak, as he waved goodbye and left me his business card.

From New Orleans, we drove to Washington DC, stopping in little towns along the way. It was the 150th anniversary of the start of the US Civil War and with memorialising underway throughout the South, it was impossible not to see all over again how racism and slavery were the ugly cornerstones on which the US was built. Eventually we arrived at Third Coast, still pondering the shocking politics of race, to a welcoming event of beer and pizza. We chitchatted with other audio lovers, all of us excited about the audio delights ahead. They were smart, interesting, likeable – and overwhelmingly *white*.

The only non-white face I saw in the room that night belonged to Christopher Johnson, then a San Francisco–based producer, whose audio feature was shortlisted for a prize at the Third Coast Competition awards, and would be played at a communal listening event the next day. Gingerly, we asked Christopher how he felt about being in such a minority as a person of colour at that event. He said he was pleased that we had raised the topic, rather than ignore it. He described, with feeling, how isolating it was to be a black producer in the extremely white world of audio production at the time. Later I tried, unsuccessfully, to get Christopher to Australia on a fellowship. In 2020 he produced the acclaimed podcast *Slow Burn* for a series that examined the life of the notorious Ku Klux Klan president, David Duke. The show made a point of not interviewing Duke himself – a silencing that symbolically perhaps mirrored the way people of colour have been sidelined by mainstream media for so long.

Diverse voices: Representation in Western podcasting

Granular data is hard to come by, but prior to *Serial*'s breakthrough, only an estimated 12 per cent of US podcast hosts were female.[8] Back on that trip in 2011, I recall I was elated to find Third Coast being run by three women: co-founders Johanna Zorn and Julie Shapiro; and producer Katie Mingle, later with the famous *99% Invisible* podcast about design, and where Christopher Johnson is now a supervising producer. In 2014, *99% Invisible* host Roman Mars would co-found Radiotopia, where Julie would become executive producer, and where one of her proudest achievements would be to launch *Ear Hustle*, a podcast hosted by two black prisoners, Earlonne Woods and Rahsaan 'New York' Thomas, along with the artist Nigel Poor. In a remarkable demonstration of podcasting's impact, Earlonne's sentence was commuted by California governor Jerry Brown, who cited Earlonne's work on the podcast as influencing his momentous decision. Earlonne continues to work on the podcast from the outside.

Julie Shapiro and her colleagues were, and are, the absolute opposite of people who sought to exploit white privilege. So how could Third Coast have been so white that year? Talking to Julie in 2021 for this book, I mentioned how jarring this apparent lack of representation now seemed. Was it that they were unaware of it as an issue? Not at all, she told me: 'We talked about it every time we put a conference list together, we saw what was lacking in it'. Yet they were hamstrung by the system they had inherited via public radio and other audio institutions:

> The professional industry we spring forth from was established in a very white-centric way. We felt limited by our options in a way. And of course, we could have gone outside that industry. And now it would be more obvious to do that because there are people from other industries around podcasting, around audio production, in a much more present way. But yeah, it was a systemic shortcoming for a long long time. And that's what's coming up now. That's what people are realising and confronting, and feeling the pain about all of those years.

Diversity at the BBC

Lack of diversity wasn't just an issue in the US audio world, of course. In the UK, the BBC created a new position, Director of Creative Diversity, in June 2019. They headhunted television presenter and author June Sarpong for the job: her book *The Power of Privilege* was described by the *Guardian* as 'a smart and digestible manual on how white people can challenge racism'. Sarpong, whose heritage is Ghanaian, will oversee the BBC's pledge to have 20 per cent of its workforce come from diverse backgrounds. Then, in mid-2021, a new unit called BBC Sounds Audio Lab launched an exciting initiative to support six new 'audio creatives' to make a podcast that would 'get the UK talking'. The program particularly welcomes 'ideas from diverse audio creators from under-represented groups across the UK including Black, Asian & Minority Ethnic; LGBTQIA+, disabled and lower socio-economic backgrounds'. Applicants must have some audio experience (one year minimum), but there is real scope for innovation. Successful applicants will be mentored and, importantly, properly paid throughout training and production. Also in 2021, former Radio Production Head at BBC Bristol Clare McGinn set up the BBC Audio Creative Development Unit 'to hatch, match and despatch big public service podcast ideas for BBC Sounds', but also to think about audio-led projects with impact outside the UK. Starting with a team of three, the CDU's remit is to build partnerships across and outside the BBC with the aim of opening doors for fresh ideas and new people. Clare told me how BBC Sounds' trans-UK model has in itself opened up a subtle correction to representation. 'What's been brilliant for BBC program makers outside of London is that there are more routes to commission for stories rooted in communities which have not been heard before. And what's emerging is really exciting.' She cites podcasts like *The Northern Bank Job*, made by BBC Northern Ireland, *Ecstasy: The Battle of Rave from Manchester*, and *Who Killed Emma?*, a gritty BBC Scotland investigation into the murder of a prostitute that treats prostitutes (the Glasgow women interviewed preferred that term to 'sex worker') with nuance and respect. 'Now production teams have the space and time to tell stories authentically with fewer filters', Clare observes.

Addressing diversity has other dimensions too, she says. 'Class and identity need to be considered.' The BBC historically shaped the broadcast sound of the nation with a preference for 'received pronunciation' ('posh' English voices and accents), particularly on national radio. This excluded and alienated many people. With podcasts, the voices and stories coming through across the BBC are changing. Check out *The YUNGBLUD Podcast* and *Songs to Live By* to hear the difference.

An independent producer (who for obvious reasons can't be named) told me that during a recent round of BBC Radio 4 offers for documentaries and arts, 'the people we deal with are virtually identical in terms of race, age, class, education (private school – Oxbridge), work experience (*Today* program news journos) and temperament.' But Clare McGinn, who grew up far from an Oxbridge (Oxford/Cambridge) background, in Belfast, cites Mohit Bakaya, current controller of Radio 4 and of Indian heritage, as someone who has been actively pressing for changes to the sound of the network. 'He has championed presenters like Grace Dent, a restaurant critic from Cumbria in the North West of England as host of the storytelling show *The Untold*; Lauren Laverne, from Sunderland in the north-east of England, took the helm at *Desert Island Discs*, and Chris Mason, a Yorkshireman, replaced Jonathan Dimbleby as presenter of the BBC's longest running political debate show *Any Questions*. And most recently, journalist Amol Rajan, a savvy working-class Londoner, has joined the prestigious *Today* program line-up.'

All of these appointments have not been without criticism from die-hard listeners who hanker for the old-world order, Clare adds. Indeed, in 2020, when Yorkshire academic Dr Katie Edwards presented a Radio 4 religious program, *Beyond Belief*, she received this snide email: 'Dear Dr Edwards ... I wish the BBC wouldn't impose their diversity agenda on the listener. You've been chosen because of the way you speak and you've obviously done very well for yourself despite your evidently difficult background. Good for you! While you have my admiration for making something of yourself, I want to hear a presenter who speaks correctly ... Congratulations on your (I'm sure very many) achievements but you do not belong on Radio 4.' Edwards, who has a first class degree and a PhD in Biblical Studies, evidently was not fazed. She is now an author, 'recovering academic' and co-host of the podcast *Noirthern*, which enthusiastically examines 'Northern noir' crime fiction.

The Equality in Audio Pact

The murder of George Floyd in Minneapolis on 25 May 2020 galvanised the simmering #BlackLivesMatter movement. The same day, in New

York's Central Park, a white woman called Amy Cooper called the police, alleging that a black man, Christian Cooper (no relation), was threatening her life. In fact, the man, a keen birdwatcher, had merely asked her to put her dog on the leash, as regulations demanded. His video of Amy Cooper's misrepresentation of the incident went viral on Twitter, fuelling intense debates over the entitlement of white people and discrimination against people of colour.

For Renay Richardson, a black British audio producer who founded the company Broccoli Productions, the two incidents were a breaking point. As she told *Hot Pod*, 'When it comes to the audio industry, I, like many black people in the industry, have been ignored when speaking of our treatment. Many of us are shut down, and many are fearful of the repercussions if we speak up'. Following a week of global unrest supporting #BlackLivesMatter, and after discussions with colleagues, Richardson decided to create 'a five-point pact that could lead to change'.

The resulting Equality in Audio Pact was concise:

1   Pay interns / No longer use unpaid interns.
2   Hire LGBTQIA+, black people, people of colour and other minorities on projects not only related to their identity.
3   If you are a company that releases gender pay gap reports, release your race pay gap data at the same time.
4   No longer participate in panels that are not representative of the cities, towns, and industries they take place in.
5   Be transparent about who works for your company, as well as their role, position and permanency.

Before going public, Richardson secured several independent companies as signatories. At around 9 am on 2 June 2020, she tweeted the sign-up form. 'I then @'d all the white people who usually ignore me. Strategic public shaming', she told *Hot Pod*. It worked. 'By the end of day one we had 53 companies signed up including Acast, Transmitter Media, and

Third Coast.' By time of writing, that had grown to over 350, including big names such as Spotify UK, Wondery, iHeartMedia and BBC Radio.

Recent initiatives at Google Podcasts

Stung by reports of the shocking lack of diversity in its own workforce, tech giant Google started to make amends by funding the Google Podcasts creator program in 2018. Partnering with Boston-based media company PRX, the plan was 'to focus on empowering and training under-represented people, offering free educational tools and showcasing their work'. In 2019, on a panel I instigated for the last ever Global Editors Network (GEN) media summit, audio veteran Mark Pagán from PRX revealed the first round of Google Podcasts creator participants. The projects included *City of Women*, 'a joyride into the minds of women and the streets of Bangalore'; *AfroQueer*, from Nairobi, Kenya, about 'queer Africans living, loving, surviving and thriving on the African continent and in the diaspora'; *Long Distance*, stories of the Filipino diaspora; *Who Taught You How to Drive?!*, 'a quirky, comical, look at identity through driving'; and *Las Raras*, Spanish-language stories of social change and minority voices from Chile. Other shows had links to Colombia, Brazil, Spain and Lebanon. These new podcasters were put through a 12-week boot camp in the US and mentored in all aspects of podcast production, from the technical to the marketing side, and each given US$12 000 to establish their show.

In 2020, a second round of the podcast creator competition selected 20 winners from Brazil, Canada, Costa Rica, Cuba, Jordan, Mexico, Nigeria, Panama, Turkey, Zambia and the United States. Shows included *Vietnamese Boat People*, tales of the almost two million people who fled Vietnam after the war, and *Leading Ladies*, featuring historical, hidden narratives of women leaders in Zambia who held prominent positions of power before colonialism.

The more the audio industry represents the actual world it
exists in – rather than just a single homogenous group of
people – the more creative and exciting it'll be.

– Eleanor McDowall, Falling Tree Productions

Pledge for change at PRX

The Google/PRX initiative is genuinely helping to empower people
from under-represented groups in podcasting. PRX is highly regarded in
public media circles as 'a non-profit media company shaping the future
of audio by producing and distributing content, building technology,
and training talent.' Described as 'a fierce champion of new voices',
its iconic shows include *This American Life*, *TED Talks Daily*, *The
Takeaway*, *Snap Judgment*, *Latino USA*, *Reveal*, *The Moth Radio Hour*
and the esteemed Radiotopia network of independent artists. So it was
a shock when, in August 2020, PRX employee Palace Shaw decided
to quit the organisation because, as a black woman, she felt alienated
and discriminated against. Shaw had been employed as the community
manager of a PRX initiative in Boston called Podcast Garage, a
community recording studio, classroom and event space for audio
storytellers of all experience levels. She emailed colleagues her reasons
for choosing unemployment at a time of pandemic and economic crisis,
later published online.

Shaw's grievances included being paid less than white, male
colleagues while doing more work than them. She reported having
her hair touched without her consent by the (white) PRX CEO, Kerri
Hoffman. Shaw accepted Hoffman's swift apology, but complained
about the incident to human resources: 'They chose to defend Kerri by
not acknowledging the obviously racialized nature of the interaction,
which I was very clear about. I was told, "I am sorry if that made you feel
othered"'. Shaw was the fourth black woman to leave PRX in less than a

year. She concluded: 'Any one of these things, the hair touching, the pay, the loss of my Black coworkers, the toxic work environment are enough reason to leave – but together they demonstrate PRX's inability to treat Black women with dignity and respect'.

Hoffman responded with a public apology, pledging to do better. 'We have to address structural racism in our culture, policies, and practices. We have deep work to do – it is hard and uncomfortable, but essential.' PRX hired a respected Boston law firm, Prince Lobel, to investigate Shaw's assertions. It 'did not uncover any evidence of unlawful discrimination or harassment', Caroline Crampton reported in *Hot Pod*. Nor did the three other employees cite 'mistreatment because they were Black women as a motivating reason for leaving PRX', PRX elaborated. It acknowledged that the investigation did, however, find 'unconscious bias and "microaggressions" that tended to make the work experience for some BIPOC employees difficult'.

In solidarity, Helen Zaltzman, UK host of the hit podcast about language, *The Allusionist*, quit the Radiotopia network. A member since its inception, she wrote that she had long felt uncomfortable about how white the network was:

> Why am I telling you about this? Well, as a message to white people in organisations which are failing on inclusion: we have to speak up, and keep speaking up; to use pester power even if we have no other power. Yes, you might feel like a jerk. That's fine! This isn't about you! Do what you can do. And if there is limited space and resources, you may have to get out of the way.

Over at podcast company Gimlet, black producer James T Green wrote a substantial public blog in February 2021 about how he was denied opportunities and pay parity with white producers (see also chapter 10).[9] Around the same time, Celeste Headlee, an award-winning, veteran black public-radio reporter, published a manifesto aimed at redressing the systemic problems around racism, inequality and lack of diversity.

'An Anti-Racist Future: A Vision and Plan for the Transformation of Public Media' is divided into five sections: amends; hiring, promotions and pay structures; training; transforming coverage; and accountability. As she writes in the introduction:

> White supremacist culture and anti-Blackness shape the policies, norms, and standards of public radio. They determine whose opinions are valued, whose voices are heard, whose stories are told and taken seriously, who is promoted, and whose resume never gets a second glance. Historically, Black on-air talent are told their dialect and speaking voices do not fit the public radio prototype. There is a strong bias against journalists who have a distinct ethnic or regional tone in their vocal delivery.[10]

It remains to be seen how much diversity and equality the audio industry landscape is willing to achieve. Radiotopia is facilitating shows by other marginalised people, such as people with disabilities, and has taken serious steps to address the diversity issue. 'We're revamping the *Showcase* series into *Radiotopia Presents* ... a space where we're really prioritizing working with BIPOC creators', says executive producer Julie Shapiro. 'We're working hard and intentionally to support more diversity in the network.' *S***hole Country* podcast, launched October 2021, is a refreshingly original example. 'An audio memoir about achieving the Ghanaian-American dream', its title derives from then President Donald Trump's disparaging 2018 description of Haiti, El Salvador and some African countries as 'shitholes'. The engaging thirty-something host, who goes by the pseudonym Afia Kaakyire, delves into family history and self-discovery, telling 'true tales dipped in entrepreneurial dreams, green card anxieties, complicated love', and more. 'She blends a subtle but killer sense of humor with sharp wit, keen details and bold moments of vulnerability', says Julie Shapiro, who is co-executive producer.

In April 2021, after a months-long consultative process, PRX appointed a new Senior Director of Diversity, Equity and Inclusion,

Dr Byron Green. Green has more than ten years' experience in running diversity programs. It's a good start.

African American academic and former NPR and commercial radio producer Kim Fox warns, however, that forging change is a shared responsibility. 'Stop putting the onus on us to fix the problem or making us in charge of diversity and inclusion,' she told me. A dynamo in the field of audio journalism education and podcasting studies (see chapter 10), Kim is a Professor of Practice, based at the American University in Cairo since 2009. She suggests a three-fold approach to rectifying 'the overbearing whiteness in podcasting': examine issues 'in the podcasting industry, in the hiring process and then in-house at media outlets and podcast production houses'.

Whiteness can be reinforced through seemingly innocuous measures such as requiring producers to have proficiency in the expensive audio production software Pro-Tools, Kim points out. 'Some people can't afford the program nor afford the resources to learn how to use it', she explains. 'In-house professional development opportunities are necessary along with leadership and mentorship initiatives.'

Kim wants to see people 'learning from the egregious patterns of behavior and microaggressions ... so that the cycle does not persist.' She adds drily: 'Rewarding bad behavior doesn't help.' Overall, Kim sounds (cautiously) optimistic. 'People who've latched on to power don't want to cede their positions, but there's a way to make space for others while maintaining your territory.' At an industry level, she welcomes recent research into the consumption habits of Black podcast listeners, which Edison has also established with US Latino audiences (see p. 243), to boost support for diverse content.[11] 'Too often the investment in non-white content is only decided when there is evidence of the potential of the investment.'

Finally, Kim wants to see a genuine commitment to change, rather than mere tokenism. 'The industry could do better by recognizing that having one Black person on their team/staff, isn't enough, nor is having just one Latino or one Asian or one queer person. We shouldn't be able to count the representation in the room.'

 ## Q&A with Patrick Abboud

Patrick (Pat) Abboud is a journalist, TV presenter, broadcaster and award-winning documentary maker. He is currently reporting and presenting for *The Project* on Network Ten while creating an eight-part true-crime podcast, *The Greatest Menace*, commissioned by Audible. In 2020 Pat did a stint hosting the ABC's *Conversations*, and he also heads up a gun team of storytellers on the ABC documentary podcast *Days like These*. He is the founder of irreverent news, satire and documentary program *The Feed* on SBS TV, and worked on *Dateline* and as host of the annual SBS Mardi Gras live TV broadcast. As a gay Australian of Palestinian and Lebanese background, Pat's unique insights on the arts and pop culture saw him curate, write and host an annual international queer cinema season on SBS, and a three-part entertainment series profiling Australian LGBTQIA+ filmmakers. As a correspondent, travelling through Europe, Asia, the USA and the Middle East, Pat has explored 53 countries.

What's your podcast The Greatest Menace about?

The Greatest Menace is an eight-part queer true-crime investigation into the world's only homosexual prison. It's a historical story with a contemporary personal narrative woven throughout. The story unfolds in a tiny Australian town with a big secret.

Why make it as a podcast – what does podcasting give you that other media formats like TV don't?

My co-producer Simon Cunich and I actually started this project as a TV documentary series and made the decision early on to switch to podcasting. We'd both been working in screen media for more than a decade and reached a point where we felt we needed to break form to push production boundaries a little further. The beauty of moving into podcasting is that we found this incredible freedom to be so much more creative. All of a sudden, there's no pictures to tell the story – you have to paint pictures with words and sounds and audio motifs. Sonically, podcasting can be so much more evocative than television. There's this deep intimacy and profound connection with characters and plot that comes with this mode of storytelling.

What have you learnt about making a narrative podcast through doing The Greatest Menace*?*

Making a story-driven series that's personal is difficult! It has taken more than three years to get the elements right – an absolute labour of love, time, commitment, passion, meticulous attention to detail and the desire to make something original that will cut through the noise. We've been living, eating and breathing this story for so long and the passion has remained the entire time. That tells me we were always onto a good story and I just hope we've found the right way to share it and build this intricate narrative that unfolds across the series. It sounds clichéd but very true for us on this project – always trust your instinct and don't feel like you have to follow storytelling 'rules'. In fact, make a point of breaking them … it's far more interesting for you and hopefully the listener.

Diversity and inclusion are hot topics in podcasting today. What's been your own experience of feeling seen and heard in the media? Is podcasting any different in this regard? How can we do better?

This is a huge question but I have a very simple answer ... Stop talking about diversity – just do it. No more check-box or token representation. Commissioners and executive producers need to acknowledge the lack of genuine opportunity for diverse storytellers. Seek them out, don't wait for them to come to you. Create pathways for these stories to be told from those with the lived experience to tell them authentically.

I chose to make this story as a narrative podcast series and share some of my experiences as a gay Arab man simply because there is such a lack of it in the wider media landscape. It felt less intimidating in a podcast language, too – I could write my own rules on what I'm comfortable with sharing. It's important to acknowledge that things are shifting. Some progressive TV networks, mainstream outlets, streaming platforms – they're finally listening. We are starting to see and hear more genuine diversity in storytelling. More of that, please! My hope is that emerging writers and storytellers also take more risks, challenge the powers that be to be more daring, and take chances, so we see bolder, less formulaic commissions that challenge the status quo.

What's the hardest thing about making a narrative podcast like The Greatest Menace?

Connecting the dots – making sure all of the storylines, characters, plot points intertwine in a way that keeps listeners stuck to your story. It's such an ongoing process of going over and over each episode to make sure that web is being woven the whole time, that you've planted seeds to keep the story evolving at the right pace – to ensure the listener is there with you every step of the way, to make them always want more. In an eight-part series, all of that has proven exceptionally difficult but we've loved the challenge. And then there's the sound design that you hope the listener indulges in with you ... that's a real craft to learn and if you get the sonics right – a strong overall sound that supports your story idea – it'll amplify the narrative.

And the most rewarding aspect?

It's an incredibly important moment in our LGBTQI+ past to unearth. The constant revelation and unexpected swerves make for a real cracker of a listen. But the most rewarding aspect for us as storytellers is knowing that hopefully we are contributing in some small part to righting a horrible injustice against the wider queer community. In some sense it feels like we are rewriting queer history. The social impact and holding those in power to account has been the driving force to us sticking with this project so long.

Any other tips and tricks for budding podcasters, especially those with non-mainstream voices?

- Don't make a podcast for the sake of making a podcast or because 'everyone's making a podcast'.
- Do your research; make sure your idea is well thought out.
- If the content of your podcast is similar to other podcasts, find ways to make yours different or unique.
- Stay true to your authentic self – tell the story the way *you* want to hear it.

- Experiment with audio and sound design – be daring sonically.

- Know your audience.

- Connect with your listeners. Build relevant content around your podcast.

- Get lots of experienced ears – strong storytellers you trust and admire – to listen and give you feedback before you put your podcast out.

- Push your creativity and enjoy the process.

Podcast growth in Latin America

Another positive change is happening in representation of the Latin American community. One of the earliest influences was *Radio Ambulante*, a narrative podcast show founded in 2011 by Carolina Guerrero, a journalist from Colombia, and Daniel Alarcón, a novelist from Peru and contributor to the *New Yorker* magazine. They were living in New York at the time and wanted to make 'uniquely Latin American stories in Spanish' for the huge Latino diaspora in the US, high-end crafted output that would bring the quality of long-form print journalism to audio. Five years in, they began to be distributed on NPR and they now employ more than 20 people, with each story taking an average of six months to be made.

I met Carolina at the GEN summit in Lisbon in 2018, when she came to my podcast storytelling workshop. She is warm, talented and driven – it's no surprise that *Radio Ambulante* is now a massive operation. 'From the beginning, we wanted our stories to have a universal appeal, so that everyone could somehow relate to them', she told *UNESCO Courier* magazine. 'They are not too newsworthy or too local – yet they are entertaining enough for a listener from the Bronx in New York to be interested in a story from Chile; or for someone from Colombia to be following a story from Guatemala.'

Radio Ambulante takes its audience very seriously. When they discovered a large percentage of listeners were non-Latinos using the podcast as a way to learn Spanish, they posted subtitled versions on YouTube. They also co-developed a dedicated language-learning app, Lupa, that combines *Radio Ambulante* stories with advanced tech features, enabling intermediate Spanish learners to rapidly become more fluent.

Other popular Spanish-language shows include *Chicas Poderosas* (Powerful Women), which tells stories of empowering women. The Chicas Poderosas organisation has local communities based in 16 countries – through South America and Central America, and in Spain, Portugal and the United States – and organises workshops, networking events and advocacy.

Among US Latinos, the hunger for content that addressed their community was evident back in the 1970s, mostly fed by community and public radio organisations. Maria Martin, then a young Mexican-American living in California, was entranced to hear bilingual songs and current affairs on her local Santa Rosa station. Soon she was a volunteer producer for a groundbreaking Hispanic women's talk show, *Somos Chicanas*. After a stint at NPR, in 1992 Martin teamed up with Texas radio station KUT and the University of Texas at Austin to develop a new half-hour news magazine called *Latino USA*. Martin was executive producer; she appointed Mexican American journalist Maria Hinojosa as host. *Latino USA* is now the longest-running Latino-focused radio/podcast in the US, is regularly in the top ten ratings and has won many awards, including a Peabody.

Latino USA is broadcast in English, but often draws on artfully integrated Spanish vernacular. As she wrote in *Reality Radio*, Martin's vision from the start was to make a program that valued craft as well as mission, and to see Latino Americans more authentically represented:

Often, when Latino communities were even considered, the focus was on viewing Hispanics as 'problem people' – that is, with the emphasis on stories about gangs and undocumented immigration. I wanted to create a radio vehicle that would portray the whole of the Latino experience, its complexity and diversity, its beauty and its pain.

Martin went on to make the major series *Después de las Guerras: Central America After the Wars* (2005), and currently directs a public-interest journalism centre based in Guatemala and in Texas. Meanwhile, in 2010, host Maria Hinojosa founded a nonprofit company, Futuro Media, which took over the running of *Latino USA*. Based in Harlem, Futuro Media makes diverse content 'in the service of empowering people to navigate the complexities of an increasingly diverse and connected world'. Among its other offerings are the political podcast *In the Thick*, the website Latino Rebels, and Futuro Studios, a creative division that produces a suite of highly produced original podcasts. They include an engaging study of Puerto Rican culture (*La Brega*), a gut-wrenching narrative podcast about young people imprisoned in the US for life (*Suave*), and *TransLash Podcast with Imara Jones*, 'where trans people and allies talk back about what matters most and discuss how to create a fairer world for all'.

In 2021, Edison, the most established podcast research company in the world, published its second report into podcast consumption habits among US Latinos.[12] It found that 36 per cent of US Latinos listened monthly to podcasts, up from 25 per cent the year before. (Overall, 40 per cent of US adults listen monthly.) While more than half of respondents said they had started listening during the COVID-19 pandemic, more than 95 per cent of monthly listeners also said they intended to keep listening post-pandemic. Interestingly, almost half reported listening while at home with family and friends, compared to only about one in five US listeners in general. In contrast, in the UK, 92 per cent of people listen alone.

Storming in from the margins

Now, the bad news: media culture and institutions have historically favoured people who are some or all of the following – white, middle class, cis gender, heterosexual, able-bodied male. The good news: podcasting is facilitating a pushback from those who do not fall into those categories. There has been an explosion of new shows from people of colour, women, the LGBQTIA+ community and people with disabilities, and from marginalised and previously unheard voices of all sorts. There are far too many such podcasts to survey here, but let me show you a tiny part of the range.

In the Middle East, the podcast *Eib* (Shame) has discussed topics that are taboo in many countries in the region, such as abortion, divorce, sexuality and rape. Produced in Jordan, it has a big listenership in neighbouring countries such as Saudi Arabia, where women's rights are still abysmal. It's part of a podcasting network called Sowt (Voice), which has also produced a podcast about statelessness (*Blank Maps*) and covered topics such as the relationship between religion and the state in the Arab world. Kerning Cultures, another big podcast network in the region, is female-led and the first venture-funded podcast company in the Middle East. It creates 'award-winning immersive Arabic and English podcasts for curious listeners', with high production standards, a blend of talk and narrative formats.

Indian podcasts have also taken off. The IVM Podcasts network, led by the ebullient Amit Doshi, has an ever-growing stable on topics 'ranging from sports to style and public policy to pop culture (and more that don't fit this alliterative sentence structure)'. They are mostly interview shows and chatcasts, come in various languages, and are slickly packaged and marketed. At the other end of the scale, *India Explained* is amateur but fun. It started as two expat Indians, one in the UK and the other in the US, ruminating on such pressing topics as why so many Indian actors have moustaches, or the three kinds of Indian uncles. But since president Narendra Modi began pursuing citizenship changes that would make Indian Muslims a clear underclass, the conversations have taken a much more serious turn, decrying Hindu jingoism and articulating clear opposition to Modi's policy on things like 'censorship of COVID-19-related news' and 'the compliance of Facebook, Twitter, and much of the Indian media in following government diktats'. In Indonesia, the NOICE audio content app claims to have close to 800 000 registered listeners, with consumption of over 100 original shows doubling to 60 minutes per day in just 12 months.[13]

Fiction podcasts are fostering expression for all kinds of new voices, in innovative ways. Malaysia launched its first 'psychological thriller' podcast in 2021, *Malpraktis Universiti*: 'Set in Kuala Lumpur at the height of the pandemic, a psychologist faces huge problems at home and begins to unravel, leading to an unexpected chain of events'. It's produced by the ZAG network, based in South-East Asia, which is 'breaking down barriers for diverse creators to bring to life fresh ideas, characters and formats through unique audio experiences'.

In Australia, *Love and Luck* is 'a slice of life queer romance story with a touch of magic', which is told via voicemails. Australia's first LGBTQIA+ audio drama podcast, it's remarkable in other ways: it's made by an all-queer, all-Melbourne crew, and written, conceptualised and co-produced by Erin Kyan, a queer, disabled trans man. And it deliberately set out to be feel-good. 'The story is about people who fall in love, learn they have magic powers, and use those powers to support and protect their community. The good guys win, no one dies, and queer people of all types are all loved and valued.'

A very different podcast whose creator is at the intersection of gay and disabled is CBC's *Disability After Dark*, in which host Andrew Gurza, a wheelchair user, 'shines a bright light on issues about sex and disability' and 'shares his lived experiences of disability, queerness, sexuality and body image in a raw, vulnerable and unapologetic fashion'. In the nonfiction world, renowned LGBTQIA+ podcasts include *Nancy* (now defunct), *Getting Curious with Jonathan Van Ness*, *Making Gay History*, *Gayish* and *Lez Hang Out*.

Culturally diverse podcasting has also taken off in Australia. *Hey Aunty* is a multicultural black women's podcast hosted by Shantel Wetherall, who has Belizean/British heritage. Launched in 2018, and in abeyance for now, it was billed as 'fireside chats with black women, fems and non-binary siblings who've been there'. It features frank and often funny interviews with women from diverse cultures on baldly described topics such as 'How'd you deal with a dickhead' and 'Should I still be code switching?'.

In the US, major podcasting networks have started to support strong narrative and chumcast podcasts hosted and/or made by black journalists and creatives. In the aftermath of the George Floyd protests, Gimlet produced *Resistance*, hosted and co-created by Saidu Tejan-Thomas Jr, a poet and journalist born in Sierra Leone and based in the US. In *Driving the Green Book*, from Amazon affiliate Macmillan Podcasts, BBC broadcaster Alvin Hall and activist/social justice trainer Janée Woods Weber retrace a travel guide called *The Negro Motorist Green Book*, a book produced at the height of segregation, and uncover powerful social history.

Acclaimed longstanding shows such as NPR's *Reveal*, hosted by Al Letson, and *Snap Judgment* with Glynn Washington continue to be popular, alongside classics such as the *New York Times* podcast *Still Processing*, in which Wesley Morris and Jenna Wortham dissect cultural issues, and other chumcasts like *Code Switch*, *The Read*, *Truth Be Told* and *Scam Goddess*. But there are lots of indie, edgy voices too, which flourish in what academic Sarah Florini calls 'a vibrant network of Black podcasters, some of whom refer to themselves as the "Chitlin' Circuit" or "urban podcasters"'.[14] See also the website Podcasts in Color, which lists around a thousand podcasts made by people of colour.

In the UK, Renay Richardson's company Broccoli Productions was founded in 2018 to tell stories that empower. As its blurb describes:

> Our name comes of course from the noble vegetable that nobody wants to eat. That's a joke, but the idea of serving up sustenance

along with our shows isn't. All Broccoli projects are guided by
our core mission to bring more minority talent both in front and
behind the mic so that whenever you listen to our shows, you'll
hear voices and experiences that sound like yours. Now go eat
your Broccoli.

Shows include *Zombiemum*, exploring mental health and parent-
hood; *Anthems*, compelling short monologues from remarkable people;
and *Human Resources*, which examines Britain's involvement with the
transatlantic slave trade and how it affects every part of the nation.

Diversity in Europe: The Prix Europa

Meanwhile, in Europe, some white folk are taking Renay Richardson's
Equality in Audio pact to heart and proactively calling out lack of
representation. One incident concerns the Prix Europa, a pan-European
broadcasting festival founded by the European Parliament, the European
Commission and the European Cultural Foundation in 1987. Each year
it awards prizes in various categories, including radio documentaries
and digital audio. In 2020, independent UK production company
Falling Tree Productions had two works shortlisted. To their dismay, the
37-member jury, comprised of representatives of European broadcast
organisations and independents, was all white. Falling Tree flagged the
Equality in Audio Pact, pointing to Item 4 about representation. But
although the Prix Europa's mission statement declares that it has 'taken
up the cause of fighting for the fellowship of Europe and all its cultural
diversity', it was not open to discussing the matter at the time. Falling
Tree withdrew its entries in protest. They were listed on the listening
schedule for festival attendees as simply 'cancelled'.

BBC Radio, also a signatory to the pact, did not boycott the event.
This, despite this statement by the then BBC Director of Radio and
Education, James Purnell, when the pact came out: 'We always consider

representation when we are invited to take part in panels, and we'll work with organisers to ensure that continues to be the case when it comes to audio industry events'. There was some ambiguity as to whether a jury was a 'panel' and whether the Prix Europa was able to monitor its participants. In the end, the BBC accepted a Special Commendation for a documentary about the Grenfell Tower fire in London, *Grenfell: Flat 142*, made by Kate Lamble for BBC Radio 4, and judged by the all-white group.

In *Hot Pod*, Renay Richardson put it bluntly: 'If your panel is all white, you're doing it wrong'. But when I contacted Prix Europa Festival Director Susanne Hoffmann, she offered some nuance. Jurors for the Prix Europa awards are made up of shortlisted entrants, not selected separately. 'Anybody can enter their production, there is no submission fee', she told me. 'From the productions entered a pre-selection is made and productions are nominated ... Our aim is to represent the *best* programmes of the year, this is why we exist, it's our essence.'

While she agreed that a 37-member all-white jury was 'unfortunate', Hoffmann noted that there was still diversity: 'they originated from 20 European countries, work for 30 different radio producing companies, as independents or on staff, as authors, directors, producers, etc. And the group didn't consist of just white men but also 27 women! I think one can call this at least in terms of gender a diverse group'. She also explained that they try to include people with a 'migration background', on the basis that a Turk in Germany, say, or a Bulgarian in Italy, might also feel marginalised. 'We will jump with joy at receiving work from diverse communities, from people with migration background, POC, LGBTQIA+, younger people, to hear these voices that haven't reached us so far', Hoffmann declares.

But such voices may need active help, such as financial support, to be able to take part. In 2021, independent Dutch audio producer Maartje Duin launched a protest action ahead of the October gathering of Prix Europa in Potsdam, Germany. 'We do not want the Prix Europa to become a Prix des Privilèges', her open letter ran. It called on Prix

Europa to ensure a more diverse pre-selection committee and suggested paying minority elements for their time as jurors. It also recommended establishing a travel and translation fund, actively recruiting entries from under-represented regions, and also putting the in situ festival online to facilitate access. Several dozen producers signed the letter (as did I), including the two Falling Tree directors, Alan Hall and Eleanor McDowall, who chose not to submit entries in 2021.

Falling Tree's stand comes at some cost, because as independent producers, they have to continuously compete for commissions, and prestigious Prix Europa awards on your CV play a part in how you are evaluated. But showing solidarity with the Equality in Audio Pact is core to their principles. 'Our values are resolutely public service values', founder Alan Hall explained. That can make things difficult at times. 'They don't transfer very easily into the commercial realm. We tend to want to make the kinds of series that only a public service broadcaster will recognise as deserving a commission.'

But even the public service broadcasters are dipping a toe into the commercial world now. In the final chapter, we'll look at how the commercialisation of podcasting may be extinguishing the very qualities that lie behind podcasting's appeal and growth.

10

Podcasting: What next?

In March 2020, as the world surfed the early waves of the COVID-19 pandemic, people started sharing images of lockdown and quarantine online. With live events cancelled, artists were stuck at home, and some began posting mini home concerts. One bunch of celebrities sang a collage version of John Lennon's *Imagine*, intended as a source of inspiration in tough times. The backlash on social media was ferocious, with people deriding the notion of rich stars singing the words 'imagine no possessions'.

In May that year, Australian celebrities featured in a video – not singing, but talking, in a parody of a public service announcement. 'We know things are hard right now', it runs. 'But now, more than ever ... it's time to think about how your choices affect others. So please. Please. Please! *Don't* start a podcast.' A breakfast radio host chimes in: 'You've probably already got a USB mic and a spare room ready to go'. 'And your mate Dave's got some interesting opinions', adds a noted TV journalist. Other famous faces chip in: 'But we're here to tell you: he doesn't. He really doesn't'. 'Don't start a podcast!' concludes a reality TV host, who happens to have his own podcast.

When I first saw the 90-second video, I laughed. Then I started getting tagged on social media by some of my students, who were outraged by what they saw as its elitist message. How dare a bunch of celebrities belittle ordinary people who are just trying to have a go? What gave them the right to shut the door just because they were already inside the room? The sketch polarised viewers. Younger people saw it as undermining the democratising role of podcasting, while older folk rolled their eyes in sympathy at the idea of stopping more boring, self-indulgent podcasts being inflicted on the world.

That some podcasts are tedious is not in question. Try *ROCpod: Talking with the Registered Organisations Commission*. It's produced by an Australian government body whose main focus, the regulation of employee and employer organisations, is actually really interesting – most of us are very concerned about our working conditions. I could imagine a show with fascinating stories of workplace stoushes and innovations, people talking about how they took on corporate bastardry or created an ideal work environment.

The title of one episode caught my eye: 'Spotlight on Whistle-blowing'. Whistleblowers have had huge impact, in all kinds of ways – think Chelsea Manning, Julian Assange, Edward Snowden and the Facebook/Cambridge Analytica scandals. This episode featured a guest academic who had conducted 'the world's leading research into public interest whistleblowing', surveying 17 000 respondents in 46 organisations. I settled in for some amazing stories. But I had to sit through 15 minutes of the 20-minute episode before I got to an anecdotal example about a guy who blew up unlawful trading at a major bank. Now, I'd have probably tried to interview that bank whistleblower, or at least include an archival clip. This guest was a public policy expert whose profile reveals remarkable achievements. But this conversation has not served him well; tighter editing would have helped.

But does it matter? Not everything in podcastland is supposed to be journalism, after all. If a *ROCpod* episode only had 60 downloads, who cares? The transcript is on the website and can be easily mined, and the Registered Organisations Commission has fulfilled its duty of interrogating policy. Part of me feels that this is what the 'long tail' of the internet is for: to accommodate all comers and give everyone a platform. The other part can't help feeling impatient. It's like knitting. By all means knit whatever items you want and invent your own designs, but don't drop stitches: get the basics right! It's about respecting your chosen outlet – which is, in the case of podcasting, the audio medium.

In late 2020 I ran a survey via social media to see how podcasters evaluated their own shows (I introduced you to some respondents in chapter 1). These independent podcasts covered the vast array of genres and topics available, from UK-based heritage conservation podcast *The C Word*, to Indian interview show *CurryUp Leadership*, an Australian cricket history called *Reverse Swept Radio*, and the business and finance advice show *Shares for Beginners*. Though their podcasts range from niche to modestly successful, all these podcasters relish the connections they make through their audio adventures: this appears to be a fundamental and universal motivation for non-corporate podcasters.

One respondent juggles an impressive array of roles. As a 'performer, writer, game designer and nerd for all seasons', Melbourne-based freelancer Ben McKenzie made a sci-fi comedy podcast called *Night Terrace*, and co-hosts the monthly book club podcast *Pratchat*. *Pratchat*, about the English author and humorist Terry Pratchett, gets around 2500–3000 downloads a month. It is crowdfunded, and it is 'the discussions and relationships with our community of listeners' that Ben loves most about podcasting. 'We tell them which book we're reading next and invite questions ... like any long-established fandom there are old-fashioned die-hards and plenty of fan wisdom, but we try to stick to our honest thoughts about the books, even when we are critical.'

To make podcasting a viable career option, Ben tells me he would like to see small independent podcasters supporting each other and organising, as a community, 'including a commitment to uplift and support diversity in hosts, subjects and producers'. At the time, I had a one-word reply – 'Radiotopia' – because Ben had just described the founding principle of the Boston-based network. But Ben was not optimistic about podcasting's future for freelancers. 'As an open platform it should present fewer barriers to creators of all backgrounds, but the reality is the medium is dominated by large studios and production companies ... Both have money and privilege to throw behind their shows.'

Ben's words were prescient. Since he wrote them, Radiotopia has lost its founder, Roman Mars, and foundational podcast, *99% Invisible*. Both have gone to SiriusXM, a satellite provider which in 2020 bought the podcast platform Stitcher for US$325 million. Roman Mars, symbol of indie podcasting in the US, will be playing alongside the likes of celebrity shows *Conan O'Brien Needs a Friend* and mega-hits *Office Ladies* and *The Sporkful*. Mars will ease the pain of his departure by donating US$1 million from the sale to Radiotopia, but the loss of *99% Invisible* is huge. Mars told the *New York Times* he was doing it to escape an increasing administrative burden. 'I've been devoted to independent podcasting for a really long time, and I still believe that there's a role for that in the world', he said. For many indie podcast fans and producers, it still felt like a sellout.

The march of corporate podcasting

Spotify, Amazon, Apple, Google and, most recently, Facebook have all muscled in on the podcasting boom. When the number of US listeners doubles in five years, and podcast advertising is up nearly 20 per cent in a year on many platforms, big money tends to sit up and take notice.

Amazon had long had a huge stake in the spoken-word online market, with its offshoot, Audible, being the world's largest purveyor of audio books since the 1990s. In 2015, on the heels of *Serial*'s success, Audible hired Eric Nuzum, former Vice President of Programming at NPR, as a senior content developer. Nuzum had overseen the rise of podcasting at NPR since 2005 and developed hit shows such as *Invisibilia*. In 2016, he launched a tranche of innovative podcasts behind the Audible paywall: a riveting fly-on-the-wall couples therapy session with charismatic Belgian counsellor Esther Perel, *Where Should We Begin*; a nuanced investigation of the porn industry by noted author Jon Ronson, *The Butterfly Effect*; and in the pipeline, an investigation into the murder of a glamorous French film producer in a picturesque

Irish village, *West Cork*. Nuzum left Audible in 2018, and the company has since developed offices in India and Australia, where it has had a slew of storytelling podcasts, and launched its first podcasts in Japan in 2020, partnering with public broadcaster NHK.

Swedish music streaming giant Spotify has stunned the podcasting world by spending almost US$1 billion on its aggressive consolidation since 2018. It has overtaken Apple in Android-dominated regions such as Latin America. In August 2021, Tom Webster of the respected Edison Research group in the US suggested Spotify had overtaken Apple Podcasts as the most-used podcast app there.[1] However, *Podnews*, 12 October 2021, carried certified data from Podtrac showing that Apple Podcasts produces seven times more streams/downloads of podcasts per user than Spotify. *Podnews* editor and prominent podcasting commentator James Cridland suggests that Apple Podcasts users are more committed podcast fans, while users of Spotify are still only occasional podcast listeners.[2] Spotify is unique, however, in that it owns so many aspects of podcast production: Anchor, a free platform for podcast creation; Gimlet, a network that creates premium content; and Megaphone (formerly Panoply), a podcast distribution and advertising sales company. As the final feather in its cap, Spotify started buying up exclusive rights to a range of podcasts: *The Ringer* from the Bill Simmons network, for fans of sport and pop culture; *The Joe Rogan Experience*, a hugely popular interview show; and story-driven network Parcast. Subsequently, it announced or released new podcasts by Kim Kardashian West and Michelle Obama; Bruce Springsteen and Barack Obama's *Renegades: Born in the USA*; *Call Your Daddy*; and, of all things, Prince Harry and Meghan Markle's *2020 Archewell Audio Holiday Special*, a deal worth a reported US$40 million but which has so far yielded only one 34-minute episode. It has also developed Spotify Original to make new podcast content, tested 90 global markets and launched (via Gimlet) a popular American fiction storytelling podcast, *Sandra*, in various languages and with cultural adaptations for Brazil, Germany, France and Mexico. The investment appears to have paid off:

Spotify reported in July 2021 that podcast listening was up by 95 per cent, and that ad revenue was up by a whopping 627 per cent, compared to the same period in 2020.

If you think it sounds like Spotify has the podcast future sewn up, think again. Eric Nuzum, now a freelance podcasting consultant, warned in his newsletter in January 2021 that there is a trade-off between the two Rs – reach and revenue:

> You can reach a lot of people *or* you can have a lot of revenue. Case in point: exclusive content. Those big [cheques] from platforms usually mean that your show is no longer available everywhere, just where the [cheque] writer wants it. Ask anyone who has ever taken one of those deals, and they'll tell you that their episodes are heard by a fraction of the people that heard them before.

James Cridland estimates that being with just Spotify loses fully 80 per cent of potential listeners.

Nuzum argues that what is more valuable to a podcaster than immediate dollars is data: information about audience that will help podcasters grow their numbers (and thereby attract advertisers). And the big-paying platforms are coy about that. As Nuzum concludes, 'The platform that figures out how to effectively and efficiently build reach – drawing more listeners to a targeted show – will be the one who wins the "platform wars". Creators will happily come to them'. Meanwhile, bespoke companies such as Chartable have emerged to fill the gap, providing podcasters with certified analytics on audience to attract advertisers, and helping advertisers understand the effectiveness of their podcast ads.

In April 2021, Apple made a long-anticipated move to monetise its widespread hosting of podcasts. Apple Podcast Subscriptions will allow podcast creators to charge listeners for a premium version of their show (extra content, ad-free, etc.). Creators pay US$19.99 a year as a flat fee for the service, and Apple takes 30 per cent of revenue the first year, dropping to 15 per cent in subsequent years. Creators also get access to crucial data: aggregated anonymised analytics such as where listeners are based, which might help them plan show tours and more. This initiative from Apple is a major shift. Though it will still offer a free catalogue of some two million podcasts, it has backed the idea of paying for podcasts for the first time. Although Apple Podcast Subscriptions is available to users in 170 countries, its iOS technology (the iPhone) is not globally dominant. Androids are more common overall, especially outside the US.

Facebook has also finally entered the podcasting arena. The data are enticing: 170 million users are connected to pages linked to a podcast, Facebook reports. In 2021, Facebook launched Live Audio Rooms, where people can host audio-only conversations, and 'Soundbites', for short podcast clips. Facebook is also launching an Audio Creator Fund. The company recently started allowing people to link their page to their podcast, which in turn will allow users to comment and share podcasts easily – a potentially huge development.

Public service broadcasters, too, are exploring the commercial side of podcasting. In the US, NPR has launched a pay-for-podcasts stream that allows you to get NPR podcasts free of ad content (usually promotions for other NPR shows). You can still get the free stream, with ads, but it's a shift in attitude. The BBC has long been funded by a licence fee paid by taxpayers, but the advent of BBC Sounds has shifted the emphasis away from the broadcaster's responsibility to their domestic, licence-paying audience, as they look towards ways of having more commercial, global impact.

The Missing Cryptoqueen (see chapter 3) has been one such success for the BBC. Everybody's on the lookout for 'the spin-off from the podcast', explains BBC executive Clare McGinn: 'Once the podcast is out there, television companies will come and they'll want the TV rights. And so *Cryptoqueen*, Jamie [Bartlett, the host] is writing a book; there's a bid for the TV drama, there's been interest from other TV companies to do their official partnership with the BBC on the documentary'. Podcasts are now partly a 'nursery' for bigger outcomes.

Podcast industry commentators

On topics related to the industry/business end of podcasting,
I recommend following these commentators, who manage to
keep abreast of this rapidly changing scene:

James Cridland is a British-born, Brisbane-based
'futurologist' with a snappy daily newsletter – *Podnews*,
packed with latest developments and job vacancies – and
a podcast, *Podland News*. His radio background dates to
the late 1980s, and in 2005 he launched the world's first
streaming radio smartphone app. These days he is an
internet strategist, keynote speaker and consultant.

Nick Quah is a Malaysian-born, US-based pod whisperer with
a deep understanding of both the creative and the business
aspects of podcasting and a distinctive, witty voice. He
charted podcasting trends for seven years in his newsletter,
Hot Pod, before selling it to Vox Media in 2021. It was taken
over by **Ashley Carman** of *The Verge*, while Quah moved to
being a full-time podcast critic at *Vulture*. Quah also hosted an
illuminating one-season podcast, *Servant of Pod*.

Eric Nuzum, based in the US, is a former Vice President of
Programming at NPR, and former executive in charge of
original audio content at Audible. He combines hands-on
knowledge of podcast production with a gruff industry voice,
and writes a newsletter, *The Audio Insurgent*.

Tom Webster, based in the US, is a Senior Vice President at
Edison Research and co-author of *The Infinite Dial*, America's
longest running research series on digital media consumption
and the gold standard for podcast consumption research. His
newsletter is called *I Hear Things*, and he writes commentary
at *Medium* <https://webby2001.medium.com>.

Other key commentators/sites

Kara Swisher, a journalist on general technology, industry and internet matters, has the podcasts *Sway* and *Pivot*, and writes for publications including the *New York Times*.

Renay Richardson is an award-winning audio producer who made the acclaimed *About Race* with Reni Eddo-Lodge. She founded Broccoli Productions, a London-based podcast production company, to empower minority talent. She also launched the Equality in Audio Pact.

Berry is a Denver-based woman who founded the directory and social media site Podcasts in Color, which lists around 1000 podcasts made by people of colour.

Minter Dial, a bilingual (French/English) veteran of leadership and branding podcasting, has hosted the *Minter Dialogue* podcast from London since 2010.

Matt Deegan co-founded the British Podcast Awards and now also runs the Australian Podcast Awards. His newsletter *Matt Deegan Writes* is a close UK take on the business side of podcasts and radio.

Rob Greenlee, a podcast industry 'evangelist and educator', is a senior executive at Libsyn, and was previously at Voxnest. He is associated with the Podcast Movement conference and The Podcast Academy.

How will podcasts find their audiences?

How does anyone get their ears on podcasts in the first place? Communal listening places already exist, of course. There are numerous podcast clubs on social media, just as there are book clubs. At one end are small, live listening groups, such as a model created by *Radio Ambulante*, which encourages people to listen to episodes as a community. Participants surveyed overwhelmingly agreed that the experience of listening together in a room and then discussing what they'd heard deepened their understanding of it. They felt able to have conversations they could not have in other spaces, including on social media.

At the other end of the spectrum, huge clubs like the *New York Times* Podcast Club on Facebook has almost 38 000 members (including me). It nominates one podcast a week for members to comment on, and offers Self-Promotion Saturday and Suggestion Sunday. The commentators come across as committed listeners, with often astute observations. Participants also ask fellow members for listening ideas within a genre and the results can be very helpful, with would-be self-publicists weeded out by admin. The Facebook group Podcasts We Listen To is 'a group for listeners by listeners', with 25 000 members, but is less structured. In general, social media sources drive 15 per cent of podcast discovery.

But almost half of listeners (46 per cent) decide on a particular podcast based on one of two things: a recommendation from family or friends, or an internet search. This data led prominent US analyst Tom Webster to urge podcasters to do three things to improve their recommendability:

1 Know who you are for, and why they are there.
2 Make your show easy to recommend.
3 Master your craft.[3]

It's sage advice. On the second point, Webster notes that while over 90 per cent of people surveyed claim to have, at some point, posted a video online, the percentage who post podcast segments is far less. This is largely because podcast producers are lazy about making audio samples of their podcasts available, Webster asserts. 'Don't leave it to your listeners to have to become audio editors. Isolate the best moments and share them', he advises. Counterintuitively, perhaps, Webster suggests that one of the best places for your podcast sample is on YouTube. While I am personally averse to screen-based sources for podcasts, others are not: almost one in five podcast listeners use YouTube to access podcasts, according to Webster's respected company, Edison Research, which has been gathering media consumption data since 1998.

Dan Misener, head of audience development at podcast agency Pacific Content, and a former columnist and producer with the Canadian Broadcasting Corporation (CBC), has done some fascinating research into how podcasts find listeners. On the mantra, 'know your audience', he offers practical advice: analyse not just what categories people listen to, but where listeners overlap with other listeners, creating what he terms podcast 'neighbourhoods'. You can get a sense of this by looking at the 'You might also like' suggestions that Apple brings up at the end of a podcast you've listened to. Their algorithms know your listening history, and by mapping where they want to take you via which show, you can discern what Misener calls 'audience affinities' that can reveal precious granular detail about gaps in the podcast market. As he told Lori Beckstead on the *New Aural Cultures* podcast:

> It's about understanding the landscape of what's already out there,
> how the audience you want to reach is already being served, and
> then offering something that is new ... and not just different
> because you think it's different, different because it actually is
> unlike anything else that people in that 'neighbourhood' are already
> listening to ... meaningfully cutting through the clutter.[4]

Packaging a podcast

Attracting listeners is also about packaging, and everything outside of the actual audio can be considered 'podcast packaging'. It sounds perverse to talk about the visual in podcasting, but as Misener notes, 'podcast listeners are going to consume your show with their eyes long before they consume a single second of audio'. Packaging matters! As Misener says, 'What is your artwork? What is the title of your show? What is the description? What are the show notes?' Misener analysed about 12 000 pieces of podcast artwork from the Top 200 podcasts in different categories on Apple. He found that a 'really deep red' was associated with the true-crime genre, blue was the colour of corporate America, while a striking 'movie poster yellow' was popular in a range of genres. As Misener points out, it's not really surprising that podcast graphic design follows certain tropes, just as book jackets do, and CDs and records once did. Interestingly, he found that podcast artwork rarely features faces, despite their proven ability to get our attention. This might be partly due to the scale of artwork viewed on a phone. The artwork has to be something that immediately signals content – hence the effectiveness of colour.

Strong branding often comes down to minute details such as title and tagline – the things you would use in your elevator pitch. Audio guru Eric Nuzum insists that you have to be able to express your podcast idea in a description that is no more than ten words long, and that description has to offer something fresh, untried. Otherwise your podcast may be too unwieldy, or derivative, to succeed. Nuzum made the comment at the Audiocraft Festival in Sydney in 2017, and used the podcast *Invisibilia* as an example, with its tagline: 'A narrative journey through the invisible forces that affect human behaviour'. The pedant in me counted the words. As Nuzum paused for breath, I interjected mildly, from the audience: 'That's 11 words!' I didn't mean to rain on his parade, but the audience cracked up. Later I saw Nuzum in the bar and he raved about his forthcoming production, *West Cork*. His descriptor:

'An unsolved murder exposes the underbelly of a rural Irish town'. That's also 11 words!

But even if he doesn't always follow his own rules, the takeaway from Nuzum's session was a good one: once you've found your motto, make sure it remains your guiding light, your 'North Star', keeping you on track as you develop your podcast's style and content, amid an ever-increasing stockpile.

Podcasts and branding

Branded content is a burgeoning podcast form. People from a journalism background may be wary of the very concept, with its PR connotation, but Dan Misener isn't fazed by it. 'When you do it right, when you actually make a show that is worth somebody's time and attention, when you offer them something that is valuable, it's often a pleasant surprise to find out that it came from a brand', he says. For instance, Pacific Content makes podcasts for the financial services company Charles Schwab. But instead of a show about the products Schwab offers, they created a show on decision making called *Choiceology*, hosted by behavioural economist Katie Milkman. There are benefits in this format for Schwab as well as for listeners, as Misener told Lori Beckstead: 'There's a benefit for the brand in terms of Schwab sort of being seen as a trusted partner ... and an authority in smart decision making'.

It's a novel way of thinking about corporate sponsorship and branding. I've heard other branded content that really works. *Business Insider*, for instance, takes an oblique approach. Its *BIQ* podcast has the tagline: '*Business Insider*'s *BIQ* asks big questions about the economy, news, and how we live'. This allows it to canvass topics from the merits of compulsory voting to the role of the now defunct Pan Am airline in Vietnam during the war. The latter episode was a riveting production, in which former airline stewards recalled poignant interactions with young GIs heading to and from a war zone, interspersed with archival audio and crafted to a high standard. And I've worked on one such podcast too: *Gertie's Law*, a podcast from the Supreme Court of Victoria in Melbourne, Australia. Launched in 2019, it was an initiative of Chief Justice Anne Ferguson, who wanted ordinary people to understand the decisions made in this great public institution. Crucially, the court hired not a lawyer but two storytellers, journalist Greg Muller (also of *Wrong Skin*) and filmmaker Evan Martin, to host and create the show. As we learn in Episode One, the title *Gertie's Law* comes from a statue that sits on top of the court of the god Themis (Greek) or Justitia (Roman), but she is known to locals as 'Gertie' – nobody knows why. Gertie also becomes an appealing image for the artwork, and that, along with the unusual title, makes her stand out on Apple Podcasts, where, at last count, she had a 4.8 out of 5 star rating from an impressive 890 reviews.

Where are podcasts headed?

Alan Hall, founder of the consistently excellent UK company Falling Tree Productions, has always tended towards the poetic aspects of audio. He comes from a background in music and to some extent he composes an audio feature or podcast episode by playing with words, actuality (tape) and music as if they were elements in an orchestra. Listen to his *The Saigon Tapes* (BBC Radio 4) to see what I mean: there is no narrator, but the music, scenes and audio-taped 'letters' between an ill-fated US soldier and his wife elevate our understanding as deftly as any host walking us through a landscape.[5]

When podcasting took off post-*Serial*, Alan was hopeful that the artier end of audio storytelling would have its heyday. 'I'd assumed close earbud listening would mean people would listen to speech content musically rather than informationally', he told me in 2016. 'I'd thought highly textured mixes and sophisticated narratives would thrive. Thus far, all the evidence suggests I was wrong. Podcast listeners seem to want a relationship with a presenter/host/storyteller rather than to immerse themselves in a sea of story/sound/visceral experience.'

Today, Alan is somewhat glumly reconciled to the explosion of market forces in his beloved audio medium. 'If the quaint old world of radio was like a museum, with curated exhibitions, or perhaps a library, then the podcast-sphere might be comparable to a book warehouse where you can access/purchase every conceivable genre', he reflects. 'One lesson of podcasting is that, to an even greater extent than previously, success is often a consequence not of the quality of the offering but of the efficacy of the marketing.'

The poetic has always had less traction than information- or personality-driven content. But just as with the old world of books, the naive romantic in me would like to think it's the artfully weighted and poetic podcasts – made with depth and nuance and insight and love – that'll remain on a listener's mental shelves.

– Alan Hall, Falling Tree Productions

In a blog in February 2021, 'Glass Walls', African American producer James T Green penned a ringing denouncement of inequity and lack of diversity at Gimlet Media, the independent podcast network created by ex-NPR producer Alex Blumberg in 2014 and immortalised in the podcast *StartUp*. Gimlet was acquired by Spotify for a staggering US$230 million in 2019 and began to ramp up production of its trademark crafted narrative podcasts. Green watched with dismay the increasing commodification of Gimlet's audio storytelling and the uncoupling of the loftier mission-driven principles of Blumberg's public radio background. 'The promise that the messiness and inefficiencies of storytelling could be simplified and reproduced as a formula' repelled him. What Green discerned is, in essence, the would-be industrialisation of empathy.

Radiotopia's Julie Shapiro also worries about the effects of corporatisation on the podcasting landscape. 'I feel like everything is getting gobbled up by the next biggest entity', she says. 'And that creates all of this fuss and noise and multiple awards and the kind of shouty, high-visibility, celebrity-laden entertainment podcasts that have really taken off.' Podcasting has become such a Thing that when Julie recently judged a fiction-writing competition, no fewer than four of the five scripts she received had characters who were podcasters. 'And I think we're gonna see more of that. It is like more of a trendy profession, an artistic expression that is more relevant now not just *for* storytelling, but *in* storytelling.'

The co-director of Falling Tree, Eleanor McDowall, is more optimistic about where podcasting is headed. She also still loves radio. 'Radio has always been the work that's paid my rent. All of my independent podcast projects (*Field Recordings*, *Radio Atlas*) just cost me money, which I invest because I want them to exist in the world', she told me. But the biggest threat to her work is burnout. 'I end up working many more days on projects than I'm paid. The lack of funding and expectation of free labour excludes so many people and builds quite a toxic culture.'

Yet podcasting is maturing fast as an industry. Increasingly I see jobs for 'podcast producer' or 'podcast editor' scroll by on social media, which wasn't happening five years ago. Those titles cover a wide range of activities, from the mundane (booking guests, uploading audio files online) to the creatively challenging. At the latter end, serious salaries are starting to be offered, commensurate with what a senior feature writer or investigative journalist could expect to earn at a traditional media organisation.

A job advertisement for a 'Lead Producer – Long-form narrative' was listed in July 2021 by Novel, a UK company that makes award-winning content for big platforms such as the BBC, iHeartRadio, Wondery, Audible and Spotify. Their preferred candidate will have 'a great ear for audio storytelling, with five years experience in narrative audio production, a solid understanding of what it takes to make impactful podcasts that gain critical acclaim and – most crucially – experience as a series or lead producer on a narrative series that they're proud of'. The list of key responsibilities is exhaustive, and includes everything from series planning and interviewing to managing budgets and sourcing music. And if that wasn't enough, they throw in 'additional skills' like 'wide ranging listening habits', writing and audio editing skills, and proficiency in creative thinking, time management and problem solving. An annual salary of £45 000 to £70 000 was offered to this overachiever (A$84 000 to $130 000), along with attractive conditions. The advertisement also notes: 'It is obvious the podcast industry needs to change and become more diverse. We are therefore particularly keen to hear from applicants that are under-represented in the industry, such as those from Black, Asian & Minority Ethnic backgrounds or those with disabilities'.

Around the same time, New York–based Pushkin Industries, co-founded by Malcolm Gladwell and Jacob Weisberg (introduced in chapter 1), advertised for a 'Development Producer'. Along with possessing a 'collaborative spirit', the successful applicant would have experience in

> hands-on production from ideation and paper development
> (treatments, outlines, etc) to pilot production (scripting, recording,
> editing) and show planning. We are looking for a highly creative
> individual with sharp audio production skills and a strong editorial
> sensibility; a cultural omnivore who is passionate, adaptable, and
> capable of working in a variety of formats.

The salary range was US$70 000 to $90 000 (A$95 000 to $123 000). The company's website notes: 'Pushkin Industries was co-founded by a person of color and is named after a bi-racial poet. Diversity is at the heart of our culture, alongside intellectual openness, respect, fairness, and ethical behavior'. It lists seven diversity principles, which cleave closely to Renay Richardson's Equality in Audio Pact (see chapter 9). Can we dare to hope that things are shifting at last?

Diversity and democracy

In the podcast landscape of the future, the dominance of English-language podcasts is likely to diminish. In India, creators are now harnessing social media, making short audio clips with search tags for discoverability, in regional and Hindi languages. Such moves are 'automatically giving voice to the under-represented', says Olya Booyar, Head of Radio at the Asia-Pacific Broadcasting Union, and a big fan of podcasting. 'In almost all of Asia, almost all podcasts are consumed via mobile phones', she points out, so in poorer countries, non-rated data – meaning phone plans that don't count social media use towards the user's download limit – 'are the key to getting podcasts out to the masses'. In some rural settings, one person with a data allowance will download a podcast, she says, then Bluetooth it to all in the village.

Such considerations make platforms like Facebook a critical force. 'To many under-developed countries in the Asia-Pacific, Facebook *is* the internet', Olya explains. In the Philippines, for instance, in the third quarter of 2020, 96 per cent of internet users aged 16 to 64 accessed Facebook, according to DataReportal. PumaPodcast, founded by veteran journalist Roby Alampay, is the country's first podcast network. It has created 17 podcasts, in English and local languages, on a wide range of topics. In a country where journalists have been labelled 'prostitutes' and 'liars' by president Rodrigo Duterte, and where the acclaimed journalist Maria Ressa is facing trumped-up charges and possible jail time, Puma's 'core values of good, independent journalism' could not be more needed.

A sobering report by Admire Mare, of the Namibia University of Science and Technology, describes the expectations for podcasting on the African continent: 'In Africa, where countless stories go unreported because of deep-seated fear of political reprisals, surveillance, repressive official secrecy laws and arbitrary arrests, podcasts were reified as alternative sites of storytelling, uncensored communication and public discourse'. But podcasting is not always a democratising force, as Mare notes. 'Instead of opening up spaces for ordinary people, the platform has been occupied by digital influencers, journalists and media organizations. As a result, podcasting has reproduced and magnified elite continuities.'[6]

Podcasting was expected to be a major disruptor, but in Africa, as in poorer parts of Asia, 'those without access to internet and digital technologies are left out of the conversation. They cannot upload and download the content', Mare writes. To use a computer with a microphone to record and edit a podcast, you need access to electricity. Even using a mobile phone to do everything, you need reliable bandwidth. And in Africa, most people still do not have access to the internet. Mare concludes: 'Cheap data and diversification into vernacular languages could radically change this'.

Collaborative podcasting models

Other models are being trialled to make podcasts more representative. Nicole Curby, a freelance Australian producer, teamed up with Mozhgan Moarefizadeh, a 29-year-old Iranian refugee stranded in Jakarta, Indonesia, in a terrible limbo. Mozghan does not have the right to work, study, marry, travel or hold a bank account. Her future is uncertain. Her situation is the result of Australia's border crackdown in 2013, and the five-part narrative podcast, *The Wait*, examines the plight of Mozghan and others like her. Beautifully crafted, with sound-rich audio scenes, actuality, archive and interviews, the podcast is co-hosted by Nicole and Mozghan.

Nicole wanted to explore 'how the consequences of Australia's border are being pushed over the horizon and into Indonesia'. For Mozghan, whose charm and vitality animate the show, the aim was humanising refugees: 'I wanted to connect with people on a personal level, so they can relate to us and feel that we're as normal as they are', she says. Nicole wants to see more of this collaborative podcast model – 'hearing people who are part of the story tell the story on their own terms, and do it with integrity and solid journalistic standards'. Audio allows this, as it 'captures the unique sounds of different voices and all the experience that is carried in them'.

Other individuals and organisations are already acting to improve representation. In 2021, Radiotopia launched a new podcast, *Blind Guy Travels*. Hosted by 23-year-old Matthew Shifrin, a blind musician, it's an engaging personal journal of navigating an unsighted world. Eleanor McDowall is another champion of people with disability in the pod space and she wants industry players to step up. 'I'd love to see a greater commitment to accessibility for D/deaf audiences – through transcripts and captioning – particularly from the big podcast distributors like the BBC.' She also wants to see 'a deepening interest in listening across languages'. It was to assist the latter that Eleanor founded *Radio Atlas*, her beautifully created website where features in many languages can be listened to in the original, while perfectly synced subtitles appear on the screen: another version of 'movies for your ears'. It's also available as a podcast, where the subtitles appear on your phone if you need them.

'There's a ton more diverse content out there now', echoes Julie Shapiro. 'And whether companies are guilt-funding or just funding, I don't care, I just want to hear it, I want to see it. And of course, it pulls more people of colour into the space because they're hearing themselves in the content that's out there.'

Diverse audiences

Podcasting sure has come a long way from the days when two white guys talked tech to a bunch of other white guys. Edison Research data in March 2021 showed that 57 per cent of monthly podcast listeners in the US are white, 16 per cent Latino, 13 per cent African American, 4 per cent Asian, and all other groups make up the remaining 10 per cent –

figures in line with ethnic representation in the general US population. 'In the near quarter of a century that *The Infinite Dial* has been the survey of record for digital audio, the space has never been more vibrant, or more diverse, than it is today', notes Tom Webster. 'Podcasting, in particular, has made great gains with women and non-White audiences, and truly reflects the diversity of America.'[7]

Difficult as it has been to get here, it feels like this awareness of the need for diversity and inclusion in our institutions, and in media, has really landed. 'It's been a remarkable moment', Julie Shapiro agrees:

> It just feels like it's taken a turn for the much better ... I'm really hopeful. Really excited. And, you know, it's kind of involved everyone – there isn't really a place where these dynamics haven't been identified. And the allyship and community that have come together online to speak out has been formidable and impressive and impactful ... It isn't like something that flared up and went away – it's the switch in the track.

Academics, education, research and podcasting

Academics are increasingly active in the podcast space, and there are any number of modestly successful academic ventures in the podsphere – usually passion projects developed by adventurous scholars, keen to share their knowledge and engage with their peers and the public. Academic podcasters are close cousins of the vast array of 'knowledge' podcasters in the ecosphere. These range from independent scholars-turned-hosts, such as the two dozen podcasters in the *Archaeology Podcast Network*, to hugely popular franchises such as Mike Duncan's *History of Rome*. The Humanities Podcast Network is a hybrid, comprising 'a group of scholars, writers, and thinkers who make podcasts', and who 'understand podcasts as a form of intellectual engagement that can expand the horizons of academic knowledge'. Its co-founders include Annie Galvin, an associate producer of *The Ezra Klein Show* at the *New York Times* who is also a literature scholar, and a host of academics in English, creative writing, philosophy and other fields.

Types of academic podcasts

The vast majority of academic podcasts follow a conversational format, such as in *Lingthusiasm*, 'a podcast that's enthusiastic about linguistics', by La Trobe University's Gretchen McCulloch and Lauren Gawne. Some universities deploy their own journalists to showcase academic research via a well-crafted podcast: take *Litmus*, from Northeastern University, Boston, in which two journalists mediate complex research. As the tagline says: 'We connect what's going on in their labs to what's going on in your life'.

At the University of Wollongong, south of Sydney, Mim Fox co-hosts *The Social Work Stories Podcast*, which 'analyses social work practice using real life case studies and replicating a clinical supervision dialogue'. The deeply personal stories, from dealing with a stillborn baby to running a suicide prevention line, garner about 10000 downloads per episode, and over two years on, total around 250000. Mim says she loves 'being able to reach people across the world and make connections both locally and internationally'. Drew Rae, a safety science researcher from Griffith University in Brisbane, co-hosts *The Safety of Work*, aimed at making safety research accessible for practitioners. Each episode is focused on a single question or piece of research, sometimes suggested by the 1000 or so listeners.

Yet only a few institutions have grappled with harnessing the full strengths of the audio medium in the service of communicating scholarly research. That's not surprising, because it usually requires this trifecta: robust interdisciplinary collaboration, a deep understanding of audio storytelling and, crucially, an ability to identify or reframe academic knowledge so that it can be absorbed aurally. The Centre for the History of the Emotions at Queen Mary University of London is one excellent example. Audio, as we have seen many times, is a splendid vector for emotion: listeners can viscerally experience its affective power. For the Centre's podcast series *The Sound of Anger*, historian Thomas Dixon teamed up with an audio producer, Natalie Steed, and other academic experts to explore the history, philosophy, science and experience of anger. They shaped deep academic knowledge into audio-friendly forms, including crafted features, interviews and even two original dramas that looked at Seneca and Darwin, in order 'to give people the tools to think through their own feelings of rage, frustration, and anger – and to reflect on whether or not they are healthy emotions'. It's a terrific series, which – to the amazement and delight of the makers – won not one but two gold awards at the British Podcast Awards 2020, for Smartest Podcast and Best Wellbeing Podcast.

Some academics have mastered the art of audio storytelling themselves to help them pursue research objectives. Barry Lam, Associate Professor of Philosophy at Vassar College, New York, used to manage a college radio station. Now he writes, edits and produces *Hi-Phi Nation*, 'a show about philosophy that turns stories into ideas'. The podcast is now so successful that it is hosted by the Slate podcast network. Others prefer to outsource the grunt work. Laurie Santos, Professor of Psychology at Yale, collaborates with Pushkin Industries to produce her phenomenally successful podcast *The Happiness Lab*, which has had more than 35 million downloads since its launch in 2019.

At the other end of the spectrum, vast numbers of academics are interested in using podcasting to assist teaching as well as research. The annual Australian Educational Podcasting Conference, launched in 2020, explores that demand, which gained added traction as so many institutions turned to online learning during the pandemic. In 2021, the conference theme was 'Engaging our hearts and minds through audio'. As a keynote speaker there, one of my topics was an analysis of my own venture into converting academic research into an award-winning narrative podcast, *Heart of Artness* (introduced in chapter 7), which examined the cross-cultural influences behind the production of contemporary Aboriginal art in Australia – influences that have important social, cultural and economic significance. My colleague, art historian Ian McLean, believes that the dozens of in-depth interviews at the heart of our podcast 'produced a more level playing field amongst our many subjects than conventional art historiographical methodology could achieve', and achieved it 'in an inclusive, inventive and collaborative way'. I also used sound lavishly to tell story: I recorded the stripping of sheets of bark in eucalypt forests to be made into an artist's canvas, women singing and dancing while painted in ochres that convey clan knowledge, a smoking ceremony performed to launch an exhibition. Curator, professor and author Margo Neale (see chapter 7) co-hosted the podcast and found the process of stewarding me through cultural protocols and towards dialogues with Indigenous communities a rewarding experience. 'At best we risk learning nothing about each other if we don't have the right kind of interaction', she reflected. 'At worst it perpetuates conflict, enhances racism and flies in the face of the whole reconciliation movement.'

Podcasting studies: A new field

Academics are coming together to form a new field: podcasting studies. There is a website, <podcaststudies.org>, where I am part of a steering group co-convened by African American Professor of Practice Kim Fox (see Chapter 9), and Richard Berry of the University of Sunderland in the UK. Kim is bringing her considerable energy to bear on researching how black podcasting can generate 'a metaphorical curriculum for blackness',[8] while also nurturing the international academic podcast community through lively Zoom meetings. Richard collates new publications, events and resources on the website; he wrote some of the earliest and most-cited articles on podcasting, and co-edited an anthology, *Podcasting: New Aural Cultures and Digital Media*. Along with Canadian academic Lori Beckstead, Richard and co-editor Dario

Llinares co-hosted the *New Aural Cultures* podcast, now rebadged as *The Podcast Studies Podcast*. It is a good way to keep up with academic debates and movements in the podcasting space.

 Kim Fox suggests the following ways in which the field of podcast studies could increase diversity:

- do an annual audit of how the podcasting community is observing Renay Richardson's Equality in Audio pact

- more collaborations on research projects with people of colour that focus on people of colour

- more research projects that are inclusive and diverse because we already see a void in diversity and inclusivity when it comes to academic research on podcasting

- encourage young and emerging scholars to conduct podcasting research

- educators to use diverse podcast case studies in their courses, for example as listening material

- if academics are producing podcasts, consider making sure the podcast hosts and production team are inclusive

One of the podcast's guests was Hannah McGregor, a Canadian academic who began the podcast *Secret Feminist Agenda* in 2017 to provide 'a weekly discussion of the insidious, nefarious, insurgent, and mundane ways we enact our feminism in our daily lives'. In a bold innovation supported by scholarly publisher Wilfrid Laurier University Press (WLU Press), McGregor had the podcast publicly peer reviewed by digital scholars, to test 'methods for podcasts to be circulated as forms of publicly engaged scholarship in their own right, rather than being understood exclusively as knowledge mobilization'. This could radically alter the way academics are evaluated for promotion and tenure, a process that relies heavily on having articles published in established scholarly print journals. Unfortunately, none of the published peer reviews of *Secret Feminist Agenda* engaged with how well or otherwise the research was communicated via the *audio medium* – an important consideration that parallels the evaluation of writing style, clarity and correctness in a print article peer review.

With Siobhan McMenemy, a senior editor at WLU Press, McGregor is pressing ahead to reimagine 'the sound of scholarship'. They co-founded the Amplify Podcast Network, 'a network of scholars, editors, audio producers, librarians, students, and arts organizers who are interested in the power and potential of podcasting as a form of scholarly communication'. One of its first productions is *The SpokenWeb Podcast*, which explores the possibilities of audio-based scholarship for engaging with audio archives. The long-term goal is 'to make peer-reviewed podcasts as easy to find as journal articles'.

Meanwhile, scholarly literature in a wide range of disciplines on podcast-related themes is growing exponentially. On the Podcast Studies website, German media researcher Nele Heise has collated an exhaustive collection of journal articles, essays, reports and other publications about podcasting. This keen academic interest is mirrored in teaching. Many universities have incorporated podcasting into the curriculum, either as a full undergraduate media/communications subject, as I did, or as a postgraduate offering, such as the Audio Literary Reportage course that Robert Boynton is developing at New York University as an adjunct to his celebrated Literary Journalism course. Since the early debates on whether podcasting was a technology, a practice, a genre or a medium, podcasting studies has become firmly established as a new field in media and communications. Podcasts are likely to become a core tool of teaching and learning at secondary and tertiary levels, studied in subjects from criminology and health sciences to arts and the humanities.

Cracking the intimacy

Will Page, a former chief economist at Spotify, pithily described podcasting as 'a transfer of ideas in an intimate setting'. Speaking in May 2021 on *Podland*, Page then warmed to his topic. 'What makes podcasts really beautiful for me is, they crack intimacy.' He's absolutely right, of course. Podcasts – the best ones – are super-intimate. That quality is so integral to the theory and practice of podcasting that I counted the words 'intimate' or 'intimacy' used 96 times across two anthologies about podcasting: the *New Aural Cultures* book mentioned above, and *Podcasting: The Audio Media Revolution*, by Martin Spinelli and Lance Dann.

But, ever the economist, Page went on: 'The internet can scale just about everything, but it can't scale intimacy. And if podcasting, as an industry, plays its cards right, it might even correct for that. We could have a huge business which preserves intimacy. That's the balancing act'.

To me, that sounds scary. If podcasting does learn to 'scale intimacy', I think it will have become hollow at its core. Intimacy in podcasting is not something you can or should commodify. It's a precious gift, born of some alchemical bond, between host and listener, voice and story.

So I will end by exploring how one podcast achieved some of the purest intimacy I've heard. It's called, appropriately enough, *Goodbye to All This*. It was written by an Australian producer at ABC Radio National, Sophie Townsend, with Eleanor McDowall as producer and Alan Hall as a listening adviser. She also had a story editor at CBC, Chris Oke, and a commissioning editor at BBC, Jon Manel.

So pace yourself, listen through – and learn from an audio storytelling great. And remember, as you wend your way through this remarkable blend of the deep and the domestic: podcasting will always be God's gift to ironing!

Goodbye to All This, with Sophie Townsend

Most episodes of Sophie's podcast begin with a clear descriptor: 'This is a story about love, loss, and coming out the other side. It's my story: *Goodbye to All This*'. In this moving and oh-so-human memoir, Sophie reflects on the untimely loss of her husband, Russell, to cancer, and the adjustments she and their two young daughters, Bear and Poppy, then aged 11 and eight, make after his death.

The intensely personal nature of this story could also have been its downfall. It could have become mawkish at one end of the tonal spectrum, or risked sounding callous at the other. Instead, it lands pitch-perfectly. She was able to achieve the right voice, partly, Sophie told me, due to timing. It happened some eight years after Russell's death, which gave her crucial emotional distance. 'I can look back on it now with clearer eyes. I think I'm less afraid than I once was of coming off too cool or too intense, and that confidence really helps too.'

She credits co-producer Eleanor McDowall with being instrumental in shaping the script. 'There are things that I feel are perfectly sensible and non-self-indulgent that she would question me on, in her gentle way, and let me go deeper into a story, or back off from it, or just understand that there was something strange about the tone', Sophie recalls. 'So I think editing helps, another trusted set of eyes helps ... examining what the essence is, what you're really trying to get out.'

Jon Manel of the BBC World Service 'asked lots of questions about the script, which always helps you understand when you're taking things for granted because you know the story so well', Sophie adds. CBC senior producer, Chris Oke, a journalist and poet, 'could see where an episode was back to front, or front-loaded (where I'd tried to explain everything I thought you needed to know before the story began) and made incredibly elegant suggestions about this'.

The 12 episodes chart the relentless narrative that is terminal illness: worry, diagnosis, impact on patient and family, treatment, death, funeral rites, coping with absence and grief, carrying on. But there are side moments too, prologues that paint small family scenes, a kind of ballast of trivia to counter the huge emotional side-swipe to come. Thus, Episode Five, 'The Crowded Goodbye', opens with Sophie ruminating on the humid horrors of a Sydney summer and how Poppy is cranky because friends won't share their frozen fruit sticks. Sophie and Russell 'nod and soothe' – and then the kicker: 'We have dinner in the living room now because it's too painful for him to sit on the kitchen chairs'. By the end of the episode, 30 minutes from now, Russell will be dead.

In the prologue, Sophie's measured voice matches a script that captures the intense way that young girls experience life, with Bear's stifled sobs presaging the death to come. The episode then opens with whirring sounds of crickets, which immediately take us to a hot summer night, and leave us, after just 30 seconds of narration, with Russell experiencing the fall from which he will not recover.

Forensic economy and virtuosic observational writing make the podcast utterly compelling. Farewelling her girls at their school in Episode Seven, Sophie remarks, quasi-cheerfully: 'They look OK. You can't tell, just by looking, that their father is dead'. In reality, Sophie was keenly aware of the need to preserve boundaries around how much of her daughters' lives and feelings she exposed. 'The girls were the trickiest part of this. I had some rules for myself about keeping the lives they led, the bits I wasn't part of, out of it', Sophie says. 'They didn't hear the episodes before they dropped. I told them they could, but they didn't want to. But I sat down with each of them and talked through the scripts, and told them about things I was saying. Most of it was OK; there were a few things that they didn't like, and I took those bits out.'

Russell's death could have made natural narrative closure, the series ending with his funeral in Episode Six. Instead, that is only a halfway point. Both Sophie and Eleanor made a deliberate decision to extend it. 'We were both interested in ... exploring loss years out from his death. And we both wanted it to be very honest and for it to go into those small moments that make up a life and say something about the bigger story.'

In Episode Ten, for instance, Sophie recounts the mundaneness of house maintenance, something Russell used to handle. The washing machine breaks down; in trying to fix it, she nearly gets electrocuted. On the day a replacement is delivered, she is beset by mounting irritations. She is late for an appointment, the delivery men get high-handed about insurance liability, and torrential rain is making everything harder. But all the tiny domestic annoyances build to a moment of revelation about grief. 'Why am I crying anyway three years after he died? And when, when is this going to stop, the way it slaps me like this? ... And when, when am I not going to feel so incredibly alone?'

Along with the spare script and attuned delivery, Eleanor's delicate sensibility and sound design elevate the podcast. There is understated and effective use of sound effects and actuality: a ticking clock, used at both a fast and slower pace, metaphorically summons the awful tedium of hours of chemotherapy. Irate beeps make an impatient taxi driver materialise, church bells elicit an Italian village. 'El's work really shaped the episodes', says Sophie. 'I rarely changed much beyond a pause or where music was sitting in the mix. Alan Hall also provided great feedback at this stage.'

Sophie actively sets out to write filmically. 'I think the art of writing visually for the ear is about action, rather than description, so that your inner eye is moving from visual to visual as the story progresses. I try to think of the way a camera might work, following the action.' This is very clear in Episode Four, when the couple get terrible news from the oncologist. 'This scene focuses on scale – the smallness of the Christmas tree in the smallness of the office is a way of making it closed-in and claustrophobic, instead of explaining that feeling. The idea I have in my head, I guess, is a sort of breadcrumb trail, where there's movement, and forward motion in a scene that takes you further into the truth of the thing.' The timing – of Sophie's script, of musical pauses, and of actual, ambient silence – is beautifully judged. When the oncologist says there is no hope and Sophie tells us flatly, 'Russell will die', there are three thrumming seconds of silence, followed by a further 14-second musical reinforcement of that pause. We need it, to absorb this crushing reality.

The music was specially composed by UK composer Jeremy Warmsley. It is tonally aligned with the writing throughout, and delivers a susurrant song at the end, a dreamy exhalation in a lilting 13/8 time signature that allows us to expel our emotions with it. 'The more I heard it ... I just couldn't imagine it without it', observes Sophie.

The script's microscopic detail, from medical treatments to takeaway meals, came from the trove of emails Sophie wrote at the time, along with notes she kept. She fact-checked medical aspects and consulted family and friends, who sometimes challenged her memory of events. 'This happened particularly when the doctor came to tell me that Russell would die in the next day or two. I remember him as curt and harsh, but my mother says he was sympathetic and kind. I tend to think she's right ... I asked lots of questions of myself about what happened when.' Episode Five ends with a montage of friends and family recounting their own memories of Russell's death. Their testimony serves to ground this traumatic event, to share the burden, as it were.

A few other voices, of friends and family, are heard at times; sometimes they are almost jarring, so completely is the listener inside Sophie's head. But her self-flagellation and despair are leavened with humour. In Episode Nine, two years after Russell's death, Sophie attempts online dating. Her first encounter, in a wine and cheese bar, is with a man who has failed to reveal he is allergic to dairy. He can only toy with a bowl of nuts as Sophie punishes him with lengthy descriptions of Russell's decline.

Sophie believes the nature of the audio medium is particularly liberating for artists who want to create deeply personal content. I will give her the final word. Somehow I can't see the internet scaling up the lightness and ephemerality she mentions – for which we can all be grateful!

I think there's something light about audio, something playful, almost. Maybe it's because it's not visual, so we don't see our work. It feels more ephemeral, more part of the air than the solid world. It feels like there's a lot of freedom in its nature. I didn't feel the need to nail a happy ending, or discover something profound for listeners, in the way I might have done in a written memoir. Audio feels scrappy and loose as a starting point. There's in fact so much precision and so much hard work that goes into it, but I come to it feeling lighter, which for me makes the work – *easier* isn't the word, but less heavy. And that lightness has given me so much.

Appendix:
Podcast recommendations
and reviews

For reliable, informed critiques of podcasts, try the following:

- *RadioDoc Review*: The journal I founded in 2014. A board of top producers and scholars nominate audio works, then the editor commissions reviews by well-credentialled people. <https://ro.uow.edu.au/rdr/>
- Bello Collective: This loose association of knowledgeable audio lovers, founded in 2017, compiles a comprehensive list of its top 100 podcasts every December and has an informative newsletter on podcasting issues and shows. <https://bellocollective.com/>
- *New Yorker*: The magazine has taken podcasting seriously ever since *Serial* dropped in 2014. Sarah Larson and others provide informed critiques. <www.newyorker.com>
- *Vulture*: Nick Quah became its full-time podcast critic in September 2021. <www.vulture.com/news/podcasts/>
- Other notable outlets for regular podcast criticism include the *Guardian* UK (Miranda Sawyer), 'Podcast Review' from the *LA Times Review of Books* and the *Atlantic*.

The recommendations here are just to give you an idea of the range of content and genres and get you started. See also the many podcasts mentioned throughout the book!

PART 1: Podcasts by genre

Narrative nonfiction – investigative journalism

CLASSICS: *In the Dark, Reveal, Hunting Warhead, Uncovered, Embedded, Trace, Catch and Kill, The Dropout, Caixin*
EXTRA:

I'm Not a Monster: This disturbing and beautifully crafted investigation explores how an all-American family ends up making propaganda videos for ISIS. A meticulously researched co-production between the BBC and PBS that plays with our sympathies and confounds expectations.

Wind of Change: Did the CIA write a power ballad that ended the Cold War? Cheeky and beautifully written, even if the ending annoys. Presented by journalist Patrick Radden Keefe.

Canary: A delicate and thorough examination of sexual assault from unusual angles, presented by Amy Brittain from *The Washington Post*.

The Greatest Menace: A combination of deep research into the horrific treatment of gay men in Australia over decades, and the moving personal story of host, Patrick Abboud. (Disclosure: I was consulting producer.)

Narrative nonfiction – true crime

CLASSICS: *Serial, Finding Cleo, Dirty John, Bowraville, Criminal, Crimetown, West Cork, Bear Brook*
EXTRA:
Unravel True Crime: Snowball: A heartwarming variation on the ruthless

con/scam artist found in *Dirty John*, this features a delightful and daggy New Zealand family in pursuit of a glamorous Californian woman who done them wrong.

The Missing Cryptoqueen: A glorious Bulgarian choir is the icing on the cake of this engrossing story of a charismatic financial scammer, Dr Ruja Ignatova, her pyramid scheme minions and her oh-so-human victims.

Nut Job: The $10 million heist you've never heard of – a rabbit hole of crime syndicates linked to almonds in California. Brilliantly synthesised as wry noir by host, Marc Fennell.

Narrative nonfiction – miscellaneous themed storytelling

CLASSIC: *Dolly Parton's America, S-Town, Heavyweight, The Heart, Radiolab, This American Life, Radio Ambulante, Snap Judgment, Invisibilia, Love Me, Love + Radio, The Moth, 9/12, Things Fell Apart*

EXTRA:

Articles of Interest: Fashion as social history and living culture.

Prison Bag: Big-hearted stories of people coping with having a loved one in prison, produced by Falling Tree Productions.

Birds Eye View: Naked stories of life inside a women's prison in northern Australia, produced by Darwin-based StoryProjects.

Hello Nature: Pakistani-born Misha Euceph only discovered national parks in her adopted US home at the age of 21. She sets off on a road trip to reclaim nature for BIPOC communities.

GOLD EPISODE: *Radiolab*: *Blame*, 'Dear Hector': A segment in which 86-year-old Hector Black tells producer Bianca Giaever how he managed to forgive the man who raped and killed his daughter. Uplifting and economically told. Sticking with *Radiolab*, another standout is 'Finding Emilie', a deeply moving story about the literal power of voice – in this case to bring a badly injured young woman back to full and loving consciousness.

Narrative nonfiction – historical storytelling

CLASSIC: *Slow Burn, Uncivil, Scene on Radio, Mobituaries, Revisionist History, Stuff the British Stole, Welcome to your Fantasy*

EXTRA:

The Apology Line: In New York in the 1970s, a man starts a telephone answering service that takes over his life, as performance art meets grim reality.

Bed of Lies: Devastating stories of how the UK police infiltrated the lives of left-wing women, even having children with them in order to spy on them.

The Service: Cold War spying shenanigans in, of all places, New Zealand.

On the Ground: In this BBC series, a female journalist viscerally revisits being embedded with British troops in Iraq when they were attacked by US allies.

Recall: How to Start a Revolution: A CBC podcast about radical and revolutionary movements in Canada in the 1960s.

Narrative nonfiction – activist

CLASSIC: *Change Makers, The Messenger, Somebody, Resistance, Be Antiracist with Ibram X. Kendi, Outrage + Optimism*

EXTRA:

Human Resources: A history of British involvement in the transatlantic slave trade, produced by Broccoli Productions.

Critical Frequency: A network of activist podcasts founded by US climate journalist Amy Westervelt and run by women. Shows examine work, environment, climate, arts, health, diversity and social justice.

Narrative news

CLASSIC: *The Daily, Post Reports, Today in Focus, 7am, Full Story, Today, Explained*

EXTRA: *5 Minutes On*: Snappy take on one issue of the day from the BBC.

Chatcasts

CLASSIC: *Slate Political Gabfest, That Peter Crouch Podcast, The Stoop, The Cut, You're Wrong About, The High Low, Still Processing, The Read*

EXTRA:

Dying for Sex: When fortysomething Molly is diagnosed with terminal cancer, she leaves her husband and dedicates her last months to flings, fetishes and wild sexting, with her non-judgmental friend Nikki as confidante and carer. A wild and unexpectedly joyful ride.

Renegades: So what if they're famous, they're also friends – and it shows. Barack Obama and Bruce Springsteen balance heart and head as they discuss the foundation themes of the US.

Dear Joan and Jericha: Deliciously bawdy 'psychosexual and sporting' advice from two pretend agony aunts, written and performed by comic actors Julia Davis and Vicki Pepperdine.

Ear Hustle: A podcast that celebrates common humanity, inside and outside prison. One host is an inmate of San Quentin prison in California, and a second is an ex-prisoner, his sentence commuted because of the podcast. Third host is artist and co-founder Nigel Poor. Diverse inmate interviews and documentary treatments add rich insight.

Conversation

CLASSIC: *Conversations* (with Richard Fidler), *WTF with Marc Maron, On Being with Krista Tippett, The Joe Rogan Experience, Death, Sex & Money, HARDtalk, Grounded with Louis Theroux*
EXTRA:
Hey Aunty: Frank and often fun discussions about being a black woman in Australia with host Shantel Wetherall, who has Belizean/British heritage and clearly relishes this chance to speak her mind.
Sway: Kara Swisher is fearless and peerless in her field: interrogating people in power, especially in tech and media. She's had Mark Zuckerberg on the ropes.
Changes with Annie Macmanus: Raw interviews rich in empathy with very real people, about turning points in their lives.
GOLD EPISODE: *In the Dark*, Season Two, 'Curtis Flowers': After two years of relentless investigation, this podcast helped overturn the wrongful conviction for murder of black American Curtis Flowers. Flowers was tried and convicted six times in Mississippi for the same crime by a vengeful white District Attorney who had black jurors struck down. In this one-hour interview, host Madeleine Baran finally meets Curtis, outside and free. He is at times sad, gentle, charming, clear-sighted and remarkably free of bitterness after losing 23 years of his life to prison. It's a powerful interview, heightened by careful placement of music for tone and timing. Now go listen to the full podcast and marvel at the dogged journalism that got Curtis there. A team of reporters moved into Curtis's hometown of Winona, Mississippi, for a year to assemble evidence and build community relationships to gather interviews and deepen the story.

Memoir

CLASSIC: *Goodbye to All This, Alone: A Love Story, Not by Accident, No Feeling Is Final, S***hole Country*
EXTRA:
Silent Waves: A remarkable journey by 25-year-old Raquel O'Brien into the troubled pathology of her family. Strong production by Georgina Savage with careful consideration of ethics and balance.
Unspeakable: A beautifully judged BBC series in which survivor Alice Musabende faces telling her boys about how her family and another million Tutsis were killed in the 1994 Rwanda genocide. Delicate, warm and moving.

Monologue

CLASSIC: *Trojan War: The Podcast, Lore, Dan Carlin's Hardcore History, The History of Rome, Revolutions*. These podcasts follow a hugely popular formula of lengthy monologues on history by white male hosts. *The Lost Archive* by historian Jill Lepore explores diverse topics, feels fresh and is much shorter.
EXTRA:
365 Stories I Want to Tell You Before We Both Die: Whimsical, sometimes provocative autobiographical musings (2–5 minutes per episode) from US filmmaker Caveh Zahedi.
Anthems: Short and stirring manifestos, speeches and stories from diverse LGBTQIA+ voices.
My Year in Mensa: Drily acerbic reflection on how a young woman, US stand-up Jamie Loftus, infiltrated the nerdy world of Mensa and uncovered a far-right subset.
HYBRID: *The Blindboy Podcast*: Irish Dadaist singer-songwriter Blindboy riffs pungently on everything under the sun, including his own mental health, before sometimes talking to a guest. F-bombs abound, used in charming vernacular harmony.

True crime – non-crafted;
monologue or chatcast

CLASSIC: *Casefile, Crime Junkie, My Favorite Murder, RedHanded, Morbid*

EXTRA: *I Catch Killers with Gary Jubelin*: A controversial ex-detective interviews coppers and other mates from a lifetime investigating crime. Raw and real.

Sword and Scale: lurid stories anchored by rich audio archive.

Fiction

CLASSIC: *Welcome to Night Vale, Homecoming, Blackout, Passenger List, The Shadows, The Truth, Carrier, Alice Isn't Dead*

EXTRA:

Love and Luck: Billed as 'Australia's first LGBT audio drama podcast' and told via voicemails. A gentle romance.

Earth Eclipsed: Immersive sci-fi story of a neuroscientist on the brink of a galaxy-changing discovery who gets kidnapped by a renegade miner.

HYBRID: *The Battersea Poltergeist*: This BBC series, described as 'a paranormal cold case', combines time-warped documentary and drama that takes you right to the scene of a 1950s haunting in London.

Poetic/creative

CLASSIC: *Short Cuts, Third Ear, Radio Atlas, Field Recordings, Constellations, Nocturne, ShortDocs, Have You Heard George's Podcast.* Also look for the work of individual creatives such as Chris Brookes, Mira Burt-Wintonick, Jesse Cox, Sharon Davis, Sherre DeLys, Cristal Duhaime, Masako Fukui, Sarah Geis, James T Green, Tim Hinman, Rikke Houd, Axel Kacoutié, Natalie Kestecher, Jaye Kranz, Nina Perry, Kaitlin Prest, Robyn Ravlich, Laura Rodero,

Sofia Saldanha, Zakia Sewell, Phil Smith, Jane Ulman, Hana Walker-Brown, Jonathan Zenti

EXTRA: *De Eso No Se Habla* (*We Don't Talk About That*): Halfway between essay and documentary, this nonfiction podcast hosted by Basque producer Isabel Cadenas Cañón 'tries to connect the dots between personal and collective silences'. The website has English transcripts to follow as you listen to the Spanish.

GOLD EPISODE: *Re:sound*, Episode 201, 'The Cathy Fitzgerald Show'. This episode of Third Coast Audio's podcast showcases the 'ethereal, Dickens-inspired works' of British producer Cathy Fitzgerald. Her BBC feature *Skylarking* is a delightful juxtaposition of the experiences of a paraglider and a prisoner.

PART 2: Categories by content

Science

CLASSIC: *Science Vs, Science Friction, Radiolab, The Infinite Monkey Cage, 13 Minutes to the Moon*

EXTRA: *Guardians of the River*: Beautifully produced and narrated stories of the passionate scientists and locals saving the Okavango Delta.

Arts and culture

CLASSIC: *Song Exploder, Scriptnotes, 99% Invisible, The New Yorker: Fiction, Sodajerker on Songwriting, Mogul, The Lonely Palette*

EXTRA: *Longform*: Running since 2012, this consistently excellent podcast has a simple but compelling premise: a weekly conversation with a nonfiction writer on how they tell stories. Features some of the biggest and brightest names in many writing genres and in satisfying depth.

Health and wellbeing

CLASSIC: *Where Should We Begin?, The Happiness Lab, We Can Do Hard Things with Glennon Doyle, Still Jill, Terrible, Thanks for Asking, Griefcast, You, Me and the Big C*

EXTRA:

Why Don't You Date Me? with Nicole Byer: Host Nicole Byer is, according to her show notes, 'smart, funny, has a fat ass and loves giving blow jobs. So the question is why is she perpetually single?' This podcast delves into topics such as racism (Nicole is black) and mental health (she has attention-deficit disorder) while being raunchy and honest, as Nicole's guests pick over her relationships.

Back from Broken: Hosted by recovering drug addict and award-winning Colorado Public Radio reporter Vic Vela, it features unflinching interviews with all kinds of people on the road back from addiction, mental illness and breakdown.

Maintenance Phase: Hosts Michael Hobbes and Aubrey Gordon debunk wellness and diet fads while fiercely interrogating misconceptions about weight and health.

News and politics

CLASSIC: *Talking Politics, Pod Save America, The United States of Anxiety, In The Thick, The Weeds, Intercepted*

EXTRA: *Pod Save the People*: Hosted by organiser and activist DeRay Mckesson, who explores news, culture, social justice, and politics with experts, influencers, and diverse local and national leaders.

Tech and media

CLASSIC: *Pivot, Recode Daily, TED Talks Technology, Tech Swamp, The Vergecast, Decoder, The Next Billion Seconds*

EXTRA: *Reply All*: Launched in 2014, this Gimlet show about the human side of the internet carved a strong niche, with hosts Alex Goldman and PJ Vogt dishing out wildly varied tech-related stories with panache. In early 2021, a series that set out to expose toxic workplace issues at the magazine *Bon Appétit* led to accusations of similar issues linked to Vogt and presenter Sruthi Pinnamaneni, who ultimately quit. After a brief hiatus, *Reply All* returned, with Goldman joined as host by Emmanuel Dzotsi, the black, British-raised journalist who co-hosted *Serial* season three. Can its pedigree survive? Even if not, the back catalogue is well worth a listen.

Business and finance

CLASSIC: *The Tim Ferriss Show, Planet Money, Freakonomics Radio, StartUp, BizChix, Brown Ambition*

EXTRA: *The Price of Football*: The financial forces and shenanigans driving the world of soccer, explained by University of Liverpool accounting lecturer Kieran Maguire.

GOLD EPISODE: *This American Life*, Episode 355, 'The Giant Pool of Money': A classic collaboration with NPR's *All Things Considered* on the housing crisis of 2008, made by Alex Davidson and Alex Blumberg. Great example of how to storify a dense financial topic.

Comedy

CLASSIC: *My Dad Wrote a Porno, The Read, The Skewer, FOGO, Beef and Dairy Network Podcast, Adam Buxton*

EXTRA: *Queers Gone By*: Caitlin Powell and Kate Butch relive films, TV shows and snacks to see if there's any way of pinpointing the things that made them the queer icons they are today.

Lost in Larrimah: Although this is also a true-crime podcast, in that it examines how one Paddy Moriarty and his dog disappeared without a trace from a tiny outback Australian town, sharp writing and observation raise a smile. It is now also a book, and has been optioned by HBO. (Disclosure: I was an adviser in the podcast's early stages.)

GOLD EPISODE: *Tim Key and Gogol's Overcoat*: This anarchic 28-minute BBC feature (reviewed in the first issue of *RadioDoc Review*) had me laughing out loud as British poet, comedian and Russophile Tim Key spins a surreal tale somewhere between fact and fiction. Key: 'I'm off on an odyssey, love'. Wife: 'Are you wearing that?'

Education and knowledge

CLASSIC: *TED Talks, Stuff You Should Know, Philosophize This!, Sideways, In Our Time, Great Lives, Emperors of Rome, Hidden Brain, Seriously, The Little Red Podcast*

EXTRA: *Queen Mary History of Emotions: The Sound of Anger*: This award-winning podcast uses the study of the past to help us understand our feelings in the present. Excellent collaboration between academics and an audio producer to convey research and knowledge effectively and engagingly.

History

CLASSIC: *You Must Remember This, You're Dead to Me, Making Gay History, A History of the World in 100 Objects, Stuff You Missed in History Class, Rear Vision, The History Listen*

EXTRA:

History Becomes Her: Host Rachel Thompson speaks to women making change now about the women of the past who paved the way for them.

History Lab: Australian academic Tamson Pietsch examines the process by which history is constructed – and delivers a good historical story.

Kids

CLASSIC: *Tai Asks Why, But Why, Mic Drop, Fairy Tales with Granny MacDuff*

EXTRA: *Fierce Girls*: Short, sound-rich stories of female heroes, many narrated by tween-aged girls.

Notes

1 Podcasting: Why, who, what

1. Chenjerai Kumanika, 'Vocal color in public radio', *The Transom Review*, vol. 15, no. 2, March 2015, <https://transom.org/wp-content/uploads/2015/01/Chenjerai-Kumanyika-Review.pdf>.

2. But note that budgets vary greatly, with travel and costs of archival material a key factor. Some top investigative journalism podcasts I know cost much less.

2 Appreciating audio storytelling: The backstory

1. For more on public broadcasting contributions, I recommend David Hendy, official historian of the BBC; Virginia Madsen, an authoritative writer on both the European radio feature tradition and Australia's Radio National; and Paddy Scannell. Michael McCauley, Jack W Mitchell and Stacey Spaulding have all written histories of NPR, while Peabody judge and academic Jason Loviglio has written penetrating analyses of its output.

2. Cited in Virginia Madsen, 'Cultural radio at the crossroads: "When I hear the word culture, I switch on my radio": Reflections on an underestimated form, "cultural radio"', *Southern Review*, vol. 39, no. 3, pp. 16–37.

3. Bill Siemering, 'National Public Radio purposes', NPR, 1970, <www.npr.org/2021/05/07/993569986/radio-with-a-purpose-bill-siemering-on-nprs-original-mission-statement>.

4. Peter M Lewis, '"A claim to be heard": Voices of ordinary people in BBC radio features', *Revue Française de Civilisation Britannique*, vol. 26, no. 1, 2021, <https://journals.openedition.org/rfcb/7681>.

5. Studs Terkel with Tony Parker, 'Interviewing an interviewer', in Robert Perks and Alistair Thomson (eds), *The Oral History Reader*, 3rd ed, Routledge, London, 2016, pp. 150–51.

6. For details of the IFC 30th anniversary collection, see Willem Davids, 'IFC 2004 – 30 years of international radio documentaries in a CD box!', IFC, 6 June 2004, <https://ifc2.wordpress.com/2004/04/05/whats-in-the-box-laurent-marceau-and-edwin-brys/>.

7. David Hendy, 'Reality radio', in Andrew Crisell (ed), *Radio: Critical Concepts in Media and Cultural Studies*, Routledge, London, 2009, pp. 220–38.

8. Seán Street, '*Poetry, Texas*: Review 1', *RadioDoc Review*, vol. 1, no. 1, 2014, <https://ro.uow.edu.au/rdr/vol1/iss1/4/>.

9. Michele Hilmes, 'Reality in sound: Problem solved?', in Jeremy Wade Morris and Eric Hoyt, (eds), *Saving New Sounds: Podcast Preservation and Historiography*, University of Michigan Press, Ann Arbor, 2021, p. 80.

3 Radio, podcasting and intimacy

1. Claudia Calhoun, 'Mysteries solved and unsolved in the search for The Missing Cryptoqueen', *RadioDoc Review*, vol. 6, no. 1, 2020, <https://ro.uow.edu.au/rdr/vol6/iss1/3/>.

2   BBC, *BBC Sounds Commissioning Brief*, BBC, 2019, <https://downloads.bbc.
co.uk/radio/commissioning/Comms_Brief_103004_BBCSounds_Podcasts_
DramaticStorytelling_2019_2020.pdf>.

3   R Murray Schafer, 'The Soundscape', in *The Sound Studies Reader* by Jonathan Sterne
(ed), Oxford, New York: Routledge, 2012, p. 102.

4   Rob Byers, *The Ear Training Guide for Audio Producers*, NPR, 31 January 2017,
<https://training.npr.org/2017/01/31/the-ear-training-guide-for-audio-producers/>.

4   The aerobic art of interviewing

1   You can compare the print versions and hear Jan's audio here: <https://transom.
org/2011/the-power-of-voice/>.

5   Milestones in the podsphere: From *Serial* to *The Daily*

1   For more on early podcasting history, see Andrew Bottomley's book *Sound Streams:
A Cultural History of Radio-Internet Convergence*, University of Michigan Press, Ann
Arbor, 2020.

2   John Biewen, Sarah Koenig and Julie Snyder, 'One story, week by week: An interview
with Sarah Koenig and Julie Snyder', in John Biewen and Alexa Dilworth (eds), *Reality
Radio: Telling True Stories in Sound*, 2nd ed, University of North Carolina Press,
Durham, 2017, p. 81.

3   In *Reality Radio*, p. 82.

4   In *Reality Radio*, p. 85.

5   Joy Wiltenburg, 'True crime: The origins of modern sensationalism', *American Historical
Review*, vol. 109, no. 5, 2004, pp. 1377–1404.

6   Nic Newman and Nathan Gallo, *Daily News Podcasts: Building New Habits in the
Shadow of Coronavirus*, research report, Reuters Institute and University of Oxford,
November 2020, <https://reutersinstitute.politics.ox.ac.uk/daily-news-podcasts-
building-new-habits-shadow-coronavirus>.

6   Podcasting as literary journalism: *S-Town*

1   Mark Kramer, 'Breakable rules for literary journalists', in Norman Sims and Mark Kramer
(eds), *Literary Journalism: A New Collection of the Best American Nonfiction*, Ballantine,
New York, 1995, pp. 21–34, <https://niemanstoryboard.org/stories/breakable-rules-
for-literary-journalists/>.

2   David Dowling and Travis Vogan, 'Can we "Snowfall" this? Digital longform and the
race for the tablet market', *Digital Journalism*, vol 3, no. 2, 2015.

3   David O Dowling and Kyle Miller, 'Immersive Audio Storytelling: Podcasting and Serial
Documentary in the Digital Publishing Industry', *Journal of Radio & Audio Media*,
vol. 26, no. 1, 2019, p.178.

4   John Hartsock, 'Svetlana Alexievich and the Nobel Prize for Literatures', *Literary
Journalism*, vol. 10, no. 2, pp 26–27, <https://s35767.pcdn.co/wp-content/
uploads/2016/03/Literary_Journalism_v10n2_Spring_2016.pdf>.

5   Whether this is legal needs to also be considered. In parts of Australia, for instance, it is
illegal to record anyone without their consent. Consent can be easily sought by asking
if it's OK to record, pressing record and repeating the question and answer on tape, as
proof of consent.

6   'Speaking with: Serial's Julie Snyder about making groundbreaking podcasts',
15 December 2016, *The Conversation*, <https://theconversation.com/speaking-with-
serials-julie-snyder-about-making-groundbreaking-podcasts-70411>.

7 Alice Lesperance, 'Growing up gay in Alabama and finding myself in S-Town', *Scalawag*, 28 May 2017, <https://scalawagmagazine.org/2017/05/growing-up-gay-in-alabama-and-finding-myself-in-s-town/>.

9 Inclusion, diversity and equality: Pushing the boundaries of podcasting

1 Belinda Duvinage, 'Spotify is gaining in importance, Apple is losing', *W&V*, 19 February 2020, <www.wuv.de/tech/spotify_gewinnt_an_bedeutung_apple_verliert>.

2 'Fiction podcasting: Growing by more than 300 percent', *Podnews*, 16 July 2021, <https://podnews.net/update/fiction-podcasting-growth>.

3 'The creepy podcast that helped overthrow a government', *Radioinfo*, 18 May 2018, <https://radioinfo.com.au/news/creepy-podcast-helped-overthrow-government/>.

4 Jiayang Fan, 'Yan Lianke's forbidden satires of China', *New Yorker*, 8 October 2018, <www.newyorker.com/magazine/2018/10/15/yan-liankes-forbidden-satires-of-china>.

5 But after taking the workshop and adjusting to Western podcasting culture, Luo Laiming (his full name) has become inspired. In 2019, he released the popular *Decoding The Art of War*, in which, with liberal use of the first person, he converts this ancient Chinese text into accessible story, to 'help you master the age-old wisdom' it contains. As the show notes cheekily note, 'follow this podcast so you no longer need to pretend you've read it.'

6 One such show, hosted by a radio journalist known as Xinran, was called *Words on the Night Breeze*. It fielded extraordinary stories, mostly from women, who described domestic violence, abuse and general repression. Xinran Xue moved to Britain, where she published a bestselling book of the stories, *The Good Women of China*, in 2002.

7 Afra Wang, 'Loud Murmurs: A feminist Chinese podcast deconstructing US pop culture', *NüVoices*, 8 October 2018, <https://nuvoices.com/2018/10/08/loud-murmurs-a-feminist-chinese-podcast-deconstructing-us-pop-culture/>.

8 Jennifer Hyland Wang, 'The perils of ladycasting', in Jeremy Wade Morris and Eric Hoyt (eds), *Saving New Sounds: Podcast Preservation and Historiography*, University of Michigan Press, Ann Arbor, 2021, p. 65.

9 James T Green, `115: Glass Walls', 28 February 2021, <https://www.jamestgreen.com/thoughts/115>.

10 Celeste Headlee, 'An anti-racist future: A vision and plan for the transformation of public media', *Medium*, 18 January 2021, <https://celesteheadlee.medium.com/an-anti-racist-future-a-vision-and-plan-for-the-transformation-of-public-media-224149ab37e6>.

11 The research, co-published by Edison Research in November 2021, shows an astonishing 50 per cent increase in weekly podcast listening among Black Americans between 2020 and 2021. Around 26 per cent of Black Americans now listen weekly to podcasts, compared to 28 per cent of all Americans. Of those who listen at home, Black Americans are twice as likely to listen with family or friends, <http://www.edisonresearch.com/wp-content/uploads/2021/11/Black-Podcast-Listener-Report-2021-for-download.pdf>.

12 Edison Research, *The Latino Podcast Listener Report 2021*, 13 July 2021, <https://www.edisonresearch.com/the-latino-podcast-listener-report-2021/>.

13 Aditya Hadi Pratama, 'Indonesian podcast app brings in ex-Googler as CEO', *Tech in Asia*, 18 August 2021, <www.techinasia.com/noice-ceo-rado-ardian-niken-sasmaya>.

14 Sarah Florini, 'The podcast "Chitlin' Circuit": Black podcasters, alternative media, and audio enclaves', *Journal of Radio & Audio Media*, vol. 22, no. 2, 2015, pp. 209–19.

10   Podcasting: What next?

1   Tom Webster, 'The most important question in podcasting', *I Hear Things*, 13 August 2021, <https://tomwebster.media/the-most-important-question-in-podcasting-2021/>.

2   James Cridland, 'US podcast app downloads and audiences: September 2021', *Podnews*, 12 October 2021, <https://podnews.net/article/podtrac-us-downloads-and-users-sep21?utm_source=podnews.net&utm_medium=email&utm_campaign=podnews.net:2021-10-12/>. Cridland also points out that Apple Podcasts has auto-downloads (Spotify doesn't), and 31 per cent of those auto-downloads are never played, if recent data around an Apple bug is correct.

3   Webster, 'The most important question in podcasting'.

4   'Branded podcasts and audience connection with Dan Misener (in conversation with Lori Beckstead)', podcast episode, *New Aural Cultures*, 5 February 2021, <https://player.fm/series/the-podcast-studies-podcast-formally-new-aural-cultures/branded-podcasts-and-audience-connection-with-dan-misener-in-conversation-with-lori-beckstead>. Now called *The Podcast Studies Podcast*.

5   For a detailed analysis of this and other audio features, see my chapter 'The invisible art of audio storytelling', in Michele Hilmes and Andrew Bottomley (eds), *The Oxford Handbook of Radio Studies*, Oxford University Press, New York, 2022.

6   Admire Mare, 'Podcasting in Africa: Current and future trends', in Yoonmo Sang, Jee Young Lee and Sora Park, *Podcast Trends and Issues in Australia and Beyond: Global Perspectives*, News & Media Research Centre, University of Canberra, 2020, pp. 28–30, <https://apo.org.au/sites/default/files/resource-files/2020-10/apo-nid308947.pdf>.

7   Edison Research, 'The Infinite Dial 2021', 11 March 2021, <www.edisonresearch.com/blog/page/4/>.

8   Kim Fox, David O Dowling and Kyle Miller, 'A curriculum for Blackness: Podcasts as discursive cultural guides, 2010–2020', *Journal of Radio & Audio Media*, vol. 27, no. 2, 2020, pp. 298–318.

Acknowledgments

In 1981, when I produced my first audio documentary, *In a Strange Land*, about the then-small community of immigrants in Ireland, I was spellbound when it went to air, imagining people listening to it all over the country. For that one half-hour, we shared a common experience. Podcasting has removed the limitations of listening at a certain time and place, but it engenders much the same sense of community that radio did. This book is dedicated first and foremost to people who love making, discussing and listening to podcasts.

The book was not my idea: I would not have dared to imagine taking on such a task as writing what has become a sort of cultural survey of the podcasting universe. The suggestion came from Phillipa McGuinness, former publisher at NewSouth, who identified the growing interest in podcasting as a new medium and pop-culture phenomenon. I am grateful to her and to the entire team at NewSouth, especially my astute and rigorous editor, Emma Driver; tireless publisher, Harriet McInerney; and excellent project manager, Sophia Oravecz. I am also indebted to my wonderful agent, Jane Novak, for her unstinting encouragement and assistance.

I am honoured to be part of a community of passionate audio storytellers who support and encourage each other. I particularly wish to thank contributors Patrick Abboud, Olya Booyar, Mark Dapin, Kim Fox, Audrey Gillan, Alan Hall, Eleanor McDowall, Clare McGinn, Margo Neale, Julie Shapiro and Sophie Townsend. I am indebted also to my friends and colleagues at *The Age* for allowing me to expose our ups and downs along the way while making *Phoebe's Fall*, *Wrong Skin* and *The Last Voyage of the Pong Su* – Richard Baker, Tom McKendrick,

Michael Bachelard, Rachael Dexter, Kate Cole-Adams, Greg Muller and all the team – thank you! I am also eternally grateful to the community of critics, scholars and producers who have built *RadioDoc Review* into the rich resource it is today, and a repository of criticism of the crafted audio storytelling form. To audio friends who have given me valuable critical feedback over the years, even (especially) when it hurt, I also say thank you: Jane Ulman, Sharon Davis, Masako Fukui, Jane Norris, Claudia Taranto, John Biewen, Fiona Martin and more.

As an academic, I have mulled over themes such as the affective power of voice, the aesthetics of audio storytelling and the intersubjective dynamics of the interview relationship before. Parts of this book have appeared in 'The Aerobic Art of Interviewing', *Asia Pacific Media Educator*, vol. 1, no. 18, 2007, pp. 147–54. I thank Bill Reynolds for editorial assistance in developing the analysis initially published as 'The Narrative Podcast as Digital Literary Journalism: Conceptualizing S-Town', *Literary Journalism Studies*, vol. 13, nos 1–2, 2021.

I wish to thank both universities with which I am affiliated, the University of Wollongong and the University of Sydney, for their support. This book is being published under the auspices of the University of Sydney, where I am developing a Hub for Innovation in Podcasting: a one-stop centre that aims to research, teach, produce and commission podcasts, and expand podcasting studies internationally. I welcome inquiries in that regard.

Finally, this book could not have happened without the unwavering support of my husband, Chris, who has put up with me wandering around the house with earphones in for years, as I listen to podcasts I am working on or evaluating or just appreciating. I dedicate this book to him and to my sons, Declan and Conor, and Alba, a recent member of the family. As in podcasting, the personal is always the most powerful.

Index

Printed and bound by CPI Group (UK) Ltd, Croydon, CR0 4YY

07/05/2024

14498532-0001